BEDSIDE MANNERS

BEDSIDE MANNERS

An Anthology of
Medical Wit and Wisdom

John Ballantyne

To my wife
Barbara
in this year of our Golden Wedding

and our daughters

Jane
anaesthetist at the Massachusetts General Hospital, Boston, USA

and

Deborah
audiologist at the University Hospital, La Sapienza, Rome, Italy

First published in Great Britain in 1995 by
Virgin Books
an imprint of Virgin Publishing Ltd
332 Ladbroke Grove
London W10 5AH

Selection, introduction and linking text
copyright © John Ballantyne 1995

Foreword copyright © Johnny Speight 1995

Copyright extracts reproduced by permission: copyright details appear
in a list of sources and acknowledgements on pages xvii–xix

The right of John Ballantyne to be identified as the author of this
work has been asserted by him in accordance with the
Copyright Designs and Patents Act 1988.

A catalogue record for this book is available from the British Library.

ISBN 0 86369 849 2

Typeset by Phoenix Photosetting, Chatham, Kent
Printed and bound in Great Britain by Bath Press Ltd

Contents

Foreword by Johnny Speight   xi
Introduction   xv
Acknowledgements   xvii

The Professions

MEDICINE

The student of medicine   *Ibn Abi Usaybia*   3
Mr Bob Sawyer   *Charles Dickens*   4
The life of medical students   *W. Somerset Maugham*   4
Medicine 1933   *Lewis Thomas*   5
Letter to Dr Coles   *William Carlos Williams*   6
Why medicine and why not?   *Peter Richards*   7
The physician   *Hippocrates*   10
Dr Thorne   *Anthony Trollope*   10
The practice   *William Carlos Williams*   15
How to be a doctor   *Stephen Leacock*   21
The status of doctors   *C.P. Snow*   24
The seven sins of medicine   *Richard Asher*   32
Doubtful character borne by the medical profession
   George Bernard Shaw   38
The medical profession   *Myles na Gopaleen*   40
Never drop dead around a specialist   *S.J. Perelman*   41
Drip feed   *Jeffrey Bernard*   42

NURSING

Nursing in the 1830s   *Sir James Paget*   44
Nurses   *Lewis Thomas*   44

DENTISTRY

'False' teeth   *Mark Twain*   50
Surgery   *Anton Chekhov*   50
Guilty gums   *E.B. White*   54
Laughing gas   *P.G. Wodehouse*   55
Nothing but the tooth   *S.J. Perelman*   57
Dentistry and doubt   *John Updike*   60

SCIENCE AND MEDICINE

Pure science   *Louis Pasteur*   67
Nature and health   *Lord Horder*   68
Are doctors men of science?   *George Bernard Shaw*   68
The doctor in the modern world   *Lord Brain*   70
Open heart university   *Spike Milligan*   70

The Doctor–Patient Relationship

GENERAL PRACTICE

Doctor and patient   *Rufus of Ephesus*   75
Family doctor   *R.K. Narayan*   75
The *objet d'art*   *Anton Chekhov*   77
The use of force   *William Carlos Williams*   81
Calling all patients   *H.C. Bosman*   85
The doctor knows best   *Damon Runyon*   88
Alf Garnett and Dr Becker   *Johnny Speight*   89
Malingering   *Theodore Dalrymple*   94

HOSPITALS

Hospital visit   *E.B. White*   96
Within limits   *Jeffrey Bernard*   97

In Sickness and In Health

HEALTH

Longevity   *Lewis Thomas*   103

Contents

No life   *Damon Runyon*   103
How to live to be 200   *Stephen Leacock*   105
Caution: living may be dangerous to your health
  Willard Espy   108

SICKNESS

Illness   *Lewis Thomas*   110
Illness is good for you   *Spike Milligan*   119

Alcohol and Tobacco

ALCOHOL

Alcoholism and alcohol   *Hugh L'Etang*   123
Rum and the Navy   *Sir Dick Caldwell*   127
Beer   *John Timbs*   129
In a pickle   *Jeffrey Bernard*   130
A cure for drinking   *Anton Chekhov*   132
The effect of alcohol on the learning abilities of the goldfish
  William Hartston   137

TOBACCO

Chain smokers respiration   *Lancet*   139
Giving it up   *Lancet*   139
The shattered health of Mr Podge   *Stephen Leacock*   140

Coughs and Sneezes and Other Diseases

COUGHS

Of coughs and sneezes   *Edward Lear*   147
Cough   *Celcus*   147
The experience of the McWilliamses with membranous croup
  Mark Twain   148
Just the one   *Jeffrey Bernard*   154

COLDS

The cold   *E.B. White*   157

Bedside Manners

Curing a cold   *Mark Twain*   158
The common cold   *Johnny Speight*   162

WIND

The wind   *Walter Harris*   164
Diary, 6 & 7 October 1663   *Samuel Pepys*   164
The illest of winds   *James Le Fanu*   165

WARTS

Warts are common enough in the Ozarks   *Vance Randolph*   167
On warts   *Lewis Thomas*   168

CANCER

Curtailing the tobacco pandemic   *Alan Blum*   172
Cancer ward   *Aleksandr Solzhenitsyn*   174
Breast cancer   *A.N. Wilson*   186

Nervous Illnesses

BRAIN TUMOUR

A journey round my skull   *Frigyes Karinthy*   201

PSYCHOLOGICAL DISTURBANCES

Hypochondria   *Smith and Jones*   208
Off colour   *Jeffrey Bernard*   211
Ode on melancholy   *John Keats*   213
Manic depression   *Spike Milligan*   214

Deafness and Tinnitus

DEAFNESS

Paracusis Willisii   *J. Trevor Hughes*   217
Visible Speech   *Eudora Welty*   218
Sophy   *Charles Dickens*   218
Laura Bridgman's story   *Charles Dickens*   220

Contents

Deafness   *David Wright*   224
Maître Florian   *Victor Hugo*   226

TINNITUS

Internal ringing of the ears   *Celcus*   229
Cricket-in-the-ear   *E.B. White*   230
The bells of hell   *James Le Fanu*   230
On his tinnitus   *Lancet*   232

Till Death Us Do Part

LAST WORDS

Death as a friend   *Oliver Wendell Holmes*   235
Errand   *Raymond Carver*   236
As I lay dying   *Willard Espy*   247
Why me?   *Damon Runyon*   248

Biographical notes   251
Index by author   265

Foreword

by Johnny Speight

It struck me recently that a good many people take up writing when they retire. Writing, it appears, is one of those trades considered to be something anyone can do. When people who have worked all their lives in some other profession and are now about to retire from it are asked what they will do now, they invariably say, 'Oh, I don't know, I think I'll take up writing.' This cavalier attitude towards writing – as something we can leave to our dotage when every other occupation is beyond us – is encouraged, I suppose, by the belief that we all have a book in us somewhere. The fact that it's probably the same book doesn't appear to matter.

Although I'm not against this writing bug for those in retirement, it's a bit irritating to discover that something I've had to struggle with for the last 40 years of my life is regarded as not much more than occupational therapy for the senior citizen. What worries me is that this attitude may be correct, and that the really sensible people don't take up writing until they have nothing better to do. I didn't take up writing myself until it was made clear to me that I was a failure as a jazz drummer. And I had already retired from a proper job in a factory to take up drumming. What I'm worried about is that maybe writing really is just something you take up after you've failed at all those other things you especially wanted to do or be.

It's a depressing thought that all you're fit for is writing. That to admit to being a writer is to admit to failure. That when friends enquire after you and are told, 'Oh, he's taken up writing,' they shake their heads pityingly and sigh, 'Oh dear. He seemed to be doing so well too.'

Most writers endeavoured to succeed at something else before they threw up the sponge and resorted to writing. George Bernard Shaw tried his hand at many things – town councillor, public speaker, living off his mother – until he was forced to take up writing for a living.

Chekhov was a doctor. It's not known how good or bad a doctor he was but most people preferred him as a writer – probably even his patients. Shakespeare wanted to be an actor but didn't have what it took. So like most failed actors he became a playwright. Then there was Stephen Leacock, a university lecturer whose only claim to fame is as a writer. And Damon Runyon – was he a failed gangster? More likely the Boswell to so many small-time crooks. It makes me wonder what our literature would have been like if all these writers had succeeded at what they first set out to be.

My friend John Ballantyne, who has retired from a very distinguished career in medicine to take up writing, has put this very good book together. It's a wonderful collection of writers who prove beyond doubt that failure can have its rewards, especially for people like me who love to read.

I have always admired the compilers of anthologies. It's a clever way of doing a book without the drudgery of writing it. And John Ballantyne is smart. What he has done is collect some of his favourite bedtime reading (which could easily become yours), most of it short essays or stories on medicine. Some of these are very funny pieces written by some of the world's great humorists and ideally suited to the insomniac who wants to laugh himself to sleep. In this collection there are stories it would take many a year of searching to find. I am a prolific reader and I haven't come across any of them before.

Leacock's story of the doctor who beat up his patients reminds me of a local doctor I knew who threw his patients over his shoulder. When the patient entered the consulting-room the doctor would offer his hand in greeting. On the patient taking it, the doctor would turn quickly and throw the patient over his shoulder, hurling him across the room. This doctor had a belief in his treatment and thought it a cure-all for most things. 'It all starts in the back,' he used to say. And, to be fair, I suppose, if his patients could survive this treatment there couldn't be a lot wrong with them. Most of his patients returned to him and those who did swore by his treatment. One thing could be said for this doctor's patients though; they were without doubt the fittest in the locality.

Years ago in the East End of London where I lived as a boy, our doctor only had two remedies – pink water or blue water. My father swore by the blue water as the most beneficial.

Our doctor's waiting-room in those days was a filthy, dirty, draughty, depressing hovel, with a one-bar gas fire you fed pennies into yourself if you wanted to keep warm. It was full of people passing around their germs and the last place to sit in if you were really ill. In fact, when the goverment brought in the National Health scheme and people began to get a reasonable sickness benefit, those who wanted a few weeks off with pay used to go and sit in his waiting-room and hope to catch something. He kept a good supply of old comics and periodicals there and quite a few people used it as a reading room. Those who could read, that is.

Before the National Health scheme you had to show him your two bob before he'd do business with you. He wouldn't give credit under any circumstances. Obviously he never had as much faith in his potions as his patients had. On a night call you would have to pass the money through his letter-box before he would come out. In fact, he'd look out of his bedroom window and you'd have to shine a torch on the money before he'd even come downstairs.

Bernard Shaw writes somewhere about an uncle of his, a doctor, who was forced by circumstances to trade with the poor and used to insist on his night patients rattling their money at the speaking tube by his front door, and worked on the principle that if you died it was the will of the Lord, and if you recovered he took the credit.

Still, our local doctor helped bring most of us into the world, kept our kidneys flushed with his coloured water, was prompt with a death certificate so that the bereaved could collect the insurance money quickly, and touted for at least one undertaker on the side. And, of course, he was poor too. No way would he have wasted time on us if he could have worked for the rich.

Anyway, most of us were very wary in those days of the rich Harley Street doctors who walked the wards in the local hospital. We were told that these rich Harley Street doctors only came down to the East End to practise on the poor. That made sense to us. Obviously they couldn't afford to risk the lives of their wealthy patients – it wasn't good business. The loss of a rich patient would be a nasty blow to the bank balance, but a dozen poor people was no skin off their nose at all. We were told that if you hadn't got a disease they gave you one, so they could have a go at curing it.

As I have said, I retired from factory work in the East End to take up writing. I was a definite failure as a poor person and have always tried to be as rich as possible because I sincerely believe I'm better suited to it. Dr Johnson said, 'Only a fool would write if it wasn't for money,' and I've always endeavoured to heed the good doctor's teaching. They say money can't buy health – but it can certainly buy a better doctor.

My good friend John Ballantyne, the author of this book, is a very fine doctor but his speciality is nose, ears and throat and as far as I can discern there is nothing much wrong with my ears, nose and throat. My problem is a dodgy leg and he knows next to nothing about legs. And besides, he has retired now to take up writing so it wouldn't help me much if he did. Like good writers, good doctors shouldn't be allowed to retire, the only exception being if they put together a good book like this.

Introduction

During a busy life in medical practice, I derived much pleasure in spare moments from reading; but periods of relaxation were few, and often confined to bedtime. Perhaps for that reason, I developed a special appetite for short stories and magazine articles and, by chance, several of them were concerned with the medical professions and with those who practise them. It is upon these that the present miscellany is based; culled from a period of over 50 years, it also contains some chapters or parts of chapters from books, and a few newspaper articles.

Most of the chosen pieces were written by professional word-smiths, including a small number by medically-qualified authors for whom the pen proved mightier than the scalpel; among these were Anton Chekhov, Oliver Wendell Holmes, W. Somerset Maugham and William Carlos Williams, the first and last of whom continued to practise medicine throughout their lives and drew inspiration for their literary output from clinical experience. However, even those pieces written by authors with medical training were penned primarily for the general reader, and I hope that the works which I have chosen will appeal to a readership well beyond the restricted confines of the medical professions themselves; they are not the conventional wisdom of standard medical textbooks but rather the unconventional ideas, and often the penetrating wit, of highly perceptive observers.

Many of the selected items belong to the twentieth century and they encompass practically every mood evoked by sickness and by those who care for the sick. Although I have indulged some of my own special interests in choosing the topics for this random collection, I have tried to cover a fairly broad canvas.

Since the short story has figured prominently in my bedtime browsing, it is not surprising that many of my chosen pieces are of American origin, not only because North America has produced some of the greatest short story writers of the present century but also because Americans are more ready than most to talk openly about medical problems, including their own.

There must be enough literature about medical matters to fill at least a dozen anthologies, and the present miscellany makes no claim to be a comprehensive collection of writings about doctors, patients and illness; but I have had to resist the temptation to include a number of literary gems, in order to avoid either excessive length (as in Anton Chekhov's *A Nervous Breakdown* or Somerset Maugham's *Sanatorium*) or undue overlap with other anthologies.

There is, of course, much sadness in sickness and this aspect of medical literature has not been overlooked; but there is also much joy in medicine, especially for its practitioners, and the professions are not alone in appreciating medical humour. Even in his last fatal illness Damon Runyon, one of the greatest of comic writers, made no concession to his own predicament when he composed his last eight stories, *Written in Sickness*.

In addition to my own personal reading, I have been introduced to medical writings not previously known to me by a number of colleagues and other friends. In particular I am pleased to acknowledge helpful suggestions about further reading from my son-in-law, Dr Andrew Brown, who directed me to writings by Samuel Pepys and P.G. Wodehouse; Norma Farnes, personal secretary for over a quarter of a century to Spike Milligan – comic writer, performer and ex-Goon – for permission to reproduce three of his short poems; Robert Greenwood, a librarian at the Royal Society of Medicine, who lent me his copy of William Carlos Williams's *Doctor Stories*; Imrich Friedmann, distinguished pathologist and close friend, who drew my attention to 'A journey round my skull' by Frigyes Karinthy; Sean Sellars, Professor of Otolaryngology in the University of Cape Town, who presented me with a volume of short stories by Herman Charles Bosman; Dr Mansfield Smith and his wife Linda, host and hostess during visits to California, who brought to my notice Eudora Welty and Lewis Thomas; Johnny Speight, who many years ago persuaded me to read George Bernard Shaw's *The Doctor's Dilemma* has written a generous foreword and has donated one of his scripts from the television series *In Sickness and in Health*; and Dr Robert Wilkins, editor of *The Doctor's Quotation Book*, from which I have borrowed a few brief items.

I am especially grateful to Lorna Russell, executive editor at Virgin Publishing, whose enthusiasm and advice have made the whole gestation period very pleasurable.

Acknowledgements

Richard Asher, 'The seven sins of medicine' from *Richard Asher Talking Sense* (Pitman Medical, 1972). Reproduced by permission of Churchill Livingstone.

Jeffrey Bernard, 'Within limits', 'Off colour', 'Drip feed', 'In a pickle' and 'Just the one' from *Low Life* © Gerald Duckworth & Co. Ltd (Pan Books Ltd, 1987). Reprinted by permission of Gerald Duckworth & Co. Ltd.

Alan Blum, 'Curtailing the tobacco pandemic' from *Cancer: Principles and Practice of Oncology* (J.P. Lippincott, 1993). Reprinted by permission of J.B. Lippincott and the author.

H.C. Bosman, 'Calling all patients' from *A Cask of Jerepigo* © Human & Rousseau, Cape Town, South Africa. Reprinted by permission of Human & Rousseau (Pty) Ltd.

Raymond Carver, 'Errand' from *Where I'm Calling From* © Raymond Carver 1988; renewed 1993 by Tess Gallagher. Reprinted by permission of International Creative Management Inc. (and Grove/Atlantic Inc.).

Anton Chekhov, 'Objet d'art' from *Anton Chekhov's Early Stories* (Oxford University Press, 1994). Translation © Patrick Miles and Harvey Pitcher 1982. 'A cure for drinking' and 'Surgery' from *Anton Chekhov's Selected Stories* (New American Library, 1960). Translation © Ann Dunnigan 1960.

Theodore Dalrymple, 'An article on malingering' from *If Symptoms Persist* (*Spectator*). Reproduced by permission of the editor.

Willard R. Espy, 'Caution: living may be dangerous to your health' and 'As I lay dying' from *An Almanac of Words at Play* © Willard R. Espy 1975 (Clarkson N. Potter Inc. 1976). Reprinted by permission of Harold Ober Associates Incorporated.

Myles na Gopaleen, 'A piece on the medical profession' from *The Best of Myles* (Pan Books Ltd, 1981).

William Hartston, 'The effect of alcohol on the learning abilities of the goldfish' from *The Drunken Goldfish and Other Irrelevant*

Scientific Research © William Hartston 1987. Reproduced by permission of Watson, Little Limited.

J. Trevor Hughes, An extract from 'Paracusis Willisii' from *Thomas Willis 1621–1675* (Royal Society of Medicine Services Limited, 1991). Reprinted by permission of Royal Society of Medicine Press Ltd.

John Keats, 'Ode on Melancholy' from *Lyric Poems* (Constable & Co., 1991). Reprinted by permission of Dover Publications Inc.

Lancet, 'Chain smokers respiration', 'Giving it up' and 'On his tinnitus' from *In England Now. 50 Years of Peripatetic Correspondence* (1989). Reprinted by permission of The *Lancet* Ltd.

Edward Lear, 'Of coughs and sneezes' from *A Book of Learned Nonsense* (edited by Peter Haining, 1992). Reprinted by permission of Mrs Vivien Noakes.

James Le Fanu, 'The illest of winds' and 'The bells of hell', from *The Sunday Telegraph*. Reprinted by permission of the author.

Hugh L'Etang, An extract from a chapter on 'Alcoholism and Alcohol' from *Fit to Lead?* (1980). Reprinted by permission of the author.

W. Somerset Maugham, An extract from *Of Human Bondage* (William Heinemann Ltd, 1915). Reprinted by permission of Reed Consumer Books Ltd.

R.K. Narayan, 'Family Doctor', from *A Story Teller's World* © R.K. Narayan 1989, 1990. Reprinted by permission of the author.

Samuel Pepys, An extract from *The Illustrated Diary of Samuel Pepys* (edited by Robert Latham) Reprinted by permission of HarperCollins Publishers.

S.J. Perelman, 'Nothing but the tooth' from *The Most of S.J. Perelman* (Methuen London Ltd, 1982). Reprinted by permission of Peters Fraser & Dunlop Group Ltd.

Vance Randolph, An extract on warts from *Ozark Superstitions* (Dover Publications Inc., 1964). Reprinted by permission of Dover Publications Inc.

Peter Richards, An extract from *Learning Medicine 1994*, published by BMJ Publishing Group (1993).

Damon Runyon, 'Why me?', 'The doctor knows best' and 'No life' from *Runyon First to Last* (Constable Publishers, 1954). Reprinted by permission of HarperCollins Publishers.

George Bernard Shaw, Extracts from the preface to *The Doctor's Dilemma* (1906). Reprinted by permission of the Society of Authors.

Mel Smith and Griff Rhys Jones. 'Hypochondria' from 'Head to

Head' (Talk Back Productions Ltd, 1992). Reprinted by permission of HarperCollins Publishers.

C.P. Snow, 'The status of doctors' from *All Heal: A Medical and Social Miscellany* (William Heinemann Ltd, 1971). Reprinted by permission of Royal Society of Medicine Press Ltd.

A. Solzhenitsyn, An extract from *Cancer ward* © The Bodley Head Ltd 1968, 1969. Reproduced by permission of Random House (UK) Ltd.

Lewis Thomas, 'On warts' from *The Medusa and the Snail* © The New England Journal of Medicine, 1979; 'Nurses' and extracts from 'Medicine 1933' and 'Endotoxin' from *The Youngest Science* © Lewis Thomas 1983. Reproduced by permission of Penguin USA and Daransoff & Verrill.

John Updike, 'Dentistry and doubt' from *The Same Door* © John Updike 1955. Reprinted by permission of Penguin Books Ltd.

Eudora Welty, A brief extract from 'First Love' from *Collected Stories* (Marion Boyars Publishers Ltd, 1981).

E.B. White, Four essays which originally appeared as 'Notes and Comments' in *The New Yorker* © 1949, 1951, 1952, 1957 E.B. White (duly renewed). (From *E.B. White: Writings from The New Yorker 1927–1976*, HarperCollins Publishers). All rights reserved.

Robert Wilkins, Extracts from *The Doctor's Quotation Book* © Robert Wilkins 1991 (published by Robert Hale Limited). Reprinted by permission of the author.

William Carlos Williams, 'The use of force' from *The Doctor Stories* (Faber & Faber Ltd). Reprinted by permission of Laurence Pollinger Ltd.

A.N. Wilson, A chapter from *The Healing Art* (1982). Reprinted by permission of Reed Consumer Books.

P.G. Wodehouse, An extract from *Laughing Gas* (Penguin Books Ltd, 1957). Reprinted by permission of Random House (UK) Ltd.

David Wright, An extract from *Deafness* (Allen Lane, The Penguin Press, 1969). Reprinted by permission of Reed Consumer Books.

If there are any omissions or misattributions of copyright, these are unintentional. Any such errors brought to the attention of Virgin Publishing will be corrected in a future edition.

THE PROFESSIONS

Medicine

The student of medicine
by Ibn Abi Usaybia

Saith Hippocrates:

'The student of medicine should be gentle by birth, excellent by nature, young in years, of moderate stature and symmetrical limbs, of good understanding and pleasant conversation, sound in judgment when consulted, chaste and courageous, no lover of money, self-controlled when angered, not apt to lose his temper even under severe provocation, and not slow of understanding.

'He should be sympathetic and kind with the sick and a faithful guardian of secrets, because many patients tell us about diseases in themselves which they do not wish to be known to others. He should be patient of insults, because many mad and melancholic persons meet us with such, wherein we should bear with them, knowing that such conduct does not proceed from them but is really caused by a disease external to their proper nature.

'His hair should be cut neatly and symmetrically, and he should neither shave it nor suffer it to grow too luxuriantly. He should neither cut his finger-nails too closely, nor suffer them to overgrow the tips of his fingers. His clothes should be white, clean and soft in texture. He should not walk hastily for this is a sign of levity, nor slowly, for this indicates faintheartedness. When summoned to a patient he should sit down cross-legged, and question him about his condition with becoming gravity and deliberation, not in a distracted and agitated manner.'

In my opinion this way, fashion and order are indeed better than any other.

~

3

Mr Bob Sawyer
from The Pickwick Papers *by Charles Dickens*

Mr Bob Sawyer, who was habited in a coarse blue coat, which, without being either a great coat or a surtout, partook of the nature and qualities of both, had about him that sort of slovenly smartness, and swaggering gait, which is peculiar to young gentlemen who smoke in the streets by day, shout and scream in the same by night, call waiters by their christian names, and do various other acts and deeds of a facetious description. He wore a pair of plaid trousers and a large double-breasted waistcoat . . . He eschewed gloves, and looked, upon the whole, something like a dissipated Robinson Crusoe.

~

The life of medical students
from Of Human Bondage *by W. Somerset Maugham*

Philip's ideas of the life of medical students, like those of the public at large, were founded on the pictures which Charles Dickens drew in the middle of the nineteenth century. He soon discovered that Bob Sawyer, if he ever existed, was no longer at all like the medical student of the present.

It is a mixed lot which enters upon the medical profession, and naturally there are some who are lazy and reckless. They think it is an easy life, idle away a couple of years; and then, because their funds come to an end or because angry parents refuse any longer to support them, drift away from the hospital. Others find the examinations too hard for them: one failure after another robs them of their nerve; and, panic-stricken, they forget as soon as they come into the forbidding buildings of the Conjoint Board the knowledge which before they had so pat. They remain year after year, objects of good-humoured scorn to younger men: some of them crawl through the examination of the Apothecaries Hall; others become non-qualified assistants, a precarious position in which they are at the mercy of their employer; their lot is poverty, drunkenness, and Heaven only knows their end. But for the most part medical students are industrious young men of the middle-class with a sufficient allowance to live in the respectable fashion they have been used to; many are the sons of doctors who have already something of the professional manner; their career is mapped out: as soon as they are qualified they propose to apply for a hospital appointment, after holding which (and perhaps a trip to the Far East as a ship's doctor), they will join their father and spend the rest of their days in a country practice. One or two are marked out as exceptionally brilliant: they will take the various prizes and scholarships which are open each year to the deserving, get one appointment after another at the hospital, go on the staff, take a consulting-room in Harley Street and, specializing in one subject or another, become prosperous, eminent, and titled.

～

Medicine 1933
from The Youngest Science *by Lewis Thomas*

The medicine we were trained to practice was, essentially, Osler's medicine. Our task for the future was to be diagnosis and explanation. Explanation was the real business of medicine. What the ill patient and his family wanted most was to know the name of the illness, and then, if possible, what had caused it, and finally, most important of all, how it was likely to turn out.

The successes possible in diagnosis and prognosis were regarded as the triumph of medical science, and so they were. It had taken long decades of careful, painstaking observation of many patients; the publication of countless papers describing the detailed aspects of one clinical syndrome after another; more science, in the correlation of the clinical features of disease with the gross and microscopic abnormalities, contributed by several generations of pathologists. By the 1930s we thought we knew as much as could ever be known about the dominant clinical problems of the time: syphilis, tuberculosis, lobar pneumonia, typhoid, rheumatic fever, erysipelas, poliomyelitis. Most of the known varieties of cancer had been meticulously classified, and estimates of the duration of life could be made with some accuracy. The electrocardiogram had arrived, adding to the fair precision already possible in the diagnosis of heart disease. Neurology possessed methods for the localization of disease processes anywhere in the nervous system. When we had learned all that, we were ready for our M.D. degrees, and it was expected that we would find out about the actual day-to-day management of illness during our internship and residency years.

We were provided with a thin, pocket-size book called *Useful Drugs*, one hundred pages or so, and we carried this around in our white coats when we entered the teaching wards and clinics in the third year, but I cannot recall any of our instructors ever referring to this volume. Nor do I remember much talk about treating disease at any time in the four years of medical school except by the surgeons, and most of their discussions dealt with the management of injuries, the drainage or removal of infected organs and tissues, and, to a very limited extent, the excision of cancers.

During the third and fourth years of school we also began to learn something that worried us all, although it was not much talked about. On the wards of the great Boston teaching hospitals – the Peter Bent Brigham, the Massachusetts General, the Boston City Hospital, and Beth Israel – it gradually dawned on us that we didn't know much that was really useful, that we could do nothing to change the course of the great majority of the diseases we were so busy analyzing, that medicine, for all its façade as a learned profession, was in real life a profoundly ignorant occupation.

Some of this we were actually taught by our clinical professors, much more we learned from each other in late-night discussions. When I am asked, as happens occasionally, which member of the Harvard faculty had the greatest influence on my education in medicine, I no longer grope for a name on that distinguished roster. What I remember now, from this distance, is the influence of my classmates. We taught each other; we may even have set careers for each other without realizing at the time that so fundamental an educational process was even going on. I am not so troubled as I used to be by the need to reform the medical school curriculum. What worries me these days is that the curriculum, whatever its sequential arrangement, has become so crowded with lectures and seminars, with such masses of data to be learned, that the students may not be having enough time to instruct each other in what may lie ahead.

～

Letter to Dr Coles
from The Doctor Stories *by* William Carlos Williams

'Look, you're not out on a four-year picnic at that medical school, so stop talking like a disappointed lover. You signed up for a spell of

6

training and they're dishing it out to you, and all you can do is take everything they've got, everything they hand to you, and tell yourself how lucky you are to be on the receiving end – so you can be a doctor, and that's no bad price to pay for the worry, the exhaustion.'

~

Why medicine and why not?
from Learning Medicine *by Peter Richards*

Why should so many school leavers, some of those finishing another degree course, and even those already established in a different career consider becoming doctors? A desire to help people is often given as a reason. But do not policemen, porters, and plumbers of sympathetic disposition do that? It surely is not necessary to become a doctor to help people. If more pastoral care is in mind why not become a priest, a social worker, or a school teacher? If a curing edge on caring is the attraction remember that doctors do not always cure. Better perhaps to become a pharmacologist developing new drugs rather than a jobbing doctor. Also understand that the cost of attempting to cure, whether by drugs or by knife, is sometimes to make worse. A doctor must accept and live with uncertainty and fallibility, inescapable parts of any walk of life but harder to bear in matters of life or death.

A love of meeting people is another common plea. Much nearer the mark was the applicant at interview who said, 'I like people,' then paused and added, 'Well, I don't like them all but I find them all interesting.' Success in many walks of life depends on an ability to communicate with all sorts of individuals. A doctor can become a trusted friend to very different people; doctors have the privilege of a passport to rich and poor alike. Unfortunately the practical domestic difficulties of one doctor providing continuity of care by day, by night, and at weekends and, in large cities, to a constantly changing population, are to some extent eroding the special relationship between doctor and patient.

An interest in how the body works in health or in disease itself often points to a career in medicine. The former interest might, however, best be served by becoming an anatomist or physiologist and devoting oneself to a lifetime study of the structure and function of the body. As for disease itself, many scientists study aspects of disease processes without having medical qualifications. Many more people

7

are curious about how the body works than either wish to or can become doctors.

More earthy considerations motivate many, although few are prepared to admit as much. Medicine has an 'up market' image, a social accolade; entry to medicine is often seen by parents, if not by their children, as the foot of a ladder leading to social advancement. Even schoolteachers are not always above pushing a pupil towards medicine because of the reflected glory of sending students to much sought after medical schools year by year – poor but inescapable reasons these. No less earthy but possibly less generative of stress is the simple search for a job which is both relatively secure and well paid. Many other careers are more or less as secure and well paid and in some respects less demanding. Nevertheless, medicine does offer a good and secure living and who knows whether an initially pragmatic motive prevents the emergence of a good doctor?

A desire for job satisfaction is often expressed at interview. Any job well done should give great satisfaction so this seems to be an insufficient reason of itself. Medicine is, however, favoured in that the routine is never without refreshing variety – the variety which is an inescapable part of mankind and womankind. Further, medicine is undoubtedly attractive as a springboard to very wide career opportunities, dealing with patients or not, as the case may be, and undertaking tasks which by and large are worldwide in their application. An international market still exists for medical graduates, albeit a shrinking one. But medicine is not unique because the world also beckons to engineers, scientists, lawyers, teachers, and nurses, to mention only a few.

Sometimes the reasons for considering medicine as a career are more personal, such as illness in the family, which has shown how much can be done to relieve suffering and anxiety, or disability such as mental handicap, which has shown how those affected can be helped to make the most of their abilities.

To be ill oneself is such a revealing experience that it prompted F.J. Ingelfinger, editor of the *New England Journal of Medicine*, then near the point of death himself, to write:

> In medical school, students are told about the perplexity, anxiety and misapprehension that may affect the patient ... and in the clinical years the fortunate and sensitive student may learn much from talking to those assigned to his supervision. But the effects of

lectures and conversations are ephemeral and are no substitute for actual experience. One might suggest, of course, that only those who have been hospitalised during their adolescent or adult years be admitted to medical school. Such a practice would not only increase the number of empathic doctors; it would also permit the whole elaborate system of medical school admissions to be jettisoned.

Few would accept personal experience of illness as the sole qualification for entry to medical school but as a supplementary qualification it has much to recommend it.

Some are drawn to medicine by the personal influence of a sympathetic local doctor or a medical relative. Admiration alone may be a slender reason for career choice, but when admiration is tempered with critical insight into what the job demands the reason is convincing. Doctors' children have a readily available opportunity to discover what medicine is about (although some do not take the trouble to find out). At the same time there is a danger that their career choice may simply represent the tramlines of unthinking predestination or the lure of easy entry into a thriving family business. At worst, a medical parent may exert pressure, a potentially deeply damaging influence on which Henry Fielding in *Tom Jones* blamed the failings of Dr Blifil, 'a gentleman who had the misfortune of losing the advantage of great talents by the obstinacy of his father, who would breed him to a profession he disliked ... the doctor had been obliged to study physick, or rather to say that he had studied it ...'

Medicine is no career for the faint hearted, nor for the weak in health, nor for complainers or clock watchers. Yet for all its demands it offers the opportunity of a deeply satisfying lifetime of service to those prepared to give themselves to it.

*

There is no royal road to learning medicine. The path is long, the demands heavy, and the sacrifices real. Learning never stops: it starts when the student is a spectator but sinks deep only when learning is through service. All doctors must continue to learn, and not only about new advances but to appreciate the limitations of all knowledge. They also need to learn humility in the face of their own imperfect understanding and their patients' courage.

The physician
by Hippocrates

The physician must have a worthy appearance; he should look healthy and be well-nourished, appropriate to his physique; for most people are of the opinion that those physicians who are not tidy in their own persons cannot look after others well. Further, he must look to the cleanliness of his person; he must wear decent clothes and use perfumes with harmless smells.

~

Dr Thorne
from Dr Thorne *by Anthony Trollope*

And thus Dr Thorne became settled for life in the little village of Greshamsbury. As was then the wont with many country practitioners, and as should be the wont with them all if they consulted their own dignity a little less and the comforts of their customers somewhat more, he added the business of a dispensing apothecary to that of physician. In doing so, he was of course much reviled. Many people around him declared that he could not truly be a doctor, or, at any rate, a doctor to be so called; and his brethren in the art living around him, though they knew that his diplomas, degrees, and certificates were all *en règle*, rather countenanced the report. There was much about this newcomer which did not endear him to his own profession. In the first place he was a newcomer, and, as such, was of course to be regarded by other doctors as being *de trop*. Greshamsbury was only fifteen miles from Barchester, where there was a regular dépôt of medical skill, and but eight from Silverbridge, where a properly established physician had been in residence for the last forty years. Dr Thorne's predecessor at Greshamsbury had been a humble-minded general practitioner, gifted with a due respect for the physicians of the county; and he, though he had been allowed to physic the servants, and sometimes the children at Greshamsbury, had never had the presumption to put himself on a par with his betters.

Then, also, Dr Thorne, though a graduated physician, though entitled beyond all dispute to call himself a doctor, according to all the laws of all the colleges, made it known to the East Barsetshire world, very soon after he had seated himself at Greshamsbury, that his rate of pay was to be seven-and-sixpence a visit within a circuit of five miles, with a proportionally increased charge at proportionally increased distances. Now there was something low, mean, unprofessional, and democratic in this; so, at least, said the children of Æsculapius gathered together in conclave at Barchester. In the first place, it showed that this Thorne was always thinking of his money, like an apothecary, as he was; whereas, it would have behoved him, as a physician, had he had the feelings of a physician under his hat, to have regarded his own pursuits in a purely philosophical spirit, and to have taken any gain which might have accrued as an accidental adjunct to his station in life. A physician should take his fee without letting his left hand know what his right hand was doing; it should be taken without a thought, without a look, without a move of the facial muscles; the true physician should hardly be aware that the last friendly grasp of the hand had been made more precious by the touch of gold. Whereas, that fellow Thorne would lug out half a crown from his breeches pocket and give it in change for a ten-shilling piece. And then it was clear that this man had no appreciation of the dignity of a learned profession. He might constantly be seen compounding medicines in the shop, at the left hand of his front door; not making experiments philosophically in materia medica for the benefit of coming ages – which, if he did, he should have done in the seclusion of his study, far from profane eyes – but positively putting together common powders for rural bowels, or spreading vulgar ointments for agricultural ailments.

A man of this sort was not fit society for Dr Fillgrave of Barchester. That must be admitted. And yet he had been found to be fit society for the old squire of Greshamsbury, whose shoe-ribbons Dr Fillgrave would not have objected to tie; so high did the old squire stand in the county just previous to his death. But the spirit of the Lady Arabella was known by the medical profession of Barsetshire, and when that good man died it was felt that Thorne's short tenure of Greshamsbury favour was already over. The Barsetshire regulars were, however, doomed to disappointment. Our doctor had already contrived to endear himself to the heir; and though there was not even then much personal love between him and the Lady Arabella, he kept his place at the great house unmoved, not only in the nursery and in the bed-rooms, but also at the squire's dining-table.

Now there was in this, it must be admitted, quite enough to make him unpopular among his brethren; and this feeling was soon shown in a marked and dignified manner. Dr Fillgrave, who had certainly the most respectable professional connexion in the county, who had a reputation to maintain, and who was accustomed to meet, on almost equal terms, the great medical baronets from the metropolis at the houses of the nobility – Dr Fillgrave declined to meet Dr Thorne in consultation. He exceedingly regretted, he said, most exceedingly, the necessity which he felt of doing so: he had never before had to perform so painful a duty; but, as a duty which he owed to his profession, he must perform it. With every feeling of respect for Lady—, – a sick guest at Greshamsbury, – and for Mr Gresham, he must decline to attend in conjunction with Dr Thorne. If his services could be made available under any other circumstances, he would go to Greshamsbury as fast as post-horses could carry him.

Then, indeed, there was war in Barsetshire. If there was on Dr Thorne's cranium one bump more developed than another, it was that of combativeness. Not that the doctor was a bully, or even pugnacious, in the usual sense of the word; he had no disposition to provoke a fight, no propense love of quarrelling; but there was that in him which would allow him to yield to no attack. Neither in argument nor in contest would he ever allow himself to be wrong; never at least to any one but to himself; and on behalf of his special hobbies, he was ready to meet the world at large.

It will therefore be understood, that when such a gauntlet was thus thrown in his very teeth by Dr Fillgrave, he was not slow to take it up. He addressed a letter to the Barsetshire Conservative *Standard*, in which he attacked Dr Fillgrave with some considerable acerbity. Dr Fillgrave responded in four lines, saying, that on mature consideration he had made up his mind not to notice any remarks that might be made on him by Dr Thorne in the public press. The Greshamsbury doctor then wrote another letter, more witty and much more severe than the last; and as this was copied into the Bristol, Exeter, and Gloucester papers, Dr Fillgrave found it very difficult to maintain the magnanimity of his reticence. It is sometimes becoming enough for a man to wrap himself in the dignified toga of silence, and proclaim himself indifferent to public attacks; but it is a sort of dignity which it is very difficult to maintain. As well might a man, when stung to madness by wasps, endeavour to sit in his chair without moving a muscle, as endure with patience and without reply the courtesies of a newspaper opponent. Dr Thorne wrote a third letter, which was too much for medical flesh and blood to bear. Dr Fillgrave answered it, not,

12

indeed, in his own name, but in that of a brother doctor; and then the war-raged merrily. It is hardly too much to say that Dr Fillgrave never knew another happy hour. Had he dreamed of what materials was made that young compounder of doses at Greshamsbury he would have met him in consultation, morning, noon, and night, without objection; but having begun the war, he was constrained to go on with it: his brethren would allow him no alternative. Thus he was continually being brought up to the fight, as a prize-fighter may be seen to be, who is carried up round after round, without any hope on his own part, and who, in each round, drops to the ground before the very wind of his opponent's blows.

But Dr Fillgrave, though thus weak himself, was backed in practice and in countenance by nearly all his brethren in the county. The guinea fee, the principle of *giving* advice and of selling no medicine, the great resolve to keep a distinct barrier between the physician and the apothecary, and, above all, the hatred of the contamination of a bill, were strong in the medical mind of Barsetshire. Dr Thorne had the provincial medical world against him, and so he appealed to the metropolis. The *Lancet* took the matter up in his favour, but the *Journal of Medical Science* was against him; the *Weekly Chirurgeon*, noted for its medical democracy, upheld him as a medical prophet, but the *Scalping Knife*, a monthly periodical got up in dead opposition to the *Lancet*, showed him no mercy. So the war went on, and our doctor, to a certain extent, became a noted character.

He had, moreover, other difficulties to encounter in his professional career. It was something in his favour that he understood his business; something that he was willing to labour at it with energy; and resolved to labour at it conscientiously. He had also other gifts, such as conversational brilliancy, an aptitude for true good fellowship, firmness in friendship, and general honesty of disposition, which stood him in stead as he advanced in life. But, at his first starting, much that belonged to himself personally was against him. Let him enter what house he would, he entered it with a conviction, often expressed to himself, that he was equal as a man to the proprietor, equal as a human being to the proprietress. To age he would allow deference, and to special recognized talent – at least, so he said; to rank, also he would pay that respect which was its clear recognized prerogative; he would let a lord walk out of a room before him if he did not happen to forget it; in speaking to a duke he would address him as his Grace; and he would in no way assume a familiarity with bigger men than himself, allowing to the bigger man the privilege of making the first advances. But beyond this he would admit that no man should walk the earth with head higher than his own.

He did not talk of these things much; he offended no rank by boasts of his own equality; he did not absolutely tell the Earl de Courcy in words, that the privilege of dining at Courcy Castle was to him no greater than the privilege of dining at Courcy Parsonage; but there was that in his manner that told it. The feeling in itself was perhaps good, and was certainly much justified by the manner in which he bore himself to those below him in rank; but there was folly in the resolution to run counter to the world's recognized rules on such matters; and much absurdity in his mode of doing so, seeing that at heart he was a thorough Conservative. It is hardly too much to say that he naturally hated a lord at first sight; but, nevertheless, he would have expended his means, his blood, and spirit, in fighting for the upper house of Parliament.

Such a disposition, until it was thoroughly understood, did not tend to ingratiate him with the wives of the country gentlemen among whom he had to look for practice. And then, also, there was not much in his individual manner to recommend him to the favour of ladies. He was brusque, authoritative, given to contradiction, rough though never dirty in his personal belongings, and inclined to indulge in a sort of quiet raillery, which sometimes was not thoroughly understood. People did not always know whether he was laughing at them or with them; and some people were, perhaps, inclined to think that a doctor should not laugh at all when called in to act doctorially.

When he was known, indeed, when the core of the fruit had been reached, when the huge proportions of that loving, trusting heart had been learned, and understood, and appreciated, when that honesty had been recognized, that manly, and almost womanly tenderness had been felt, then, indeed, the doctor was acknowledged to be adequate to his profession. To trifling ailments he was too often brusque. Seeing that he accepted money for the cure of such, he should, we may say, have cured them without an offensive manner. So far he is without defence. But to real suffering no one found him brusque; no patient lying painfully on a bed of sickness ever thought him rough.

~

The practice
from The Autobiography *by William Carlos Williams*

It's the humdrum, day-in, day-out, everyday work that is the real satisfaction of the practice of medicine; the million and a half patients a man has seen on his daily visits over a forty-year period of weekdays and Sundays that make up his life. I have never had a money practice; it would have been impossible for me. But the actual calling on people, at all times and under all conditions, the coming to grips with the intimate conditions of their lives, when they were being born, when they were dying, watching them die, watching them get well when they were ill, has always absorbed me.

I lost myself in the very properties of their minds: for the moment at least I actually became *them*, whoever they should be, so that when I detached myself from them at the end of a half-hour of intense concentration over some illness which was affecting them, it was as though I were re-awakening from a sleep. For the moment I myself did not exist, nothing of myself affected me. As a consequence I came back to myself, as from any other sleep, rested.

Time after time I have gone out into my office in the evening feeling as if I couldn't keep my eyes open a moment longer. I would start out on my morning calls after only a few hours' sleep, sit in front of some house waiting to get the courage to climb the steps and push the front-door bell. But once I saw the patient all that would disappear. In a flash the details of the case would begin to formulate themselves into a recognizable outline, the diagnosis would unravel itself, or would refuse to make itself plain, and the hunt was on. Along with that the patient himself would shape up into something that called for attention, his peculiarities, her reticences or candors. And though I might be attracted or repelled, the professional attitude which every physician must call on would steady me, dictate the terms on which I was to proceed. Many a time a man must watch the patient's mind as it watches him, distrusting him, ready to fly off at a tangent at the first opportunity; sees himself distrusted, sees the patient turn to someone else, rejecting him.

More than once we have all seen ourselves rejected, seen some hard-pressed mother or husband go to some other adviser when we know that the advice we have given him has been correct. That too is part of the game. But in general it is the rest, the peace of mind that comes from adopting the patient's condition as one's own to be struggled with toward a solution during those few minutes or that hour or those trying days when we are searching for causes, trying to relate this to that to build a reasonable basis for action which really gives us our peace. As I say, often after I have gone into my office harassed by personal perplexities of whatever sort, fatigued physically and mentally, after two hours of intense application to the work, I came out at the finish completely rested (and I mean rested) ready to smile and to laugh as if the day were just starting.

That is why as a writer I have never felt that medicine interfered with me but rather that it was my very food and drink, the very thing which made it possible for me to write. Was I not interested in man? There the thing was, right in front of me. I could touch it, smell it. It was myself, naked, just as it was, without a lie telling itself to me in its own terms. Oh, I knew it wasn't for the most part giving me anything very profound, but it was giving me terms, basic terms with which I could spell out matters as profound as I cared to think of.

I knew it was an elementary world that I was facing, but I have always been amazed at the authenticity with which the simple-minded often face that world when compared with the tawdriness of the public viewpoint exhibited in reports from the world at large. The public view which affects the behavior of so many is a very shabby thing when compared with what I see every day in my practice of medicine. I can almost say it is the interference of the public view of their lives with what I see which makes the difficulty, in most instances, between sham and a satisfactory basis of thought.

I don't care much about that, however. I don't care a rap what people are or believe. They come to me. I care for them and either they become my friends or they don't. That is their business. My business, aside from the mere physical diagnosis, is to make a different sort of diagnosis concerning them as individuals, quite apart from anything for which they seek my advice. That fascinates me. From the very beginning that fascinated me even more than I myself knew. For no matter where I might find myself, every sort of individual that it is possible to imagine in some phase of his development, from the highest to the lowest, at some time exhibited himself to me. I am sure I have seen them all. And all have contributed to my pie. Let the successful carry off their blue ribbons; I have known the unsuccessful, far better persons than their more lucky brothers. One can laugh at them both, whatever the costumes they adopt. And when one is able to reveal them to themselves, high or low, they are always grateful as they are surprised that one can so have revealed the inner secrets of another's private motives. To do this is what makes a writer worth heeding: that somehow or other, whatever the source may be, he has gone to the base of the matter to lay it bare before us in terms which, try as we may, we cannot in the end escape. There is no choice then but to accept him and make him a hero.

All day long the doctor carries on this work, observing, weighing, comparing values of which neither he nor his patients may know the significance. He may be insensitive. But if in addition to actually being an accurate craftsman and a man of insight he has the added quality of – some distress of mind, a restless concern with the . . . If he is not satisfied with mere cures, if he lacks ambition, if he is content to . . . If there is no content in him and likely to be none; if in other words, without wishing to force it, since that would interfere with his lifelong observation, he allows himself to be called a name! What can one think of him?

He is half-ashamed to have people suspect him of carrying on a clandestine, a sort of underhand piece of spying on the public at large. They naively ask him, 'How do you do it? How can you carry on an active business like that and at the same time find time to write? You must be superhuman. You must have at the very least the energy of two men.' But they do not grasp that one occupation complements the other, that they are two parts of a whole, that it is not two jobs at all, that one rests the man when the other fatigues him. The only person to feel sorry for is his wife. She practically becomes a recluse. His only fear is that the source of his interest, his daily going about among human beings of all sorts, all ages, all conditions will be terminated. That he will be found out.

As far as the writing itself is concerned it takes next to no time at all. Much too much is written every day of our lives. We are overwhelmed by it. But when at times we see through the welter of evasive or interested patter, when by chance we penetrate to some moving detail of a life, there is always time to bang out a few pages. The thing isn't to find the time for it – we waste hours every day doing absolutely nothing at all – the difficulty is to catch the evasive life of the thing, to phrase the words in such a way that stereotype will yield a moment of insight. That is where the difficulty lies. We are lucky when that underground current can be tapped and the secret spring of all our lives will send up its pure water. It seldom happens. A thousand trivialities push themselves to the front, our lying habits of

17

everyday speech and thought are foremost, telling us that *that* is what 'they' want to hear. Tell them something else. You know you want to be a successful writer. This sort of chitchat the daily practice of medicine tends drastically to cure.

Forget writing, it's a trivial matter. But day in day out, when the inarticulate patient struggles to lay himself bare for you, or with nothing more than a boil on his back is so caught off balance that he reveals some secret twist of a whole community's pathetic way of thought, a man is suddenly seized again with a desire to speak of the underground stream which for a moment has come up just under the surface. It is just a glimpse, an intimation of all that which the daily print misses or deliberately hides, but the excitement is intense and the rush to write is on again. It is then we see, by this constant feeling for a meaning, from the unselected nature of the material, just as it comes in over the phone or at the office door, that there is no better way to get an intimation of what is going on in the world.

We catch a glimpse of something, from time to time, which shows us that a presence has just brushed past us, some rare thing – just when the smiling little Italian woman has left us. For a moment we are dazzled. What was that? We can't name it; we know it never gets into any recognizable avenue of expression; men will be long dead before they can have so much as ever approached it. Whole lives are spent in the tremendous affairs of daily events without even approaching the great sights that I see every day. My patients do not know what is about them among their very husbands and children, their wives and acquaintances. But there is no need for us to be such strangers to each other, saving alone laziness, indifference and age-old besotted ignorance.

So for me the practice of medicine has become the pursuit of a rare element which may appear at any time, at any place, at a glance. It can be most embarrassing. Mutual recognition is likely to flare up at a moment's notice. The relationship between physician and patient, if it were literally followed, would give us a world of extraordinary fertility of the imagination which we can hardly afford. There's no use trying to multiply cases, it is there, it is magnificent, it fills my thoughts, it reaches to the farthest limits of our lives.

What is the use of reading the common news of the day, the tragic deaths and abuses of daily living, when for over half a lifetime we have known that they must have occurred just as they have occurred given the conditions that cause them? There is no light in it. It is trivial fill-gap. We know the plane will crash, the train be derailed. And we know why. No one cares, no one can care. We get the news and discount it, we are quite right in doing so. It is trivial. But the hunted news I get from some obscure patients' eyes is not trivial. It is profound: whole academies of learning, whole ecclesiastical hierarchies are founded upon it and have developed what they call their dialectic upon nothing else, their lying dialectics. A dialectic is any arbitrary system, which, since all systems are mere inventions, is necessarily in each case a false premise, upon which a closed system is built shutting those who confine themselves to it from the rest of the world. All men one way or another use a dialectic of some sort into which they are shut, whether it be an Argentina or a Japan. So each group is maimed. Each is enclosed in a dialectic cloud, incommunicado, and for that reason we rush into wars and prides of the most superficial natures.

Do we not see that we are inarticulate? That is what defeats us. It is our inability to communicate to another how we are locked within ourselves, unable to say the simplest thing of importance to one another, any of us, even the most valuable, that makes our lives like those of a litter of kittens in a wood-pile. That gives the physician, and I don't mean the high-priced psychoanalyst, his opportunity; psychoanalysis amounts to no more than another dialectic into which to be locked.

The physician enjoys a wonderful opportunity actually to witness the words being born. Their actual colors and shapes are laid before him carrying their tiny burdens which he is privileged to take into his care with their unspoiled newness. He may see the difficulty with which they have been born and what they are destined to do. No one else is present but the speaker and ourselves, we have been the words' very parents. Nothing is more moving.

But after we have run the gamut of the simple meanings that come to one over the years, a change gradually occurs. We have grown used to the range of communication which is likely to reach us. The girl who comes to me breathless, staggering into my office, in her underwear a still breathing infant, asking me to lock her mother out of the room; the man whose mind is gone – all of them finally say the same thing. And then a new meaning begins to intervene. For under that language to which we have been listening all our lives a new, a more profound language, underlying all the dialectics offers itself. It is what they call poetry. That is the final phase.

It is that, we realize, which beyond all they have been saying is what they have been trying to say. They laugh (For are they not laughable?); they can think of nothing more useless (What else are they but the same?); something made of words (Have they not been trying to use words all their lives?). We begin to see that the underlying meaning of all they want to tell us and have always failed to communicate is the poem, the poem which their lives are being lived to realize. No one will believe it. And it is the actual words, as we hear them spoken under all circumstances, which contain it. It is actually there, in the life before us, every minute that we are listening, a rarest element – not in our imaginations but there, there in fact. It is that essence which is hidden in the very words which are going in at our ears and from which we must recover underlying meaning as realistically as we recover metal out of ore.

The poem that each is trying actually to communicate to us lies in the words. It is at least the words that make it articulate. It has always been so. Occasionally that named person is born who catches a rumor of it, a Homer, a Villon, and his race and the world perpetuates his memory. Is it not plain why? The physician, listening from day to day, catches a hint of it in his preoccupation. By listening to the minutest variations of the speech we begin to detect that today, as always, the essence is also to be found, hidden under the verbiage, seeking to be realized.

But one of the characteristics of this rare presence is that it is jealous of exposure and that it is shy and revengeful. It is not a name that is bandied about in the market place, no more than it is something that can be captured and exploited by the academy. Its face is a particular face, it is likely to appear under the most unlikely disguises. You cannot recognize it from past appearances – in fact it is always a new face. It knows all that we are in the habit of describing. It will not use the same appearance for any new materialisation. And it is our very life. It is we ourselves, at our rarest moments, but inarticulate for the most part except when in the poem one man, every five or six hundred years, escapes to formulate a few gifted sentences.

The poem springs from the half-spoken words of such patients as the physician sees from day to day. He observes it in the peculiar, actual conformations in which its life is hid. Humbly he presents himself before it and by long practice he strives as best he can to interpret the manner of its speech. In that the secret lies. This, in the end, comes perhaps to be the occupation of the physician after a lifetime of careful listening.

How to be a doctor

from Literary Lapses *by Stephen Leacock*

Certainly the progress of science is a wonderful thing. One can't help feeling proud of it. I must admit that I do. Whenever I get talking to anyone – that is, to anyone who knows even less about it than I do – about the marvellous development of electricity, for instance, I feel as if I had been personally responsible for it. As for the linotype and the aeroplane and the vacuum house-cleaner, well, I am not sure that I didn't invent them myself. I believe that all generous-hearted men feel just the same way about it.

However, that is not the point I am intending to discuss. What I want to speak about is the progress of medicine. There, if you like, is something wonderful. Any lover of humanity (or of either sex of it) who looks back on the achievements of medical science must feel his heart glow and his right ventricle expand with the pericardiac stimulus of a permissible pride.

Just think of it. A hundred years ago there were no bacilli, no ptomaine poisoning, no diptheria, and no appendicitis. Rabies was but little known, and only imperfectly developed. All of these we owe to medical science. Even such things as psoriasis and parotitis and trypanosomiasis, which are now household names, were known only to the few, and were quite beyond the reach of the great mass of the people.

Or consider the advance of the science on its practical side. A hundred years ago it used to be supposed that fever could be cured by the letting of blood; now we know positively that it cannot. Even seventy years ago it was thought that fever was curable by the administration of sedative drugs; now we know that it isn't. For the matter of that, as recently as thirty years ago, doctors thought that they could heal a fever by means of low diet and the application of ice; now they are absolutely certain that they cannot. This instance shows the steady progress made in the treatment of fever. But there has been the same cheering advance all along the line. Take rheumatism. A few generations ago people with rheumatism used to have to carry round potatoes in their pockets as a means of cure. Now the doctors allow them to carry absolutely anything they like. They may go round with their pockets full of water-melons if they wish to. It makes no difference. Or take the treatment of epilepsy. It used to be supposed that the first thing to do in sudden attacks of this kind was to unfasten the patient's collar and let him breathe; at present, on the contrary, many doctors consider it better to button up the patient's collar and let him choke.

In only one respect has there been a decided lack of progress in the domain of medicine, that is in the time it takes to become a qualified practitioner. In the good old days a man was turned out thoroughly equipped after putting in two winter sessions at a college and spending his summers in running logs for a sawmill. Some of the students were turned out even sooner. Nowadays it takes anywhere from five to eight years to become a doctor. Of course, one is willing to grant that our young men are growing stupider and lazier every year. This fact will be corroborated at once by any man over fifty years of age. But even when this is said it seems odd that a man should study eight years now to learn what he used to acquire in eight months.

However, let that go. The point I want to develop is that the modern doctor's business is an extremely simple one, which could be acquired in about two weeks. This is the way it is done.

The patient enters the consulting-room. 'Doctor,' he says, 'I have a bad pain.' 'Where is it?' 'Here.' 'Stand up,' says the doctor, 'and put your arms up above your head.' Then the doctor goes behind the patient and strikes him a powerful blow in the back. 'Do you feel that,' he says. 'I do,' says the patient. Then the doctor turns suddenly and lets him have a left hook under the heart. 'Can you feel that,' he says viciously, as the patient falls over on the sofa in a heap. 'Get up,' says the doctor, and counts ten. The patient rises. The doctor looks him over very carefully without speaking, and then suddenly fetches him a blow in the stomach that doubles him up speechless. The doctor walks over to the window and reads the morning paper for a while. Presently he turns and begins to mutter more to himself than the patient. 'Hum!' he says, 'there's a slight anaesthesia of the tympanum.' 'Is that so?' says the patient, in an agony of fear. 'What can I do about it, doctor?' 'Well,' says the doctor, 'I want you to keep very quiet; you'll have to go to bed and stay there and keep quiet.' In reality, of course, the doctor hasn't the least idea what is wrong with the man; but he *does* know that if he will go to bed and keep quiet, awfully quiet, he'll either get quietly well again or else die a quiet death. Meantime, if the doctor calls every morning and thumps and beats him, he can keep the patient submissive and perhaps force him to confess what is wrong with him.

'What about diet, doctor?' says the patient, completely cowed.

The answer to this question varies very much. It depends on how the doctor is feeling and whether it is long since he had a meal himself. If it is late in the morning and the doctor is ravenously hungry, he says: 'Oh, eat plenty, don't be afraid of it; eat meat, vegetables, starch, glue, cement, anything you like.' But if the doctor has just had lunch and if his breathing is short-circuited with huckleberry-pie, he says very firmly: 'No, I don't want you to eat anything at all: absolutely not a bite; it won't hurt you, a little self-denial in the matter of eating is the best thing in the world.'

'And what about drinking?' Again the doctor's answer varies. He may say: 'Oh, yes, you might drink a glass of lager now and then, or, if you prefer it, a gin and soda or a whisky and Apollinaris, and I think before going to bed I'd take a hot Scotch with a couple of lumps of white sugar and bit of lemon-peel in it and a good grating of nutmeg on the top.' The doctor says this with real feeling, and his eye glistens with the pure love of his profession. But if, on the other hand, the doctor has spent the night before at a little gathering of medical friends he is very apt to forbid the patient to touch alcohol in any shape, and to dismiss the subject with great severity.

Of course, this treatment in and of itself would appear too transparent, and would fail to inspire the patient with a proper confidence. But nowadays this element is supplied by the work of the analytical laboratory. Whatever is wrong with the patient, the doctor insists on snipping off parts and pieces and extracts of him and sending them mysteriously away to be analysed. He cuts off a lock of the patient's hair, marks it, 'Mr Smith's Hair, October, 1910.' Then he clips off the lower part of the ear, and wraps it in paper, and labels it, 'Part of Mr Smith's Ear, October, 1910.' Then he looks the patient up and down, with the scissors in his hand, and if he sees any likely part of him he clips it off and wraps it up. Now this, oddly enough, is the very thing that fills the patient up with that sense of personal importance which is worth paying for. 'Yes,' says the bandaged patient, later in the day to a group of friends much impressed, 'the doctor thinks there may be a slight anaesthesia of the prognosis, but he's sent my ear to New York and my appendix to Baltimore and a lock of my hair to the editors of all the medical journals, and meantime I am to keep very quiet and not exert myself beyond drinking a hot Scotch with lemon and nutmeg every half-hour.' With that he sinks back faintly on his cushions, luxuriously happy.

And yet, isn't it funny?

You and I and the rest of us – even if we know all this – as soon as we have a pain within us, rush for a doctor as fast as a hack can take us. Yes, personally, I even prefer an ambulance with a bell on it. It's more soothing.

~

The status of doctors
Lecture given at the Royal Society of Medicine, London, 18 May
1966 by C.P. Snow

The reason I presume to talk to you is that for a long time I had to think about the status of engineering. This was something I had to do in my civil service career and, later on, in my spell in Government. In this country far too few people are becoming engineers and the few who do are not honoured, rewarded or esteemed very much by society. This is a real weakness on our part, as against other comparable countries; it is a great problem which none of us knows how to solve. But until we do solve it we are at a major economic disadvantage. During the course of my thoughts on engineers I have compared the engineering profession with the medical profession. Some of the facts about the two are not dissimilar: some of the education is not dissimilar, and one or two of the criticisms I am going to make of medical education may be applied equally to engineering education; and we are as short of doctors as we are of engineers.

Status is a very odd concept; it is a very subjective concept. None of us knows quite what it means, but it means something important. Although it is important in drawing people into a profession, it appears not to be by any means the most important single factor. For instance, in this country the Bar has traditionally had a very high status. The rewards are extremely high; even a moderately successful junior at the Bar makes more money than any but a handful of doctors or engineers. Yet at the present time there is a really chronic shortage of persons wanting to become barristers.

The status of both doctors and engineers in this country leaves much to be desired – more so for engineers than for doctors. Like engineers, doctors have a really serious professional training, and they have a much longer history. There were professional doctors in ancient Egypt. At Salerno, one of the oldest universities in the world, instruction was confined to medicine; this was the first of the universities of Europe, before Paris or Oxford.

It occurred to me to think about status in the three countries in which I have lived for any length of time – this country, the United States and the Soviet Union. There is the status accorded by general opinion – what the whole community thinks of these professions; and there is the status of what might be called informed or academic opinion. These may be somewhat different.

I will start with a very objective fact: there are still marriage brokers in New York. A marriage broker charges $300 if your daughter marries a doctor, $400 if she marries an attorney, $300 if she marries an engineer. These figures come from the Jewish marriage market in New York, and they seem to me to indicate roughly the relative status of these professions.

Not long ago the National Science Foundation in the United States did an opinion poll among the general population on the status of occupations, and the order was: first, doctors; second, scientists; third, politicians and academics who, oddly enough, got mixed up together; and then engineers a long way behind. I think we can take for granted that in the United States the status of doctors, so far as they have any status at all, is very high; it is not quite so high among academic opinion, for reasons I will come to, the main one being that doctors make far too much money.

In the Soviet Union the position is reversed: engineers have by far the highest social prestige, scientists are some way down the scale, doctors very much further down. In January 1966 the greatest of contemporary Soviet engineers, a man called Korolev, died of cancer at the age of 60. He had a state funeral and 40,000 people were reported to have attended. Would any doctor have a funeral of that size? This was the man behind the whole Russian space programme; he was a genuine and serious engineer.

In this country I think the order is somewhat different. Here the prestige order is, probably: first, scientists, largely owing to the traditional English respect for the high academics, the repute of the Royal Society, and so forth; second, doctors; third, engineers. I think most people in this country would accept that scientists are widely respected; doctors, although my friends tell me their prestige is going down, I think still come second; engineers, unfortunately for our economic future, are very low down.

Why is this? The answers, I suspect, are very complicated. We are all prudish about this, we find it hard to be honest, we do not even know what is the truth. But assuming we are not going to have complete egalitarianism (for which, as Bernard Shaw used to say, there is something to be said, in fact a good deal to be said), then I suspect that we leave to chance more than with other things the rewards for people in arduous, responsible professions that require long training.

When the Review Committee issued its report a friend of mine in the House of Commons criticized the awards for doctors on the ground that the industrial working class would take this very hard. On many things I agree with him, but not on this: I believe that society is perfectly prepared, in a country like ours, to accept at least modest differentials without much trouble, and we have to think what these differentials should be. Obviously, putting it harshly and crudely, we cannot afford to lose 300 doctors a year any more than we can lose a rather smaller number of good engineers.

Doctors' pay in the United States is very good. In the midwest I have seen suburbs inhabited by rich doctors and nobody else, which means that they are not terribly popular with the academic community, and this has probably separated them from the rest of society in a way which I think undesirable. I do not want to go into American medical politics but it is certainly true that doctors there are not regarded with unqualified enthusiasm by the society which they purport to serve.

In Russia, doctors' pay is genuinely poor, much less than that of engineers or scientists. In this country, I would say the pay of scientists, doctors and engineers is very close together, they are in the same professional belt. I do not believe you can distinguish within 10% at any level. Granted equality of training and equality of talent, then so far as I know the rate of pay on all sides should be the same. But an apparently highly paid profession like the Bar is not attracting candidates either quantitatively or qualitatively.

In this country, although there is a parallel between doctors and engineers, there is no doubt that doctors are more esteemed than engineers; doctors have a higher place in the popular imagination and I think also in the more esoteric imagination. A novelist can bring a doctor into a novel without any trouble at all, people know who he is; but try bringing an engineer into a novel and it is terribly difficult – they have not got recognition symbols in the way the medical profession has.

It is, I think, true that neither the engineering profession nor the medical profession plays its part in public life in the way that I certainly would like them to. Clearly it is to be expected that most people who have the professional training will in fact become doctors and engineers and nothing else; but it is true of many other professions, such as the law and science, that some members filter out great virtue and value to the community in other areas of activity. This does not happen in this country with engineers, and only to a limited extent with doctors.

Let me give an example: this is not a political speech in any sense, but I congratulate the Conservative Party on trying to get on good terms with the academic community. They are trying to set up committees, drawn of course from dons, which can give them academic advice, which will reach the universities of the country. The Labour Party did this in 1945 and many of the ideas which are now coming from the Labour Party sprang from this kind of academic advice. No one has thought of bringing in engineers, and certainly not doctors, to this kind of relation with politics. Why? Both professions have extremely intelligent, very widely experienced people, of sober judgement and so on, and yet the idea is effectively unthinkable. Dons are one thing and engineers and doctors are clearly another. We shall not get these great professions into their right perspective until it is automatic that they give advice on all kinds of things outside their ordinary workaday life, as we think of dons or economists giving advice.

In the same way I should like to see a tiny sprinkle of people leaving the medical profession and taking their part in public life, and far more engineers than now doing exactly the same thing. Again, it does not happen: there are a few doctors in the House of Commons, there are one or two in administration, but surprisingly few. This is not so in the Soviet Union: Kosygin is an engineer, Brezhnev is an engineer, Gromyko is an engineer; it seems that there is a level of professional infiltration into government which we completely lack, and I think this may become a serious weakness in the western world. I want not only engineers in the layer of government, but doctors also. I think they have a great deal of human wisdom to contribute, without which we shall be genuinely impoverished in any process of decision-making which we can foresee.

I am surprised that medical education has turned out to be a less good humane education than might have been expected. It has obviously become, for some reason, entirely professional, and that applies equally to some of the deficiencies of engineering education. Engineering education in this country is all right, it has produced

27

relatively good engineers, but nothing beyond. Medical education, to an extent, suffers from the same faults.

Doctors, in my experience, are better citizens than most of us; despite their temptations, they are relatively honest and upright and make relatively good husbands. They are pillars of society and yet there is a weakness; I believe the weakness to an extent springs from the temperament of those who elect to be doctors, but much more from the way they are trained. Doctors, like engineers, appear to be remarkably conformist, conformist in their young manhood, conformist in their professional life. The more I have thought of medical education the more I think that speculative and rebellious intelligence is surprisingly neglected – that part of the intelligence which makes people question, often foolishly, often nihilistically, often unrewardingly, but makes them question the whole of the axioms of the life which they lead. I believe this part is as deficient in medical education and in the medical profession as it is in the engineering profession. This is entirely contrary to what happens in pure science. Pure scientists are an awful nuisance – they are so as young men, and they are not much less of a nuisance until they are very old indeed; and yet they are intensely valuable because their speculative and rebellious intelligence is never quenched, it is encouraged by the process, it is there all the time; and that is why any government at any time is going to have scientists probably playing a really active part within it.

I was once a tutor at Cambridge and I loved my medical students for whom I was responsible. But compared with the rest of the students in the college they were, together with the engineers, by far the most conservative part of the whole body of students. These were people who would never do anything which was intellectually rebellious. Some of them made nuisances of themselves on Boat Race night and May Week nights, drank hard, chased girls; that was fun, they were hearty, cheerful characters who would make good citizens; but they did not, as I dearly should have liked them to do, question the assumptions in the way my scientific students did.

It is not that I want all medical students immediately to belong to the left wing organizations of our universities. What I want is a scatter. It is bad for any profession if all its entrants are automatically more conformist and more conservative than their contemporaries. This is happening now to medical students and engineering students. Statistically there is no doubt about it, these are the people who by the standards of modern student society are on the conservative side, and they never budge. It seems to me that the medical profession should think a little about this education. What is lacking? These people are no different from others. Of my pupils some had a sense of genuine dedication, a vocation, some came in because their fathers were doctors, a surprisingly large number, I remember. They were good human material, but they were never given much chance to think. I would have thought that preclinical education was extremely dull. Medical education wants some re-thinking, it wants some adjuncts probably entirely outside medical subjects, and to give these people something to make their imagination work, or it will never work again in their lives.

Engineers likewise start with a highly disciplined course, highly professional from the outset, and never have a chance to stretch their speculative intelligence until they become old men. I would like to see both disciplines have something like social history, economics, as a compulsory part of the pre-professional stage. This would mean they would have to think, be exposed to argument and know what it means, know that in fact traditional instruction is not the only thing in the world.

I do not think doctors suffer from the other great weakness of engineers, that is, their complete lack of verbalism. Engineers can often be extremely clever but they cannot spell and they cannot speak. The doctors I have known are extremely articulate. I suspect the descriptive processes they have to go through, both themselves and presumably with their patients, are extremely good verbal training, and I do not think it is an accident that the one thing the medical profession has done, apart from producing doctors, is to produce writers. I do not think it is an accident that there are almost no engineering writers, and very few from the scientific professions. On the other hand, the medical profession has produced some really good writers in the last hundred years.

I will not reproach doctors for lack of verbiage, which is one of the defects of the engineering profession, but I do reproach them for the lack of speculative intelligence in medical education.

This situation is not helped by the extreme specialization from which we are all suffering. We try to squeeze into a qualifying graduate course a content which thirty years ago would have been thought impossible. (Sir J. Chadwick once told me he thought the practical content of a physics Part II at Cambridge was about twice what it was in his time). This is true not only in medicine and engineering but in academic life generally. There must be qualifying examinations, possibly less factual but more scientific than at present; and then post-graduate courses should be added. We cannot possibly, when there is an accumulation of knowledge which is going to increase exponentially for a long time, expect our bright children to go into medicine and qualify between 21 and 24 without strain and without loss. The brightest ones will not do it: if given the choice they will prefer something like economics.

That brings me to what is really the core of what I want to say. If we get the education right, I believe we shall get some part of the status of the medical profession right. Here I am thinking very largely of general practitioners, since the real problem is the function of the general practitioner in society. Here we have two things, one is the esteem in which society holds doctors, and the other is the part which the doctor gives to society. I am not going to be hypocritical; I believe it is a one-sided contract, more one-sided than most of us realize. Any possible system that I can imagine is going to require a doctor to give more to society than society can give him, of that I am quite sure; in other places I have been I have known this is true. The work is always there, intolerably arduous, intolerably responsible, much more so than in most professions and whatever the rewards, they will not be sufficient. This will always be true. If I were a doctor I should not think this entirely to my disadvantage: I should feel my conscience was pretty clear because of it. But, that being said, our general practitioners do seem to have a unique function in society, through the possibility that they may be nuclei which can to some extent help avoid or help minimize the fractionization which is going on in the whole of advanced life, in the whole of advanced society, and in particular in the whole of advanced England. I believe that some kind of foci are going to be desperately significant.

None of us knows what is happening to our society; in many material ways people are living more comfortably than they have ever lived in the whole of human history. That is obvious, and yet there are great dangers. I doubt if we have the social insight to see how deep these dangers are, but we can see their efflorescence in the increase of crime and juvenile delinquency and so on. The kind of forces which bind society together are getting very weak. This is a thing which my Russian friends are constantly worried about, and some of their activities which puzzle us are explained by this reason. In this country and in America, modern life is becoming entirely deprived of any sense of community. There is no wise man, the religion which was preached is no longer listened to. We have to find people who are respected, who are on the spot, who are sensible and who can perform some kind of function of religion. I believe that general practitioners have always understood this, and certainly in the suburb where I was born, the one person I knew when I was a child, who was educated and relatively humane and wanted the children of the parish to get on, was the local GP. I do not think he was a very clever GP, though he kept us all alive, but he was a nice and good man, in one of the early suburbs of a provincial town. How are we going to continue and possibly develop this particular spiritual and social function of general practitioners? I do not know, but I know it is desperately important. I know also that there are organizational reasons which make it very difficult. I cannot go into that, except to say that obviously people with thousands and thousands of patients cannot possibly practice, in the sense I mean, very effectively.

I want to go on with something else, not the organizational problem, but the conflict between this social function of the general practitioner as I conceive it, and the claims of scientific medicine. It seems to me that if we think only of scientific medicine, only of how people's bodies are actually working and how they are to be made to work, it is possible to imagine a system from which the human and social leadership might easily be eliminated within a generation. You would have an immense computer service, with very large groups of general practitioners working comparatively anonymously and, in cases where the computer showed any sign of doubt, at once rushing patients off to the nearest specialist. To an extent this happens in America and in other societies. I believe it is a perfectly efficient way of conducting a large part of medicine. But I believe it may take away the unique contribution which medicine can bring to our world. People want not only to be kept alive and working properly, they want to be cheered, they want some sort of stimulus some sort of contact, they want, in fact, a leader. Here we have to resolve an extremely delicate and very difficult balance between what scientific medicine requires and what the personal relation between physician and patient also requires.

I do not begin to know the answer. This is a matter for medical persons who know all the real facts and all the real possibilities of scientific medicine and all the real resources of computerized knowledge. But I am sure there is a problem and I am perfectly clear that if the personal side is left out we shall be desperately at fault. Let me remind

31

you of a popular television programme called 'Dr Finlay's Casebook', which is enshrined very deeply in the hearts of people; it shows something which people need – not only want, but need – a real friend, in a society which is constantly getting further from any kind of personal relationship. This we must not lose, and this is what doctors can uniquely give.

~

The seven sins of medicine
from Richard Asher Talking Sense *by Richard Asher*

There is an unlimited number of medical sins, but I am going to catalogue and comment on seven of them in the hope that those students who wish to avoid them may do so and those who wish to indulge in them may enlarge their repertoire or refine their technique. The seven sins are obscurity, cruelty, bad manners, over-specialisation, love of the rare, stupidity, and sloth.

OBSCURITY

Both in writing and in lecturing clear style and short words are best. Obscurity is bad, not only because it is difficult to understand but also because it is confused with profundity, just as a shallow muddy pool may look deep. Here is an example from a recent article. The writers wanted to say: 'We judge men's health by their working-places and their homes', but they imbedded their meaning in this sentence: 'It is generally accepted that the evaluation of the nutritional status of a community should include assessments of the environmental conditions under which individual members live and work.' As Mr Ivor Brown has pointed out, such writing produces a slow weak ooze of words instead of a keen forceful jet. The double negative is a common way of making a simple statement harder to understand, and if we read 'It is by no means far from infrequently that the absence of tubercle bacilli is not invariably detected', few of us can say whether tubercle bacilli are present or not (nor do we care).

I warn students taking histories against turning the simple English of their patients into the jargon of their textbooks. If a patient says 'if I go half-way up a hill I feel I'm done for', these very words should appear in the notes rather than 'The patient complains that during ambulation up a moderate incline he suffers a feeling of impending dissolution'.

CRUELTY

Cruelty is probably the most important and prevalent sin in the list I have chosen. Usually it is due to thoughtlessness, and not deliberate.

Mental cruelty is common and arises in three ways: (1) by saying too much; (2) by saying too little; and (3) by the patient being forgotten. By saying too much we often burden a patient with a load of anxiety which adds to the illness we are trying to relieve. Many times I have seen patients who felt well till they were told they had high blood-pressure or a heart murmur, and since that time have been afflicted with every grievous symptom which could be gathered from hearsay, from patent medicine advertisements, and from 'The Home Doctor'. Before telling a patient anything of his illness it is essential to consider whether it will help him or harm him, and with a little practice one soon learns what it is wise to say.

By saying too little one can cause the fear of the unknown; the gaps may be filled in by the patient with alarming inventions and superstitions. That is why some explanation should be given to the patient who is discharged from hospital, both so that some of his groundless fears are removed and so that if he gets under the care of another doctor he can give a moderately accurate account of what he has had. The doctor should know what fears and superstitions are common among patients so that he may allay them and prevent mental cruelty. For example, a patient with shingles has nearly always been told by his grandmother that 'if they meet in the middle you die', and the assurance that neither will they meet nor will he die may give him much relief. Patients with mild arthritis are usually terrified of becoming 'crippled with rheumatism', and, similarly, many patients with bronchitis dread tuberculosis; in these cases reassurance is more important than medicine, and it is the doctor's duty to dig out these fears if possible.

Lastly, forgetting the patient. I refer to that kind of bedside teaching and discussion where the patient is treated as if he were unconscious, or discussed as if he already lay on the necropsy slab. It must be remembered that patients have ears, and that sotto-voice murmurings about polysyllabic diseases strike needless terror into their hearts.

Physical cruelty: over-investigation is a form of physical cruelty. If a man is dying of secondary cancer and the primary cancer will soon be discovered at necropsy, it is cruel to make his last days uncomfortable by playing at 'hunt the primary' as one might play 'hunt the slipper', and it gives extra work to the radiologists and pathologists. Patients dying of heart-failure are happier without cardiac catheters, arterial punctures, and other tests beloved of those who judge a patient with heart-failure by his cardiac output in litres per minute rather than by the number of stairs he can climb.

Here are some minor cruelties which can easily be avoided. Do not give mersalyl in the evening, so keeping the patient awake passing urine all night. Do not do a fractional test-meal on a patient with pernicious anaemia when he is admitted with a haemoglobin in the twenties; put his haemoglobin up with liver treatment first – his achlorhydria will keep. Do not play at 'pushing the parkinsonian'; there are enough signs of parkinsonism to diagnose a case without pushing him in the back to see how far he totters forward. Do not put sticking plaster on hairy limbs; you can easily shave them first. Do not wheel elaborate trolleys to a patient's bedside and start sticking needles in him until you have given him a word of reassurance and explanation.

BAD MANNERS

If students do not learn good manners while they are learning medicine they will be at a great disadvantage in dealing with patients, nurses, and colleagues.

Towards patients. I once asked a student to examine the abdomen of a patient lying in an outpatient cubicle. He dashed into the cubicle where she lay, flung back the blanket, plumped his hand on her abdomen, shouted 'Gosh, what a beauty' (he was referring to the patient's enlarged spleen and not to her personal appearance), and dashed out again. Such behaviour must be condemned.

Other forms of bad manners are: (1) impatience in taking a history from a slow-witted patient; (2) making jokes at the expense of the patient; and (3) reading the patient's newspaper which lies on his bed and displays headlines far more exciting than the story the patient is telling.

Towards nurses. Students will find that a courteous good morning to the sisters makes their access to patients and to ward equipment much easier. (In America the remark 'Good morning, sister', is equivalent to saying 'How goes it, honey?' and should be avoided.) Too many students or house-men call for a nurse in the manner of an impatient diner calling for a waiter.

Towards medical staff. Years ago a student would take his hands out of his pockets even if a registrar passed him, and almost grovel at the sight of a chief. Perhaps the senior staff had too much majesty and pomp in those days, but the pendulum has swung in the other direction today. At any rate, I advise students not to examine an abdomen with one hand in the pocket, because it is an inefficient way of palpating; it will irritate physicians and give a bad impression in the examination hall. In general, students should aim at a reasonable respect for their seniors but avoid an oily deference. I further caution them against bad manners when they become more senior, and suggest such courtesies as asking their colleagues' permission before seeing a case in their wards, and writing and congratulating them on their publications or appointments.

OVER-SPECIALISATION

It is right that a doctor should have special interest and knowledge about one subject. It is wrong for him to show special indifference and ignorance about all other subjects. A good doctor should be a jack-of-all-trades and master of one. For example, a surgeon should be able to advise a patient with simple obesity about her diet and not refer her to an endocrine clinic; a gynaecologist should be capable of treating a mild iron-deficiency anaemia without referring her to an anaemia clinic; and a physician ought to squash a small ganglion on the back of the hand with his thumbs (or bible). I have known an eye surgeon after seeing a case of retinitis pigmentosa write in the notes: 'This might be part of the Laurence-Moon-Biedl syndrome; is there any evidence of polydactyly?' For an ophthalmologist to feel himself incapable of counting fingers is surely the limit of over-specialisation; and, if nothing is done to stop this tendency, we shall have one physician who specialises in the first heart sound, and the other who is only concerned with the second.

Perhaps the worst feature of specialisation is that it makes doctors feel they are doing wrong to deal with even the simplest case if it lies within the protected area of somebody else's specialty. Particularly is this the case with psychiatry, which is regarded by other doctors with a mixture of suspicion, reverence, and ridicule. In Noel Coward's *Blithe Spirit* a character, referring to psychotherapy, says: 'I refuse to go through months of expensive humiliation in order to find that at the age of ten I was desperately in love with my rocking-horse.' A surgeon or a physician faced with a patient exhibiting some 'functional' symptoms is likely to take a similar attitude, feeling that the origin of the simplest psychoneurotic symptoms lies buried in an uncharted swamp in which only the expert can poke with impunity – a swamp crawling with complexes and repressions, where nothing is what it seems and everything symbolises something indecent. This is a foolish attitude to take; a sensible physician or surgeon should be able to give wise counsel in the simpler case of neurosis.

Further, there is a complication of specialisation – that it allows bees to remain undisturbed within their masters' bonnets so that the allergist looks at the world through allergic-coloured glasses and beams myopically at a world where everything is allergic.

LOVE OF THE RARE (SPANOPHILIA)

This sin is more prevalent among students, because they lack the experience that teaches which illnesses are common and which are rare. It is responsible for the failure of bookworms to pass exams. Headache and vomiting are more often due to migraine than to cerebral tumour; nose-bleeding is more often due to picking the nose than to multiple hereditary haemorrhagic telangiectasis; and wasting of the small muscles of the hand occurs in old age and rheumatoid arthritis more often than in motor-neurone disease or cervical rib.

COMMON STUPIDITY

By this I mean the opposite of common sense – common nonsense in fact. There are many kinds of this particular sin, but I think the commonest type is what might be called therapeutic automatism. No illness has a rigid code of treatments which must be advised in all circumstances; one must cut one's therapeutic coat according to the mental and economic cloth of one's patient. It is mere foolishness to order an elaborate dict for a busy working-class woman with instructions to add on the fourth day 1¾ oz of steamed red mullet to the graduated scheme prescribed. I saw the finest example of therapeutic automatism as a medical student when I was skating one winter on the local squire's pond, watching all the quality displaying their skill. A woman fell and broke her tibia. I longed to treat her, but I was only a student. 'She mustn't be moved till the doctor comes; we must treat her for shock,' cried all the bystanders. It was only at the last moment that these zealous first-aiders were persuaded to abandon their treatment and drag the lady off the ice; otherwise the patient, together with a valuable collection of furs, might have been lost. I mention this to show that patients should never be treated by rote and rule, for there may be special circumstances.

SLOTH

Medical sloth can be physical or mental. Physical sloth exists more than we like to admit. When bloodbanks and standard apparatus made transfusion quick and easy, the number of transfusions quadrupled in a few years, which makes it regrettably apparent that the easiness of treatment rather than its urgency may decide whether or not it is given.

Physical sloth: this often causes the omission of blood-pressure estimations, ophthalmoscopy, or rectal examination, and leads to lapses in aseptic ritual (if a lumbar-puncture needle touches the bedclothes, it is tempting to pretend not to notice it). Physical sloth may also affect the overworked nurse who, tired of counting respirations, adds one more twenty to the row of twenties already on the chart, and this may stretch the doctor's powers of belief greatly.

Mental sloth: this is commoner and more important. Especially in history-taking is sloth the great danger. If the day is hot, the patient deaf, the doctor in a hurry, and the history garnished with reminiscences and irrelevances, it requires enormous patience and concentration to distil the essence from it. One form of unconscious sloth is worth special mention. Do not accept the patient's diagnosis when taking a history – find out his symptoms. Rheumatic fever at the age of 10 years is important, but the patient's statement that he had it needs amplification. He may have been one day in bed with a pain in the ankle which his aunt said was rheumatic fever or, on the other hand, may have been twelve weeks in bed with flitting joint pains of great severity starting after a sore throat. Similarly with diet (so important a part of the history in cases of anaemia), do not write 'adequate' or 'fair', but find out what exactly your patient eats at each meal, and you will be astonished how many women are living on bread and margarine and countless cups of tea.

Lastly, beware of sloth in thinking. If you are too lazy to think for yourselves, you will fall an easy prey to the less thoughtful papers and publications, blindly accepting the myth and mumpsimus against which John Forbes has so ably warned us. If you cultivate a healthy doubt (without being unduly sceptical) you may have the experience of the Queen of the Fairies in *Iolanthe*:

> 'On fire that glows
> With heat intense
> I turn the hose
> Of common sense
> And out it goes
> At small expense.'

Please adopt this attitude with everything I have said, and realise that much of it may be nonsense.

~

Doubtful character borne by the medical profession
from the preface to The Doctor's Dilemma
by George Bernard Shaw

Again I hear the voices indignantly muttering old phrases about the high character of a noble profession and the honor and conscience of its members. I must reply that the medical profession has not a high character; it has an infamous character. I do not know a single thoughtful and well-informed person who does not feel that the tragedy of illness at present is that it delivers you helplessly into the hands of a profession which you deeply mistrust, because it not only advocates and practises the most revolting cruelties in the pursuit of knowledge, and justifies them on grounds which would equally justify practising the same cruelties on yourself or your children, or burning down London to test a patent fire extinguisher, but, when it has shocked the public, tries to reassure it with lies of breath-bereaving brazenness. That is the character the medical profession has got just now. It may be deserved or it may not: there it is at all events: and the doctors who have not realized this are living in a fool's paradise. As to the honor and conscience of doctors, they have as much as any other class of men, no more and no less. And what other men dare pretend to be impartial where they have a strong pecuniary interest on one side? Nobody supposes that doctors are less virtuous than judges; but a judge whose salary and reputation depended on whether the verdict was for plaintiff or defendant, prosecutor or prisoner, would be as little trusted as a general in the pay of the enemy. To offer me a doctor as my judge, and then weight his decision with a bribe of a large sum of money and a virtual guarantee that if he makes a mistake it can never be proved against him, is to go wildly beyond the ascertained strain which human nature will bear. It is simply unscientific to allege or believe that doctors do not under existing circumstances perform unnecessary operations and manufacture and prolong lucrative ill-nesses. The only ones who can claim to be above suspicion are those who are so much sought after that their cured patients are immedi-ately replaced by fresh ones. And there is this curious psychological fact to be remembered: a serious illness or a death advertizes the doc-tor exactly as a hanging advertizes the barrister who defended the person hanged. Suppose, for example, a royal personage gets some-thing wrong with his throat, or has a pain in his inside. If a doctor effects some trumpery cure with a wet compress or a peppermint lozenge nobody takes the least notice of him. But if he operates on the throat and kills the patient, or extirpates an internal organ and keeps the whole nation palpitating for days whilst the patient hovers in pain and fever between life and death, his fortune is made: every rich man who omits to call him in when the same symptoms appear in his household is held not to have done his utmost duty to the patient. The wonder is that there is a king or queen left alive in Europe.

∼

The medical profession
from The Best of Myles *by Myles na Gopaleen*

The medical profession, remember, wasn't always the highly organ-ised racket that it is today. In your grandfather's time practically anybody could take in hand (whatever that means) to be a physician or surgeon and embark on experiments which frequently involved terminating other people's lives. Be that as it may, certain it is that Chapman in his day was as fine a surgeon as ever wore a hat. Chapman took in hand to be an ear nose and throat man and in many an obscure bedroom he performed prodigies which, if reported in the secular press, would have led to a question in the House. Keats, of course, always went along to pick up the odd guinea that was going for the anaesthetist. Chapman's schoolday lessons in carpentry often saved him from making foolish mistakes.

On one occasion the two savants were summoned to perform a delicate antrum operation. This involved opening up the nasal passages and doing a lot of work in behind the forehead. The deed was done and the two men departed, leaving behind a bleeding ghost suffering severely from what is nowadays called 'postoperative debility'. But through some chance the patient lived through the night, and the following day seemed to have some slim chance of surviving. Weeks passed and there was no mention of his death in the papers. Months passed. Then Chapman got an unpleasant surprise. A letter from the patient containing several pages of abuse, obviously written with a hand that quivered with pain. It appeared that the patient after 'recovering' somewhat from the operation, developed a painful swelling at the top of his nose. This condition progressed from pain to agony and eventually the patient took to consuming drugs made by his brother, who was a blacksmith. These preparations apparently did more harm than good and the patient had now written to Chapman demanding that he should return and restore the patient's health and retrieve the damage that had been done; otherwise that the brother would call to know the reason why.

'I think I know what is wrong with this person,' Chapman said. 'I missed one of the needles I was using. Perhaps we had better go and see him.' Keats nodded.

When they arrived the patient could barely speak, but he summoned his remaining strength to utter a terrible flood of bad language at the selfless men who had come a long journey to relieve pain. A glance by the practised eye of Chapman revealed that one of the tiny instruments had, indeed, been sewn up (inadvertently) in the wound, subsequently causing grandiose suppurations. Chapman got to work again, and soon retrieved his property. When the patient was re-sewn and given two grains, the blacksmith brother arrived and kindly

offered to drive the two men home in his trap. The offer was grate-
fully accepted. At a particularly filthy part of the road, the blacksmith
deliberately upset the trap, flinging all the occupants into a morass of
muck. This, of course, by way of revenge, accidentally on purpose.

That evening Chapman wore an expression of sadness and depression. He neglected even to do his twenty lines of Homer, a nightly
chore from which he had never shrunk in five years.

'To think of the fuss that fellow made over a mere needle, to think
of his ingratitude,' he brooded. 'Abusive letters, streams of foul language, and finally arranging to have us fired into a pond full of filth!
And all for a tiny needle! Did you ever hear of such vindictiveness!'

'He had it up his nose for you for a long time,' Keats said.

~

Never drop dead around a specialist
from The Most of S.J. Perelman *by S.J. Perelman*

Tennis . . . produced an incident not without drama just before I left
Martha's Vineyard. I was playing doubles against a pair of people,
one of them a New York dermatologist, one very hot afternoon. My
partner was a 62-year-old grain broker from Chicago, an excellent
player but inclined to overdo. He'd already played three sets that
afternoon, but as there was a gallery of attractive ladies, he wouldn't
quit . . .

Well our opponents, sensing my inadequacy at the net, kept lobbing
my partner in the rear court and after some exhausting footwork he
caved in with a thrombosis . . . The ironic part of the thing though
was that the dermatologist didn't want to get involved. No doctor
likes to be confronted with a dead patient and he kept saying that
somebody ought to call a doctor, meaning a general practitioner.

While all the excitement was going on, the next team of players
arrived, one of them a fancy surgeon. He was appealed to, took a quick
look at the victim and said, 'Get a doctor, somebody! Forty love!'

Well, we were just braiding our arms to carry the sufferer into a
hotel room nearby so that he wouldn't spoil everybody's fun by dying
in the middle of the set, when another doc pulled up in a car. This one
was a pediatrician, and we fully expected him to shear off and say he
treated only measles.

Luckily, a bystander managed to get hold of an ordinary three-dollar medico and my partner will be back in the wheat pit gouging his associates before the snow flies. I guess the moral is, never drop dead around a specialist.

~

Drip feed
from Low Life *by Jeffrey Bernard*

I wasn't feeling very well last week. My man who dealt with my chest complaint implied that I might have lung cancer and the thought didn't concentrate the mind, as Doctor Johnson said, but dulled it and made the approach to this wretched typewriter something of an obstacle course. But last Monday, during a visit to Brompton Chest Hospital, a specialist told me that I had nothing 'sinister'. I drew a great breath of relief which made me cough for five minutes. Now this specialist struck me as being something of a shrewd nut. He guessed that I had the odd cigarette and cocktail, and how can you tell that looking at a bronzed Greek god across a desk in a consulting room? God only knows. What did fascinate me was the sight of my heart on the X-ray screen. It's there all right and it looks a lot bigger than it feels. Furthermore, it is not broken as I'd thought it was in an emotional accident I had in 1972 when Juliet told me for the last time, 'You make me sick.'

But what a bloody miracle this body is. If you fed into a cow or a horse what some of us consume in one day, what on earth would happen? I'd very much like to wake up one morning with a cow of the Friesian variety and walk her down to Soho to the Coach & Horses, stopping on the way to buy twenty Players, ply her with vodkas until closing time, whip her off to an Indian restaurant, take her up to the Colony Room Club till 5.30 and then to the Yorkminster, Swiss Tavern, Three Greyhounds, get beaten up by Chinese waiters at midnight, have a row with a taxi driver, set the bed on fire, put it out with tears and then wake up on the floor. Could you then milk the said cow? I doubt it.

During one of my animal visits to the great Fred Winter's yard I said to him, 'Good God, Fred, your horses look magnificent. Beautifully fit.' 'Of course they do, you twit,' he said. 'They don't sit up all night drinking gin and tonic and playing cards.' Anyway, although the past four months have been a bore and then a fright for me, I shall never be converted to jogging, wheat germ, deep-breathing exercises, free-range women or press-ups. It's put-downs and not press-ups that keep a man on his toes. But, as I say, this body never ceases to amaze me. It's very rebellious. It won't lie down. Now that the right lung is mere scar tissue it comes up with another card. The legs and feet are aching and it's got to be circulatory problems. The eyes are deteriorating all the time and what is in good nick doesn't get put to the test as often as it did in the old days or would wish to now. And one of the problems of losing weight is that you get a bony arse and the only thing I can sit on in comfort is a bar stool.

But the crunch is, I suppose, the brain. It's never had more than two or three tracks but they are now in need of repair and like British Rail I shall devote future Sundays to repairing them with Perrier water, the Oxford Dictionary, sackcloth, and ashes. The old nonsense about dying brain cells isn't nonsense. I'm starting a book (I shall bore you with excerpts in the near future) and the difficulty is not being able to remember anything before last Tuesday except for the odd bet, lady, fight and unpaid bill. The fact that my hands tremble indicates no more than a sensitive nature but the fact that my head trembles too has initiated my making another appointment at St Stephen's.

Talking of St Stephen's, I must mention the Registrar, Dr McNab, who nursed me through my pneumonic and pleuristic days. I have always held that ninety nine per cent of the medical profession were, and are, idiots: the playing God with the white coat and talking to you with the sing-song voice as though you were a twelve-year-old half-wit. But this man, like the specialist at the Brompton chest pad, has restored faith. Not often is it that you meet a man you can immediately trust. Very few spring to mind. I can now add Doctors McNab and Collins to the list comprising the first Duke of Wellington, Mr Micawber, Rocky Graziano, Fred Winter, my brothers, my ex-wife Ashley and the breakfast television weather forecaster on BBC. I used to think that you could go into the jungle with my old doctor in Suffolk but he died of drink having told me for five years to abstain.

Nursing

Nursing in the 1830s
by Sir James Paget

I believe, indeed, that fifty years ago the admission of young ladies to be nurses in this [St Bartholomew's] or any similar hospital could not have been seriously proposed. It would have been called indecent, audacious, unprincipled, and I know not what besides; and the notion of their being associated with medical students would have been deemed utterly vile; nothing but vile mischief would have been foretold of it.

~

Nurses
from The Youngest Science by Lewis Thomas

When my mother became a registered nurse at Roosevelt Hospital, in 1903, there was no question in anyone's mind about what nurses did as professionals. They did what the doctors ordered. The attending physician would arrive for his ward rounds in the early morning, and when he arrived at the ward office the head nurse would be waiting for him, ready to take his hat and coat, and his cane, and she would stand while he had his cup of tea before starting. Entering the ward, she would hold the door for him to go first, then his entourage of interns and medical students, then she followed. At each bedside, after he had conducted his examination and reviewed the patient's progress, he would tell the nurse what needed doing that day, and she would write it down on the part of the chart reserved for nursing notes. An hour or two later he would be gone from the ward, and the work of the rest of the day and the night to follow was the nurse's frenetic occupation. In addition to the stipulated orders, she had an endless list of routine things to do, all learned in her two years of nursing school: the beds had to be changed and made up with fresh sheets by an exact geometric design of folding and tucking impossible for anyone but a trained nurse; the patients had to be washed head to foot; bedpans had to be brought, used, emptied, and washed; temperatures had to be taken every four hours and meticulously recorded on the chart; enemas were to be given; urine and stool samples collected, labeled, and sent off to the laboratory; throughout the day and night, medications of all sorts, usually pills and various vegetable extracts and tinctures, had to be carried on trays from bed to bed. At most times of the year about half of the forty or so patients on the ward had typhoid fever, which meant that the nurse couldn't simply move from bed to bed in the performance of her duties; each typhoid case was screened from the other patients, and the nurse was required to put on a new gown and wash her hands in disinfectant before approaching the bedside. Patients with high fevers were sponged with cold alcohol at frequent intervals. The late-evening back rub was the rite of passage into sleep.

In addition to the routine, workaday schedule, the nurse was responsible for responding to all calls from the patients, and it was expected that she would do so on the run. Her rounds, scheduled as methodical progressions around the ward, were continually interrupted by these calls. It was up to her to evaluate each situation quickly: a sudden abdominal pain in a typhoid patient might signify intestinal perforation; the abrupt onset of weakness, thirst, and pallor meant intestinal hemorrhage; the coughing up of gross blood by a tuberculous patient was an emergency. Some of the calls came from neighboring patients on the way to recovery; patients on open wards always kept a close eye on each other: the man in the next bed might slip into coma or seem to be dying, or be indeed dead. For such emergencies the nurse had to get word immediately to the doctor on call, usually the intern assigned to the ward, who might be off in the outpatient department or working in the diagnostic laboratory (interns of that day did all the laboratory work themselves; technicians had not yet been invented) or in his room. Nurses were not allowed to give injections or to do such emergency procedures as spinal punctures or chest taps, but they were expected to know when such maneuvers were indicated and to be ready with appropriate trays of instruments when the intern arrived on the ward.

It was an exhausting business, but by my mother's accounts it was the most satisfying and rewarding kind of work. As a nurse she was a low person in the professional hierarchy, always running from place to place on orders from the doctors, subject as well to strict discipline from her own administrative superiors on the nursing staff, but none of this came through in her recollections. What she remembered was her usefulness.

Whenever my father talked to me about nurses and their work, he spoke with high regard for them as professionals. Although it was clear in his view that the task of the nurses was to do what the doctor told them to, it was also clear that he admired them for being able to do a lot of things he couldn't possibly do, had never been trained to do. On his own rounds later on, when he became an attending physician himself, he consulted the ward nurse for her opinion about problem cases and paid careful attention to her observations and chart notes. In his own days of intern training (perhaps partly under my mother's strong influence, I don't know) he developed a deep and lasting respect for the whole nursing profession.

I have spent all of my professional career in close association with, and close dependency on, nurses, and like many of my faculty colleagues, I've done a lot of worrying about the relationship between medicine and nursing. During most of this century the nursing profession has been having a hard time of it. It has been largely, although not entirely, an occupation for women, and sensitive issues of professional status, complicated by the special issue of the changing role of women in modern society, have led to a standoffish, often adversarial relationship between nurses and doctors. Already swamped by an increasing load of routine duties, nurses have been obliged to take on more and more purely administrative tasks: keeping the records in order; making sure the supplies are on hand for every sort of ward emergency; supervising the activities of the new paraprofessional group called LPNs (licensed practical nurses), who now perform much of the bedside work once done by RNs (registered nurses); overseeing ward maids, porters, and cleaners; seeing to it that patients scheduled for X rays are on their way to the X-ray department on time. Therefore, they have to spend more of their time at desks in the ward office and less time at the bedsides. Too late maybe, the nurses have begun to realise that they are gradually being excluded from the one duty which had previously been their most important reward but which had been so taken for granted that nobody mentioned it in listing the duties of a nurse: close personal contact with patients. Along with everything else nurses did in the long day's work, making up for all the tough and sometimes demeaning jobs assigned to them, they had the matchless opportunity to be useful friends to great numbers of human beings in trouble. They listened to their patients all day long and through the night, they gave comfort and reassurance to the patients and their families, they got to know them as friends, they were depended on. To contemplate the loss of this part of their work has been the deepest worry for nurses at large, and for the faculties responsible for the curricula of the nation's new and expanding nursing schools. The issue lies at the center of the running argument between medical school and nursing school administrators, but it is never clearly stated. Nursing education has been upgraded in recent years. Almost all the former hospital schools, which took in high school graduates and provided an RN certificate after two or three years, have been replaced by schools attached to colleges and universities, with a four-year curriculum leading simultaneously to a bachelor's degree and an RN certificate.

The doctors worry that nurses are trying to move away from their historical responsibilities to medicine (meaning, really, to the doctors' orders). The nurses assert that they are their own profession, responsible for their own standards, co-equal colleagues with physicians, and they do not wish to become mere ward administrators or technicians (although some of them, carrying the new and prestigious title of 'nurse practitioner,' are being trained within nursing schools to perform some of the most complex technological responsibilities in hospital emergency rooms and intensive care units). The doctors claim that what the nurses really want is to become substitute psychiatrists. The nurses reply that they have unavoidable responsibilities for the mental health and well-being of their patients, and that these are different from the doctors' tasks. Eventually the arguments will work themselves out, and some sort of agreement will be reached, but if it is to be settled intelligently, some way will have to be found to preserve and strengthen the traditional and highly personal nurse-patient relationship.

I have had a fair amount of firsthand experience with the issue, having been an apprehensive patient myself off and on over a three-year period on the wards of the hospital for which I work. I am one up on most of my physician friends because of this experience. I know some things they do not know about what nurses do.

One thing the nurses do is to hold the place together. It is an astonishment, which every patient feels from time to time, observing the affairs of a large, complex hospital from the vantage point of his bed, that the whole institution doesn't fly to pieces. A hospital operates by the constant interplay of powerful forces pulling away at each other in different directions, each force essential for getting necessary things done, but always at odds with each other. The intern staff is an almost irresistible force in itself, learning medicine by doing medicine, assuming all the responsibility within reach, pushing against an immovable attending and administrative staff, and frequently at odds with the nurses. The attending physicians are individual entrepreneurs trying to run small cottage industries at each bedside. The diagnostic laboratories are feudal fiefdoms, prospering from the insatiable demands for their services from the interns and residents. The medical students are all over the place, learning as best they can and complaining that they are not, as they believe they should be, at the epicenter of everyone's concern. Each individual worker in the place, from the chiefs of surgery to the dieticians to the ward maids, porters, and elevator operators, lives and works in the conviction that the whole apparatus would come to a standstill without his or her individual contribution, and in one sense or another each of them is right.

My discovery, as a patient first on the medical service and later in surgery, is that the institution is held together, *glued* together, enabled to function as an organism, by the nurses and by nobody else.

The nurses, the good ones anyway (and all the ones on my floor were good), make it their business to know everything that is going on. They spot errors before errors can be launched. They know everything written on the chart. Most important of all, they know their patients as unique human beings, and they soon get to know the close relatives and friends. Because of this knowledge, they are quick to sense apprehensions and act on them. The average sick person in a large hospital feels at risk of getting lost, with no identity left beyond a name and a string of numbers on a plastic wrist-band, in danger always of being whisked off on a litter to the wrong place to have the wrong procedure done, or worse still, *not* being whisked off at the right time. The attending physician or the house officer, on rounds and usually in a hurry, can murmur a few reassuring words on his way out the door, but it takes a confident, competent, and cheerful nurse, there all day long and in and out of the room on one chore or another through the night, to bolster one's confidence that the situation is indeed manageable and not about to get out of hand.

Knowing what I know, I am all for the nurses. If they are to continue their professional feud with the doctors, if they want their professional status enhanced and their pay increased, if they infuriate the doctors by their claims to be equal professionals, if they ask for the moon, I am on their side.

Dentistry

*'All this fuss about sleeping together. For physical pleasure
I'd sooner go to my dentist any day.'*

Evelyn Waugh

'False' teeth
from The Damned Human Race *by Mark Twain*

Man seems to be a rickety poor sort of a thing, any way you take him;
a kind of British Museum of infirmities and inferiorities. He is always
undergoing repairs. A machine that was as unreliable as he is would
have no market.

The higher animals get their teeth without pain or inconvenience.
Man gets his through months and months of cruel torture; and at a
time of life when he is but ill able to bear it. As soon as he has got
them they must all be pulled out again, for they were of no value in
the first place, not worth the loss of a night's rest. The second set will
answer for a while, by being reinforced occasionally with rubber or
plugged up with gold; but he will never get a set which can really be
depended on till a dentist makes him one. This set will be called 'false'
teeth – as if he had ever worn any other kind.

~

Surgery
from Selected Stories *by Anton Chekhov*

Azemstvo hospital. In the absence of the doctor, who has gone off to
get married, the patients are received by his assistant, the feldscher
Kuryatin, a stout man of about forty, whose face wears an expression
of amiability and a sense of duty. He is dressed in a shabby pongee

jacket, frayed woolen trousers, and between the index and middle fingers of his left hand carries a cigar that gives off a stench.

Into the waiting room comes the sexton, Vonmiglasov. He is a tall,
heavy-set old man, wearing a brown cassock with a wide leather belt.
He has a cataract on his right eye, which is half-closed, and on his
nose there is a wart that from a distance resembles a large fly. He
stands for a moment trying to locate an ikon; unable to discover one,
he crosses himself before a bottle of carbolic acid, then takes a loaf of
communion bread out of a red handkerchief and, with a bow, places
it before the feldscher.

'A-a-a-h ... greetings,' yawns the feldscher. 'What brings you
here?'

'A blessed Lord's day to you, Sergei Kuzmich. I've come to your
worship – verily and in truth is it said in the Psalter: "Thou givest
them tears to drink in great measure." The other day I sat down to
drink tea with my old woman and – dear Lord! – not a drop, nothing
could I swallow. I was ready to lie down and die! One little sip and
there was no bearing it. And it's not just the tooth itself, but this
whole side – it aches and aches! It goes right into my ear, if you will
excuse me, as if a tack or some such object was in there. Such shooting pains, such shooting pains! I sinned and I transgressed, shamefully
have I besmirched my soul with sins, and in slothfulness have I passed
the days of my life! It's for my sins, Sergei Kuzmich, for my sins! His
Reverence rebuked me after the liturgy: "You're stammering, Yefim,
you talk through your nose. You sing and nobody can make out a
word you say." ... And how do you think I can sing if I can't open my
mouth? It's all swollen, if you will excuse me, and not having slept all
night –'

'Hmmm ... yes. Sit down. Open your mouth.'

Vonmiglasov does as he is told. Kuryatin knits his brows and begins
his examination. Among the teeth, all yellowed by time and tobacco,
he discovers one that is ornamented with a gaping hole.

'Father deacon told me to use an application of vodka and horse-
radish – that didn't help. Glikeria Anisimovna, God grant her health,
gave me a little thread from Mount Athos to wear, and she told me to
rinse the tooth with warm milk. Although I did put on the little
thread, as for the milk, I did not take that – I'm a God-fearing man, I
keep the fast.'

'Superstition.' The feldscher pauses. 'It has to be pulled, Yefim
Mikheich.'

'You know best, Sergei Kuzmich. That's what you've been trained for, to understand this business; to know whether to pull it or use drops or something else. It's for this that you, our benefactors, have been put here, God give you health, in order that, day and night, till they lay us in our coffins, we should pray for you, our fathers –'

'It's nothing,' says the feldscher modestly. He goes to one of the cupboards and begins rummaging among the instruments. 'Surgery is nothing; it's all a matter of a firm hand. Quick as you can spit! The other day the landowner Alexander Ivanich Yegipetsky came here to the hospital, like you, also with a tooth. He's an educated man, asks all kinds of questions, goes into everything, wants to know the how and the what of things. He shook my hand and called me by my full name. He lived in Petersburg for seven years and hobnobbed with all the professors. I spent a long time over him. "In Christ's name, pull it out for me, Sergei Kuzmich!" Why not? It can be pulled. But – this business has to be understood; without understanding – impossible. There are teeth and teeth. One you pull with forceps, another with molar forceps, and a third with a key. To each according.'

The feldscher takes up the molar forceps, dubiously gazes at the instrument for a moment, then puts it down and takes up the forceps.

'Now, sir, open your mouth wide,' he says, approaching the sexton with the forceps. 'We'll have that out quick as you can spit! I only have to cut the gum a little, get leverage on a vertical axis, and that's all.' He cuts the gum. 'And that's all.'

'You are our benefactor! We are benighted fools, but the Lord has enlightened you –'

'Well, don't make a speech just because you have your mouth open. That will pull easily. There are some that give trouble; nothing but roots to them. This will – quick as you can spit!' He lays down the forceps. 'Don't twitch! Sit still! . . . In the twinkling of an eye.' Then, getting leverage: 'The important thing is to get a deep enough hold,' pulling, 'so that you don't break the crown.'

'Our Father! – Holy Mother! – O-o-o-h!'

'Don't do that – don't do that! What's the matter with you? Don't grab me! Let go my hands!' Beginning to pull again. 'In a minute – now – *now*! . . . You know, this business is not so simple.'

'Fathers! Saints!' screams Vonmiglasov. 'Ministering angels! Oh! O-o-o-h! Pull – pull! Why do you have to take five years?'

'It's a question of – surgery. Impossible to do it all at once. Now – *now* –'

Vonmiglasov's knees come up to his elbows, his eyes bulge, his fingers twitch, and his breath comes in gasps; perspiration breaks out on his crimson face and tears stand in his eyes. Kuryatin breathes audibly, shifting his weight from one foot to the other, and pulls. An agonising half minute passes . . . and the forceps slip off the tooth. The sexton jumps up, thrusts his fingers into his mouth, and feels the tooth intact.

'But you pulled it!' he cries in a wailing, and at the same time, derisive voice. 'May they pull you like that in the next world! We humbly thank you. If you don't know how to pull a tooth, then don't do it! I'm seeing stars!'

'And why did you grab hold of me?' The feldscher is furious. 'I'm pulling and you're shoving my hands away and saying stupid things. *Fool!*'

'You're a fool, yourself!'

'Do you think, you peasant, that it's easy to pull a tooth? Just try it! It's not like climbing up into a belfry and rattling off a few chimes! "If you don't know how, if you don't know how!"' he mimics. 'Look, an expert has turned up! How do you like that? When I pulled Mr Yegipetsky's tooth – Alexander Ivanich, that is – he didn't say anything, not a word! He's a better man than you are, he didn't grab me. Sit down. *Sit down*, I tell you!'

'I'm still seeing stars – let me catch my breath! Oh!' Vonmiglasov sits down. 'Don't drag it out so long, just pull it. Don't drag on it so, give it one quick yank!'

'Teach your grandmother to suck eggs! Oh, Lord, the ignorance of the people! Live with them and you go out of your mind. Open your mouth.' He inserts the forceps. 'Surgery is no joke, brother. It's not like reading the Scriptures from the pulpit!' Getting leverage: 'Don't jerk! The tooth appears to have been neglected for a long time. The roots go deep.' Pulling: 'Don't move! There – there – don't move – now – *now* –' A crunching sound is heard. 'I knew it!'

For a moment Vonmiglasov sits motionless, as if numb. He is stunned and stares blankly into space, his white face covered with sweat.

'Perhaps I ought to have used the molar forceps,' mumbles the feldscher. 'What a mess!'

Coming to himself, the sexton puts his fingers into his mouth. In place of the defective tooth he feels two sharp stumps.

'You mangy devil!' he cries. 'They planted you on this earth, you fiend, for our destruction!'

'Go on, curse me some more,' mutters the feldscher, putting the forceps into the cupboard. 'Ignoramus! They didn't treat you to the rod sufficiently at your seminary. Mr Yegipetsky – Alexander Ivanich, that is – lived seven years in Petersburg, he's a cultured man. One suit costs him a hundred rubles – and he didn't swear. What sort of peahen are you? Don't worry, you won't die!'

The sexton takes the communion bread from the table and, holding his hand to his cheek, goes on his way.

~

Guilty gums
from Writings from the New Yorker 1927–1976 *by*
E.B. White

Now that children's teeth can be protected by adding fluorine to their drinking water, dentists are casting around for some new place to sink their drills. It looks as though they may have found it, too. Last week, Dr Robert S. Gilbert told his fellow-dentists that a patient's open mouth is a stage on which is enacted the drama of his emotional life. Plenty of people who complain of toothache are just upset, and he (Gilbert) has himself cured a man whose teeth were hurting because of guilt feelings about a dead sister. This is wonderful news, this broadening of the scope of dentistry. We, in our own lifetime, have seen dentistry come a long way. We recall clearly the days when a cavity was a hole that a dentist could feel by poking about with his pry. Then came X-ray, and a cavity was something that the dentist could see on the negative but the patient couldn't, and dentists would drill according to a plotted position on a chart, crashing their way through fine, sturdy old walls of enamel to get to some infinitesimal weakness far within. Now dentists are in search of guilt, not caries, and go rummaging around among the gums for signs of emotional instability. The toothpaste people will undoubtedly follow along – guilt paste, fear paste, and old Doc Lyon's psychosomatipowder.

~

Laughing gas
from Laughing Gas *by P.G. Wodehouse*

I.J. Zizzbaum proved to be rather a gloomy cove. He looked like a dentist with a secret sorrow. In reply to my 'Good afternoon,' he merely motioned me to the chair with a sombre wave of the hand. One of those strong, silent dentists.

I, on the other hand, was at my chattiest. I am always that way when closeted with a molar-mangler. I dare say it's the same with you. I suppose one's idea is that if one can only keep the conversation going, the blighter may get so interested that he will shelve the dirty work altogether in favour of a cosy talk. I started in right away.

'Hullo, hullo, hullo. Here I am. Good afternoon, good afternoon. What a lovely day, what? Shall I sit here? Right ho. Shall I lean my head back? Right ho. Shall I open my mouth? Right ho.'

'Wider, please,' said I.J. Zizzbaum sadly.

'Right ho. Everything set for the administration of the old laughing gas? Good. You know,' I said, sitting up, 'it's years since I had gas. I can't have been more than twelve. I know I was quite a kid, because it happened when I was at a private school, and of course one leaves one's private school at a very tender age. And, talking of kids, who do you think I met in the waiting-room? None other than little Joey Cooley. And it's an odd coincidence, but he's having gas, too. Shows what a small world it is, what?'

I broke off, abashed. It did not need the quick wince of pain on I.J. Zizzbaum's mobile face to tell me that I had made a bloomer and said the tactless thing. I could have kicked myself.

Because it had suddenly flashed upon me what the trouble was and why he was not this afternoon the sunny I.J. Zizzbaum whose merry laugh and gay quips made him, no doubt, the life and soul of the annual dentists' convention. He was brooding on the fact that the big prize in the dentistry world, the extraction of little Joey Cooley's bicuspid, had gone to his trade rival, B.K. Burwash.

No doubt he had been listening in on all that interviewing and camera-clicking, and the shrill cries of the human interest writers as they went about their business must have made very bitter hearing – rubbing it in, I mean to say, that old Pop Burwash was going to get his name on the front page of all the public news-sheets and become more or less the World's Sweetheart, while all he, Zizzbaum, could expect was my modest fee.

It was enough to depress the most effervescent dentist, and my heart bled for the poor bloke. I hunted in my mind for some soothing speech that would bring the roses back to his cheeks, but all I could think of was a statement to the effect that recent discoveries in the Congo basin had thrown a new light on something or other. I had this on the authority of the *National Geographic Magazine*.

It didn't seem to cheer him up to any marked extent. Not interested in the Congo basin, probably. Many people aren't. He simply sighed rather heavily, levered my jaws a bit farther apart, peered into the abyss, sighed again as if he didn't think highly of the contents, and motioned to his A.D.C. to cluster round with the gas-bag.

And presently, after a brief interlude during which I felt as if I was being slowly smothered where I sat, I was off.

I don't know if you are familiar with this taking-gas business. If you are, you will recall that it has certain drawbacks apart from the sensation of being cut off in your prime by stoppage of the windpipes. It is apt to give you unpleasant dreams and visions. The last time I had had it, on the occasion which I had mentioned in my introductory remarks, I remember that I had thought somebody was shoving me down into the sea, and I had a distinct illusion of being pried asunder by sharks.

This time, the proceedings were still rummy, but not quite so bad as that. The sharks were not on the bill. The stellar role was played by little Joey Cooley.

It seemed to me that he and I were in a room rather like the waiting-room, only larger, and as in the real waiting-room, there were two doors, one on each side.

The first was labelled:

I.J. ZIZZBAUM

The other:

B.K. BURWASH

And the Cooley kid and I were jostling one another, trying to get through the Zizzbaum door.

Well, any chump would have seen that that wasn't right. I tried to reason with the misguided little blighter. I kept saying: 'Stop shoving, old sport; you're trying to get into the wrong room,' but it wasn't any use – he simply shoved the more. And presently he shoved me into an arm-chair and told me to sit there and read the *National Geographic Magazine*, and then he opened the door and went through.

After that, things got blurred for a while. When they clarified somewhat, I was still sitting in a chair, but it was a dentist's chair, and I realized that I had come out from under the influence.

~

Nothing but the tooth
from The Most of Perelman *by S.J. Perelman*

I am thirty-eight years old, have curly brown hair and blue eyes, own a uke and a yellow roadster, and am considered a snappy dresser in my crowd. But the thing I want most in the world for my birthday is a free subscription to *Oral Hygiene*, published by Merwin B. Massol, 1005 Liberty Avenue, Pittsburgh, Pa. In the event you have been repairing your own teeth, *Oral Hygiene* is a respectable smooth-finish technical magazine circulated to your dentist with the compliments of his local supply company. Through its pages runs a recital of the most horrendous and fantastic deviations from the dental norm. It is a confessional in which dentists take down their back hair and stammer out the secrets of their craft. But every time I plunge into its crackling pages at my dentist's, just as I get interested in the story of the Man with the Alveolar Dentures or Thirty Reasons Why People Stay Away from Dentists, the nurse comes out slightly flushed and smoothing her hair to tell me that the doctor is ready. Last Thursday, for example, I was head over heels in the question-and-answer department of *Oral Hygiene*. A frankly puzzled extractionist, who tried to cloak his agitation under the initials 'J.S.G.,' had put his plight squarely up to the editor: 'I have a patient, a woman of 20, who has a full complement of teeth. All of her restorations are gold foils or inlays. She constantly grinds her teeth at night. How can I aid her to stop grinding them? Would it do any good to give her a vellum rubber bite?' But before I could learn whether it was a bite or just a gentle hug the editor recommended, out popped Miss Inchbald with lipstick on her nose, giggling, 'The Doctor is free now.' 'Free,' indeed – 'running amok' would be a better way to put it.

I had always thought of dentists as of the phlegmatic type – square-jawed sadists in white aprons who found release in trying out new kinds of burs on my shaky little incisors. One look at *Oral Hygiene* fixed that. Of all the inhibited, timorous, uncertain fumble-bunnies who creep the earth, Mr Average Dentist is the worst. A filing clerk is a veritable saber-toothed tiger by comparison. Faced with a decision, your dentist's bones turn to water and he becomes all hands and feet. He muddles through his ordinary routine with a certain amount of bravado, plugging a molar here with chewing gum, sinking a shaft in a sound tooth there. In his spare time he putters around his laboratory making tiny cement cupcakes, substituting amber electric bulbs for ordinary bulbs in his waiting room to depress patients, and jotting down nasty little innuendoes about people's gums in his notebook. But let an honest-to-goodness sufferer stagger in with his face out of drawing, and Mr Average Dentist's nerves go to hell. He runs sobbing to the 'Ask *Oral Hygiene*' department and buries his head in the lap of V. C. Smedley, its director. I dip in for a typical sample:

Question – A patient of mine, a girl, 18, returned from school recently with a weird story of lightning having struck an upper right cuspid tooth and checked the enamel on the labial surface nearly two-thirds of the way from the incisal edge toward the neck. The patient was lying on a bed looking out an open window during an electric storm, and this one flash put out the lights of the house, and at the same time, the patient felt a burning sensation (like a burning wire) along the cuspid tooth. She immediately put her tongue on the tooth which felt rough, but as the lights were out she could not see it so she went to bed. (A taste as from a burnt match accompanied the shock.)

Next morning she found the labial of the tooth black. Some of the color came off on her finger. By continually brushing all day with the aid of peroxide, salt, soda and vinegar she removed the remainder of the black after which the tooth was a yellow shade and there was some roughness on the labial surface.

Could the lightning have caused this and do you recommend smoothing the surface with discs? – R. D. L., D.D.S., Oregon.

Well, Doctor, let us take your story step by step. Miss Muffet told you the sensation was like a burning wire, and she tasted something like a burnt match. Did you think, by any chance, of looking into her mouth for either wire or matches? Did you even think of looking into her mouth? I see no mention of the fact in your letter. You state that she walked in and told you the story, that's all. Of course it never occurred to you that she had brought along her mouth for a reason. Then you say, 'she removed the remainder of the black after which the tooth was a yellow shade.' Would it be asking too much of you to make up your mind? Was it a tooth or a yellow shade? You're quite sure it wasn't a Venetian blind? Or a gaily striped awning? Do you ever take a drink in the daytime, Doctor?

Frankly, men, I have no patience with such idiotic professional behavior. An eighteen-year-old girl walks into a dentist's office exhibiting obvious symptoms of religious hysteria (stigmata, etc.) She babbles vaguely of thunderstorms and is patently a confirmed drunkard. The dentist goes to pieces, forgets to look in her mouth, and scurries off to *Oral Hygiene* asking for permission to smooth her surface with discs. It's a mercy he doesn't take matters into his own hands and try to plow every fourth tooth under. This is the kind of man to whom we entrust our daughters' dentures.

There is practically no problem so simple that it cannot confuse a dentist. For instance, thumb-sucking. 'Could you suggest a method to correct thumb and index finger sucking by an infant of one year?' flutters a Minnesota orthodontist, awkwardly digging his toe into the hot sand. Dr Smedley, whose patience rivals Job's, has an answer for everything: 'Enclose the hand by tying shut the end of the sleeve of a sleeping garment, or fasten a section of a pasteboard mailing tube to the sleeping garment in such a position as to prevent the bending of the elbow sufficiently to carry the thumb or index finger to the mouth.' Now truly, Dr Smedley, isn't that going all the way around Robin Hood's barn? Nailing the baby's hand to the high-chair is much more cozy, or, if no nail is available, a smart blow with the hammer on Baby's fingers will slow him down. My grandfather, who was rather active in the nineties (between Columbus and Amsterdam avenues – they finally got him for breaking and entering), always used an effective method to break children of this habit. He used to tie a Mills grenade to the baby's thumb with cobbler's waxed thread, and when the little spanker pulled out the detonating pin with his teeth, Grandpa would stuff his fingers into his ears and run like the wind. Ironically enough, the people with whom Grandpa now boards have the same trouble keeping him from biting his thumbs, but overcome it by making him wear a loose jacket with very long sleeves, which they tie to the bars.

I have always been the mildest of men, but you remember the old saying, 'Beware the fury of a patient man.' (I remember it very well and put my finger on it instantly, page 269 of Bartlett's book of quotations.) For years I have let dentists ride roughshod over my teeth; I have been sawed, hacked, chopped, whittled, bewitched, bewildered, tattooed, and signed on again; but this is cuspid's last stand. They'll never get me into that chair again. I'll dispose of my teeth as I see fit, and after they're gone, I'll get along. I started off living on gruel, and, by God, I can always go back to it again.

~

Dentistry and doubt
from Forty Stories *by John Updike*

Burton knew what the dentist would notice first: the clerical collar. People always did. The dentist was standing not quite facing the door, as if it had just occurred to him to turn away. His eyes, grey in a rose, faintly moustached face, clung to Burton's throat a moment too long for complete courtesy before lifting as he said, 'Hello!' Shifting his feet, the dentist thrust out an unexpectedly soft hand.

He noticed next that Burton was an American. In Oxford, Burton had acquired the habit of speaking softly, but susurration alone could not alter the proportionate emphasis of vowel over consonant, the slight drag at the end of each sentence, or any of the diphthongal peculiarities that betray Americans to the twittering English. As soon as Burton had returned the greeting, with an apology for being late (he did not blame the British buses, though they were at fault), he fancied he could hear the other man's mind register 'U.S.A. . . . pioneer piety . . . R.C.? Can't be; no black hat . . . frank enough smile . . . rather heavy tartar on the incisors.'

He motioned Burton to the chair and turned to a sink, where he washed his hands without looking at them. He talked over his shoulder. 'What part are you from?'

'Of the States?' Burton enjoyed saying 'the States'. It sounded so aggregate, so ominous.

'Yes. Are you Canadian?'

'No, I'm from Pennsylvania.' Burton had never had such a good view from a dentist's chair. A great bay window gave on a small back yard. Black shapes of birds fluttered and jiggled among the twigs of two or three trees – willows, he guessed. Except for the birds, the trees were naked. A wet-wash sky hung, it seemed, a few feet behind the net of limbs. A brick wall looked the shade of rust, and patches of sky hinted at blue, but there was little colour in any of it.

'Pennsylvania,' the dentist mused, the latter syllables of the word amplifying as he drew closer. 'That's in the East?'

'It's a Middle Atlantic state. You know where New York City is?'

'Roughly.'

'It's a little west of that, more or less. It's a neutral sort of state.'

'I see.' The dentist leaned over him, and Burton received two wonderful surprises when he opened his mouth: the dentist said 'Thank you'; and the dentist had something on his breath that, without being either, smelled sweet as candy and spicy as cloves. Peering in, he bumped a mirror across Burton's teeth. An electric reflector like an eye doctor's was strapped to his head. Outside, the black birds did stunts among the twigs. The dentist's eyes were not actually grey; screwed up, they seemed more brown, and then, as they flicked towards the tool tray, rather green, like pebbles on the bed of a fast-running creek. He scraped at an eye-tooth, but with such tact that Burton felt nothing. 'There's certainly one,' he said, turning to make a mark on a clean card.

Burton took the opportunity to rid himself of a remark he had been holding in suspension. 'More than ninety per cent of the world's anthracite comes from Pennsylvania.'

'Really?' the dentist said, obviously not believing him. He returned his hands, the tools in them, to in front of Burton's chin. Burton opened his mouth. 'Thank you,' the dentist said.

As he peered and picked and made notations, a measure of serenity returned to Burton. That morning, possibly because of the scheduled visit to a foreign dentist, the Devil had been very active. Scepticism had mingled with the heat and aroma of his bed; it had dripped from the cold ochre walls of his digs; it had been the substance of his dreams. His slippers, his bathrobe, his face in the mirror, his books – black books, brown ones, C.S. Lewis, Karl Barth, *The Portable Medieval Reader*, Raymond Tully, and Bertrand Russell lying together as nonchalantly as if they had been Belloc and Chesterton – stood witness to a futility that undercut all hope and theory. Even his toothbrush, which on good days presented itself as an acolyte of matinal devotion, today seemed an agent of atheistic hygiene, broadcasting the hideous fact of germs. The faucet's merry gurgle had sounded over Burton's sudden prayers.

The scent of candy and cloves lifted. The dentist, standing erect, was asking. 'Do you take novocain?'

Burton hesitated. He believed that one of the lazier modern

61

assumptions was the identification of pain with evil. Indeed, in so far as pain warned us of corruption, it was good. On the other hand, relieving the pain of others was an obvious virtue – perhaps the *most* obvious virtue. And to court pain was as morbid as to chase pleasure. Yet to flee from pain was clearly cowardice.

The dentist, not hinting by his voice whether he had been waiting for an answer several seconds or no time at all, asked, 'Does your dentist at home give you novocain?'

Ever since Burton was a little boy in crusty dungarees, Dr Gribling had given him novocain. 'Yes.' The answer sounded abrupt, impolite. Burton added, 'He says my nerves are exceptionally-large.' It was a pompous thing to say.

'We'll do the eye-tooth,' the dentist said.

Burton's heart beat like a wasp in a jar as the dentist moved across the room, did unseeable things by the sink, and returned with a full hypodermic. A drop of fluid, by some miracle of adhesion, clung trembling to the needle's tip. Burton opened his mouth while the dentist's back was still turned. When at last the man pivoted, his instrument tilting up, a tension beneath his moustache indicated surprise and perhaps amusement at finding things in such readiness. 'Open a little wider, please,' he said. 'Thank you.' The needle moved closer. It was under Burton's nose and out of focus. 'Now, this might hurt a little.' What a kind thing to say! The sharp prick and the consequent slow, filling ache drove Burton's eyes up, and he saw the tops of the bare willow trees, the frightened white sky, and the black birds. As he watched, one bird joined another on the topmost twig, and then a third joined these two and the twig became radically crescent, and all three birds flapped off to where his eyes could not follow them.

'There,' the dentist sighed, in a zephyr of candy and cloves.

Waiting for the novocain to take effect, Burton and the dentist made conversation.

'And what brings you to Oxford?' the dentist began.

'I'm doing graduate work.'

'Oh? What sort?'

'I'm doing a thesis on a man called Richard Hooker.'

'Oh?' The dentist sounded as incredulous as he had about Pennsylvania's anthracite.

Richard Hooker – 'pious, peaceable, primitive', in Walton's phrase – loomed so large in Burton's world that to doubt Hooker's existence was in effect to doubt the existence of Burton's world. But he added the explanatory 'An English divine' without the least bit of irritability or condescension. The lesson of humility was one that had come rather easily to Burton. He recognised, however, that in his very thinking of his own humility he was guilty of pride, and his immediate recognition of it as pride was foundation for further, subtler egotism.

He would have harried the sin to its source had not the dentist said, 'A divine is a church writer?'

'That's right.'

'Could you quote me something he wrote?'

Burton had expected, and was prepared to answer, several questions ('When did he live?' '1554 to 1600.' 'What is the man's claim to fame?' 'He attempted to reconcile Christian – that is, Thomist – political theory with the actual state of things under the Tudor monarchy; he didn't really succeed, but he did anticipate much of modern political thought.' 'What is your thesis?' 'Mostly an attempt to get at reasons for Hooker's failure to come to grips with Renaissance Platonism.'), but he was unprepared for this one. Scraps and phrases – 'visible Church', 'law eternal', 'very slender ability', 'Popish superstition', the odd word 'scrupulosity' – came to mind, but no rounded utterance formed itself. 'I can't think of anything right now,' he apologized, touching his fingers to his collar and, as still sometimes happened, being taken aback by the hard, unbroken edge they met.

The dentist did not seem disappointed. 'Feel numb yet?' he asked.

Burton tested and said, 'Yes.'

The dentist swung the drilling apparatus into place and Burton opened his mouth. 'Thank you.' The novocain had taken. The drilling at the tooth seemed vastly distant, and it hurt no more than the explosion of a star, or the death of an elephant in India, or, Burton realized, the whipping of a child right next door. Pain. The problem presented itself. He slipped into the familiar arguments he used with himself. Creation is His seeking to make souls out of matter. Morally, matter, *per se*, is neutral – with form imposed upon it, good, but in any case its basic nature is competitive. No two things can occupy the same place at the same time. Hence, pain. But we must act with non-material motives. What was His journey on earth but a flouting of competitive values? And then there is the Devil. But with the Devil the whole cosmos became confused, and Burton's attention, by default, rested on the black birds. They kept falling out of the sky and the tree-tops, but he noticed few ascending.

The dentist changed his drill. 'Thank you.' There were things

Burton could comprehend. And then there were things he could not –
his aeon-long wait as life struggled up from the atom. With what
emotion did He watch all those preposterous, earnest beasts labour
up out of the swamp and aimlessly perish on the long and crooked
road to Man? And the stars, so far off, the comedy of waste spaces –
theologians had always said infinite, but could they have meant *that*
infinite? Once, Burton had asked his father if he believed in purgatory.
'Of course I do,' he had snapped, jabbing towards the floor with his
pipe-stem. '*This* is purgatory.' Remembering the incident so depressed
Burton that when the drill broke through the shell of anaesthetic and
bit his nerve, it came in the shape of an answer, and he greeted the
pain with something like ecstasy.

'There,' the dentist said. 'Would you care to wash out, please.' He
swung the drilling apparatus over to one side, so Burton could see it
wouldn't be used any more. He was so kind.

'There seem to be a lot of birds in your back yard,' Burton said to
him.

'We have a feeding station,' the dentist said, grinding the silver for
the filling in a thick glass cup.

'What are those black birds?'

'Starlings. A greedy bird. They take everything they can away from
the wren.'

For the first time, Burton noticed some smaller shapes among the
branches, quicker, but less numerous and less purposeful than the
black birds. He watched one in particular, swivelling on his perch,
now a formless blob, like a big bud, the next moment in vivid profile,
like a Picasso ceramic. As he watched the bird, his mind emptied
itself, and nothing, not even the squeaking of the silver, disturbed it.

When he again became conscious, it was of the objects on the tray
before him as things in which an unlimited excitement inhered; the
tweezers, the picks, the drill burrs, the celluloid container of cotton,
the tiny cotton balls, the metal cup where a flame could burn, the
enamelled construction beside him housing a hundred useful devices,
the tiled walls, the window frame, the things beyond the window – all
travelled to his senses burdened with delight and power. The sensation was one that Burton had frequently enjoyed in his childhood and
more and more rarely as he aged. His urge to laugh, or to *do* something with the objects, was repressed, and even the smile he gave the
dentist was lost, for the man was concerned with keeping a dab of
silver on the end of a minute golf-club-shaped tool.

Burton received the silver. He thought of the world as being, like all music, founded on tension. The tree pushing up, gravity pulling down, the bird desiring to fill the air, the air compelled to crush the bird. His head brimmed with irrelevant recollections: a rubber Donald Duck he had owned, and abused, as an infant; the grape arbour in his parents' back yard; the respect his father commanded throughout his town; Shibe Park in sunlight; Max Beerbohm's sentence about there always being a slight shock in seeing an envelope of one's own after it has gone through the post.

The dentist coughed. It was the sound not of a man who has to cough but of one who has done his job, and can cough if he pleases. 'Would you like to wash out, please?' He gestured towards a glass filled with pink fluid, which up to this time Burton had ignored. Burton took some of the liquid into his mouth (it was good, but not as good as the dentist's breath), sloshed it around, and, as silently as possible, spat it into the impeccable basin. 'I'm afraid three or four trips are called for,' the dentist said, studying his card.

'Fine.'

The dentist's moustache stretched fractionally. 'Miss Leviston will give you the appointments.' One by one, he dropped the drill burrs into a compartmented drawer. 'Do you have any idea why your teeth should be so, ah, indifferent?'

Burton concentrated. He yearned to thank the man, to bless him even, but since there was no conventional way to do that, he would show his gratitude by giving everything the dentist said his closest attention. 'I believe Pennsylvania has one of the worst dental records of any state.'

'Really? And why should that be?'

'I don't know. I think the Southern states have the best teeth. They eat fish, or turnip tops, or something with lots of calcium in it.'

'I see.' The dentist moved aside so Burton could climb out of the chair. 'Until next time, then.'

Burton supposed they would not shake hands twice in one visit. Near the doorway, he turned. 'Oh, Doctor, uh . . .'

'Merritt,' the dentist said.

'I just thought of a quotation from Hooker. It's just a short sentence.'

'Yes?'

' "I grant we are apt, prone, and ready, to forsake God; but is God as ready to forsake us? Our minds are changeable; is His so likewise?" '

Dr Merritt smiled. The two men stood in the same position they had hesitated in when Burton entered the room. Burton smiled. Outside the window, two wrens, one by pretending to locate a crumb and the other by flicking a real crumb away, outmanoeuvred a black bird.

Science and Medicine

'There is something fascinating about Science. One gets such wholesome returns of conjecture out of such a trifling investment of fact.'

Mark Twain

'The great tragedy of science: the slaying of a beautiful hypothesis by an ugly fact.'

Thomas Huxley

Pure science
by Louis Pasteur

Without theory, practice is but routine born of habit. Theory alone can bring forth and develop the spirit of invention. It is to you especially that it will belong not to share the opinion of those narrow minds who disdain everything in science which has not an immediate application. You know Franklin's charming saying? He was witnessing the first demonstration of a purely scientific discovery, and people round him said: 'But what is the use of it?' Franklin answered: 'What is the use of a new-born child?' Yes, gentlemen, what is the use of a new-born child? And yet, perhaps, at that tender age, germs already existed in you of the talents which distinguish you! In your baby boys, fragile beings as they are, there are incipient magistrates, scientists, heroes as valiant as those who are now covering themselves with glory under the walls of Sebastopol. And thus, gentlemen, a theoretical discovery has but the merit of its existence: it awakens hope, and that is all. But let it be cultivated, let it grow, and you will see what it will become.

Nature and health
by Lord Horder

But let me remind you that health does not necessarily depend upon science at all. There were millions of healthy persons living before science, as we understand it today, existed. Though a large number of our forebears died prematurely from diseases which we have learnt to prevent, or to control, by science, many of them who escaped fatal disease, enjoyed even without the help of science as perfect health as we can ever hope to do. We mustn't mistake the explanation which science gives us as to why these folk were healthy for any supposed scientific methods that kept them healthy. Our ancestors didn't follow any scientific methods. To tell the truth, nature taught man how to be healthy long before science discovered the laws of health.

~

Are doctors men of science?
from the preface to The Doctor's Dilemma
by George Bernard Shaw

I presume nobody will question the existence of a widely spread popular delusion that every doctor is a man of science. It is escaped only in the very small class which understands by science something more than conjuring with retorts and spirit lamps, magnets and microscopes, and discovering magical cures for disease. To a sufficiently ignorant man every captain of a trading schooner is a Galileo, every organ-grinder a Beethoven, every piano-tuner a Helmholtz, every Old Bailey barrister a Solon, every Seven Dials pigeon-dealer a Darwin, every scrivener a Shakespeare, every locomotive engine a miracle, and its driver no less wonderful than George Stephenson. As a matter of fact, the rank and file of doctors are no more scientific than their tailors; or, if you prefer to put it the reverse way, their tailors are no less scientific than they. Doctoring is an art, not a science: any layman who is interested in science sufficiently to take in one of the scientific journals and follow the literature of the scientific movement, knows more about it than those doctors (probably a large majority) who are not interested in it, and practise only to earn their bread. Doctoring is not even the art of keeping people in health (no doctor seems able to advise you what to eat any better than his grandmother or the nearest

68

quack): it is the art of curing illnesses. It does happen exceptionally that a practising doctor makes a contribution to science (my play describes a very notable one); but it happens much oftener that he draws disastrous conclusions from his clinical experience because he has no conception of scientific method, and believes, like any rustic, that the handling of evidence and statistics needs no expertness. The distinction between a quack doctor and a qualified one is mainly that only the qualified one is authorized to sign death certificates, for which both sorts seem to have about equal occasion. Unqualified practitioners now make large incomes as hygienists, and are resorted to as frequently by cultivated amateur scientists who understand quite well what they are doing as by ignorant people who are simply dupes. Bone-setters make fortunes under the very noses of our greatest surgeons from educated and wealthy patients; and some of the most successful doctors on the register use quite heretical methods of treating disease, and have qualified themselves solely for convenience. Leaving out of account the village witches who prescribe spells and sell charms, the humblest professional healers in this country are the herbalists. These men wander through the fields on Sunday seeking for herbs with magic properties of curing disease, preventing childbirth, and the like. Each of them believes that he is on the verge of a great discovery, in which Virginia Snake Root will be an ingredient, heaven knows why! Virginia Snake Root fascinates the imagination of the herbalist as mercury used to fascinate the alchemists. On week days he keeps a shop in which he sells packets of penny-royal, dandelion, &c., labelled with little lists of the diseases they are supposed to cure, and apparently do cure to the satisfaction of the people who keep on buying them. I have never been able to perceive any distinction between the science of the herbalist and that of the duly registered doctor. A relative of mine recently consulted a doctor about some of the ordinary symptoms which indicate the need for a holiday and a change. The doctor satisfied himself that the patient's heart was a little depressed. Digitalis being a drug labelled as a heart specific by the profession, he promptly administered a stiff dose. Fortunately the patient was a hardy old lady who was not easily killed. She recovered with no worse result than her conversion to Christian Science, which owes its vogue quite as much to public despair of doctors as to superstition. I am not, observe, here concerned with the question as to whether the dose of digitalis was judicious or not: the point is, that a farm laborer consulting a herbalist would have been treated in exactly the same way.

The doctor in the modern world
from Doctors Past and Present *by Lord Brain*

The great scientific developments in medicine have had indirect effects which have profoundly influenced the relationship between the doctor and the public. The very successes of medicine themselves have given rise to new problems. We frequently hear of the miracles of modern medicine. This description is used by journalists and not by doctors. Nevertheless, it does cause difficulties for the presumed miracle-workers. First, it creates an atmosphere in which the public comes to take miracles so much as a matter of course that it begins to view with suspicion the miracle worker whose miracles fail to come off. In other words, people are led to expect too much, and are not aware, as doctors are only too well aware, of the limitations of their science and their art. It is easy to be wise after the event, but we all know that owing to the limitations of the human mind, by which I mean not merely our inevitable ignorance but our failure sometimes to use to the best advantage the available knowledge, mistakes in diagnosis are bound to occur. The greater the potentialities for treatment, however, the more tragic may be the consequences of mistakes. Furthermore, the achievements of modern medicine are based upon techniques of diagnosis whose daring would have astonished our forefathers, and drugs of a potency many times greater than any known before, and these carry their own risks; so that, while on the credit side of the ledger are thousands of lives saved, on the debit side must be placed the few lives lost as a result of the methods employed.

~

Open heart university
by Spike Milligan, March 1977

Dedicated to BBC-TV Open University

We've come a long way
          said the Cigarette Scientist
as he destroyed a live rabbit
          to show the students how it worked.

He took its heart out
        plugged it into an electric pump
        that kept it beating for nearly two hours.

I know rabbits who can keep their hearts
        beating for nearly seven years

And look at the electricity they save.

THE
DOCTOR–PATIENT
RELATIONSHIP

General Practice

Doctor and patient
by Rufus of Ephesus

One must put questions to the patient, for thereby certain aspects of the disease can be better understood, and the treatment rendered more effective. And I place the interrogation of the patient himself first, since in this way you can learn how far his mind is healthy or otherwise; also his physical strength and weakness; and you can get some idea of the disease and the part affected. For, if his answers are given in a consecutive way, and from memory, and are relevant and if he shows no hesitancy either in judgement or utterance; if he answers according to his natural bent; that is to say, if, being in other ways well-bred, he answers gently and politely; or if, on the other hand, being naturally bold or timid, he answers in a bold or timid way, one may then look on him as being at least sound mentally. But if you ask him one thing and he answers another; and if in the middle of speaking his memory fails him; if again, his enunciation is tremulous and hesitating, and he exhibits complete changes of manner; all these are signs of mental inadequacy. In this way one also appreciates deafness in a patient; if he does not hear, one must in addition inquire of those about him whether he was in any way deaf before, or whether it is the disease that has made him so. This is a very important diagnostic point.

~

Family doctor
from A Story-Teller's World *by R.K. Narayan*

I fear the grand old institution of 'family doctor' is now gone. I say 'doctor', rather than 'physician' or 'surgeon', since no one ever bothered about such distinctions in the good old times. 'Doctor' was a generic term without a category or classification, and also the family doctor of pre-War years lived up to our expectations of his being an all-round healer.

That was before medical science developed complex branches. There was little popular writing on health, disease and sudden mortality: too much information has now created hypochondriacs who suspect the worst at the least sympton of pain and rush to the doctor for an opinion, who cannot help suggesting, 'Why don't you go through a complete check-up and see me again?' The man appears again before his doctor in due course, clutching a sheaf of documents and papers, like a habitual litigant at a lawyer's office, to be assured by the doctor in most cases, 'You are fine. Nothing to worry about.'

The present-day doctor has to make sure that he has scientific backing before pronouncing an opinion. But the old family doctor gave the same cheerful verdict spontaneously, intuitively, without much ado. Probing and scanning being unheard of, he had to depend for diagnosis on a stethoscope, thermometer and a flashlight, and probably a spoon to hold down the tongue for examining a throat. Also, by tapping the abdomen and chest with two fingers, he could judge from the subtle resonance what might be right and wrong under the skin. His final advice would be, 'Avoid buttermilk and drink plenty of water,' or he might sit down and write a prescription, perhaps in Latin, with an air of one composing a sonnet, to be interpreted only by the pharmacist later, who would fill an eight-ounce bottle with a colourful mixture labelled properly. A bazaar doctor of my acquaintance, whose clients were mostly villagers, wrote his prescriptions in not less than twenty minute lines and then turned the sheet sideways and wrote also on the margin while his patients looked on solemnly, in profound admiration.

Tablets and antibiotics in aluminium strips were unknown in those days. In case of pneumonia, I remember fermentation with what seemed to be warmed-up horse manure (judging from the pervasive odour) was recommended. For eye trouble, which is nowadays handled by specialists with extreme delicacy, our doctor would just turn up the patient's eye-lids and rub on silver nitrate every morning while the patient groaned and squirmed. Occasionally, in an emergency, the doctor would also hold down the patient and incise an abscess with a scalpel and soak the wound in tincture iodine while the patient screamed and cursed and tried to knock down the doctor. However, relief was definite in most cases, achieved through an unflinching faith in the family doctor and the doctor's faith that we would not so easily crumble or collapse, which speaks for the hardihood of the human constitution.

There was an indefinable quality and sustenance in the relationship between a doctor and his patient, which is missing today. Nowadays every doctor is hard-pressed for time with an unrelenting 'Kumbh Mela' crowd at his door night and day. The doctor-patient relationship has become literally mechanical. At a busy doctor's establishment, you will come face to face with the doctor, if at all, only at the end of a long journey through a number of secretaries, technicians and assistants.

I have come to this conclusion after a recent experience with an ear specialist after a great deal of importuning over the phone. At the waiting hall, by the time my name was called, I had finished reading cover to cover several old issues of a ladies' journal heaped on the table. I presented myself at a ticket window. On the other side a lady was sitting and questioned me as to what was wrong and took down dictation while I narrated my troubles through the grill. Next, I was ushered into the presence of the doctor who studied my card, examined my ear and gestured to me to follow his assistant. I found myself in a chamber of electronics. The operators seated me on a stool and turned switches off and on after fitting an ear-phone to me, and finally produced a chart on graph paper. Back to the doctor, who studied the chart, handed me a printed message which just confirmed that I was having an ear problem, but assured that it was inevitable at my age, and concluded with the advice that I take B-Complex daily. I wanted clarification on some points in the printed message but I realized that the next patient was already breathing down my neck. And 'I came out by the same door as in I went', my head throbbing with unasked questions.

~

The objet d'art
from Early Stories *by Anton Chekhov*

Holding under his arm an object carefully wrapped up in No. 223 of the *Stock Exchange Gazette*, Sasha Smirnoff (an only son) pulled a long face and walked into Doctor Florinsky's consulting-room.

'Ah, my young friend!' the doctor greeted him. 'And how are we today? Everything well, I trust?'

Sasha blinked his eyes, pressed his hand to his heart and said in a voice trembling with emotion.

'Mum sends her regards, Doctor, and told me to thank you . . . I'm a mother's only son and you saved my life – cured me of a dangerous illness . . . and Mum and me simply don't know how to thank you.'

'Nonsense, lad,' interrupted the doctor, simpering with delight. 'Anyone else would have done the same in my place.'

'I'm a mother's only son . . . We're poor folk, Mum and me, and of course we can't pay you for your services . . . and we feel very bad about it, Doctor, but all the same, we – Mum and me, that is, her one and only – we do beg you most earnestly to accept as a token of our gratitude this . . . this object here, which . . . It's a very valuable antique bronze – an exceptional work of art.'

'No, really,' said the doctor, frowning. 'I couldn't possibly.'

'Yes, yes, you simply must accept it!' Sasha mumbled away as he unwrapped the parcel. 'If you refuse, we'll be offended, Mum and me . . . It's a very fine piece . . . an antique bronze . . . It came to us when Dad died and we've kept it as a precious memento . . . Dad used to buy up antique bronzes and sell them to collectors . . . Now Mum and me are running the business . . .'

Sasha finished unwrapping the object and placed it triumphantly on the table. It was a small, finely modelled old bronze candelabrum. On its pedestal two female figures were standing in a state of nature and in poses that I am neither bold nor hot-blooded enough to describe. The figures were smiling coquettishly, and altogether seemed to suggest that but for the need to go on supporting the candlestick, they would leap off the pedestal and turn the room into a scene of such wild debauch that the mere thought of it, gentle reader, would bring a blush to your cheek.

After glancing at the present, the doctor slowly scratched the back of his ear, cleared his throat and blew his nose uncertainly.

'Yes, it's a beautiful object all right,' he mumbled, 'but, well, how shall I put it? . . . You couldn't say it was exactly tasteful . . . I mean, décolleté's one thing, but this is really going too far . . .'

'How do you mean, going too far?'

'The Arch–Tempter himself couldn't have thought up anything more vile. Why, if I were to put a fandangle like that on the table, I'd feel I was polluting the whole house!'

'What a strange view of art you have, Doctor!' said Sasha, sounding hurt. 'Why, this is a work of inspiration! Look at all that beauty and elegance – doesn't it fill you with awe and bring a lump to your throat? You forget all about worldly things when you contemplate beauty like that . . . Why, look at the movement there, Doctor, look at all the air and *expression*!'

'I appreciate that only too well, my friend,' interrupted the doctor, 'but you're forgetting, I'm a family man – think of my small children running about, think of the ladies.'

'Of course, if you're going to look at it through the eyes of the masses,' said Sasha, 'then of course this highly artistic creation does appear in a different light . . . But you must raise yourself above the masses, Doctor, especially as Mum and me'll be deeply offended if you refuse. I'm a mother's only son – you saved my life . . . We're giving you our most treasured possession . . . and my only regret is that we don't have another one to make the pair . . .'

'Thank you, dear boy, I'm very grateful . . . Give Mum my regards, but just put yourself in my place – think of the children running about, think of the ladies . . . Oh, all right then, let it stay! I can see I'm not going to convince you.'

'There's nothing to convince me of,' Sasha replied joyfully. 'You must stand the candelabrum here, next to this vase. What a pity there isn't the pair! What a pity! Goodbye, then, Doctor!'

When Sasha had left, the doctor spent a long time gazing at the candelabrum, scratching the back of his ear and pondering.

'It's a superb thing, no two ways about that,' he thought, 'and it's a shame to let it go . . . But there's no question of keeping it here . . . Hmm, quite a problem! Who can I give it to or unload it on?'

After lengthy consideration he thought of his good friend Harkin the solicitor, to whom he was indebted for professional services.

'Yes, that's the answer,' the doctor decided. 'As a friend it's awkward for him to accept money from me, but if I make him a present of this object, that'll be very *comme il faut*. Yes, I'll take this diabolical creation round to him – after all, he's a bachelor, doesn't take life seriously . . .'

Without further ado, the doctor put on his coat, picked up the candelabrum and set off for Harkin's.

'Greetings!' he said, finding the solicitor at home. 'I've come to thank you, old man, for all that help you gave me – I know you don't like taking money, but perhaps you'd be willing to accept this little trifle . . . here you are, my dear chap – it's really rather special!'

When he saw the little trifle, the solicitor went into transports of delight.

'Oh, my word, yes!' he roared. 'How do they think such things up? Superb! Entrancing! Wherever did you get hold of such a gem?'

Having exhausted his expressions of delight, the solicitor glanced round nervously at the door and said:

'Only be a good chap and take it back, will you? I can't accept it . . .'

'Why ever not?' said the doctor in alarm.

'Obvious reasons . . . Think of my mother coming in, think of my clients . . . And how could I look the servants in the face?'

'No, no, no, don't you dare refuse!' said the doctor, waving his arms at him. 'You're being a boor! This is a work of inspiration – look at the movement there . . . the *expression* . . . Any more fuss and I shall be offended!'

'If only it was daubed over or had some fig leaves stuck on . . .'

But the doctor waved his arms at him even more vigorously, nipped smartly out of the apartment and returned home, highly pleased that he'd managed to get the present off his hands . . .

When his friend had gone, Harkin studied the candelabrum closely, kept touching it all over, and like the doctor, racked his brains for a long time wondering what was to be done with it.

'It's a fine piece of work,' he reflected, 'and it'd be a shame to let it go, but keeping it here would be most improper. The best thing would be to give it to someone . . . Yes, I know – there's a benefit performance tonight for Shashkin, the comic actor. I'll take the candelabrum round to him as a present – after all, the old rascal loves that kind of thing . . .'

No sooner said than done. That evening the candelabrum, painstakingly wrapped, was presented to the comic actor Shashkin. The whole evening the actor's dressing-room was besieged by male visitors coming to admire the present; all evening the dressing-room was filled with a hubbub of rapturous exclamations and laughter like the whinnying of a horse. Whenever one of the actresses knocked on the door and asked if she could come in, the actor's husky voice would immediately reply:

'Not just now, darling, I'm changing.'

After the show the actor hunched his shoulders, threw up his hands in perplexity and said:

'Where the hell can I put this obscenity? After all, I live in a private apartment – think of the actresses who come to see me! It's not like a photograph, you can't shove it into a desk drawer!'

'Why not sell it, sir?' advised the wig-maker who was helping him off with his costume. 'There's an old woman in this area who buys up bronzes like that . . . Just ask for Mrs Smirnoff – everyone knows her.'

The comic actor took his advice . . .

Two days later Doctor Florinsky was sitting in his consulting-room with one finger pressed to his forehead, and was thinking about the acids of the bile. Suddenly the door flew open and in rushed Sasha Smirnoff. He was smiling, beaming, and his whole figure radiated happiness . . . In his hands he was holding something wrapped up in newspaper.

'Doctor!' he began, gasping for breath. 'I'm so delighted! You won't believe your luck – we've managed to find another candelabrum to make your pair! . . . Mum's thrilled to bits . . . I'm a mother's only son – you saved my life . . .'

And Sasha, all aquiver with gratitude, placed the candelabrum in front of the doctor. The doctor's mouth dropped, he tried to say something but nothing came out: he was speechless.

~

The use of force
from The Doctor Stories *by William Carlos Williams*

They were new patients to me, all I had was the name, Olson. 'Please come down as soon as you can, my daughter is very sick.'

When I arrived I was met by the mother, a big startled looking woman, very clean and apologetic who merely said, 'Is this the doctor?' and let me in. In the back, she added, 'You must excuse us, doctor, we have her in the kitchen where it is warm. It is very damp here sometimes.'

The child was fully dressed and sitting on her father's lap near the kitchen table. He tried to get up, but I motioned for him not to bother, took off my overcoat and started to look things over. I could see that they were all very nervous, eyeing me up and down distrustfully. As often, in such cases, they weren't telling me more than they had to, it was up to me to tell them; that's why they were spending three dollars on me.

The child was fairly eating me up with her cold, steady eyes, and no expression to her face whatever. She did not move and seemed, inwardly, quiet; an unusually attractive little thing, and as strong as a heifer in appearance. But her face was flushed, she was breathing rapidly, and I realized that she had a high fever. She had magnificent blonde hair, in profusion. One of those picture children often reproduced in advertising leaflets and the photogravure sections of the Sunday papers.

'She's had a fever for three days,' began the father, 'and we don't know what it comes from. My wife has given her things, you know, like people do, but it don't do no good. And there's been a lot of sickness around. So we tho't you'd better look her over and tell us what is the matter.'

As doctors often do I took a trial shot at it as a point of departure. Had she had a sore throat?

Both parents answered me together, 'No . . . No, she says her throat don't hurt her.'

'Does your throat hurt you?' added the mother to the child. But the little girl's expression didn't change nor did she move her eyes from my face.

'Have you looked?'

'I tried to,' said the mother, 'but I couldn't see.'

As it happens we had been having a number of cases of diphtheria in the school to which this child went during that month and we were all, quite apparently, thinking of that, though no one had as yet spoken of the thing.

'Well,' I said, 'suppose we take a look at the throat first.' I smiled in my best professional manner and asking for the child's first name I said, 'Come on, Mathilda, open your mouth and let's take a look at your throat.'

Nothing doing.

'Aw, come on,' I coaxed, 'just open your mouth wide and let me take a look. Look, I said opening both hands wide, I haven't anything in my hands. Just open up and let me see.'

'Such a nice man,' put in the mother. 'Look how kind he is to you. Come on, do what he tells you to. He won't hurt you.'

At that I ground my teeth in disgust. If only they wouldn't use the word 'hurt' I might be able to get somewhere. But I did not allow myself to be hurried or disturbed but speaking quietly and slowly I approached the child again.

As I moved my chair a little nearer suddenly with one catlike movement both her hands clawed instinctively for my eyes and she almost reached them too. In fact she knocked my glasses flying and they fell, though unbroken, several feet away from me on the kitchen floor.

Both the mother and father almost turned themselves inside out in embarrassment and apology. 'You bad girl,' said the mother, taking her and shaking her by one arm. 'Look what you've done. The nice man . . .'

'For heaven's sake,' I broke in, 'don't call me a nice man to her. I'm here to look at her throat on the chance that she might have diphtheria and possibly die of it. But that's nothing to her. Look here, I said to the child, we're going to look at your throat. You're old enough to understand what I'm saying. Will you open it now by yourself or shall we have to open it for you?'

Not a move. Even her expression hadn't changed. Her breaths however were coming faster and faster. Then the battle began. I had to do it. I had to have a throat culture for her own protection. But first I told the parents that it was entirely up to them. I explained the danger but said that I would not insist on a throat examination so long as they would take the responsibility.

'If you don't do what the doctor says you'll have to go to the hospital,' the mother admonished her severely.

Oh yeah? I had to smile to myself. After all, I had already fallen in love with the savage brat, the parents were contemptible to me. In the ensuing struggle they grew more and more abject, crushed, exhausted while she surely rose to magnificent heights of insane fury of effort bred of her terror of me.

The father tried his best, and he was a big man but the fact that she was his daughter, his shame at her behavior and his dread of hurting her made him release her just at the critical moment several times when I had almost achieved success, till I wanted to kill him. But his dread also that she might have diphtheria made him tell me to go on, go on though he himself was almost fainting, while the mother moved back and forth behind us raising and lowering her hands in an agony of apprehension.

'Put her in front of you on your lap,' I ordered, and held both her wrists.

But as soon as he did the child let out a scream. 'Don't, you're hurting me. Let go of my hands. Let them go I tell you.' Then she shrieked terrifyingly, hysterically. 'Stop it! Stop it! You're killing me!'

Do you think she can stand it, doctor!' said the mother.

'You get out,' said the husband to his wife. 'Do you want her to die of diphtheria?'

'Come on now, hold her,' I said.

Then I grasped the child's head with my left hand and tried to get the wooden tongue depressor between her teeth. She fought, with clenched teeth, desperately! But now I also had grown furious – at a child. I tried to hold myself down but I couldn't. I know how to expose a throat for inspection. And I did my best. When finally I got the wooden spatula behind the last teeth and just the point of it into the mouth cavity, she opened up for an instant but before I could see anything she came down again and gripping the wooden blade between her molars she reduced it to splinters before I could get it out again.

'Aren't you ashamed to act like that in front of the doctor?'

'Get me a smooth-handled spoon of some sort,' I told the mother. 'We're going through this.' The child's mouth was already bleeding. Her tongue was cut and she was screaming in wild hysterical shrieks. Perhaps I should have desisted and come back in an hour or more. No doubt it would have been better. But I have seen at least two children lying dead in bed of neglect in such cases, and feeling that I must get a diagnosis now or never I went at it again. But the worst of it was that I too had got beyond reason. I could have torn the child apart in my own fury and enjoyed it. It was a pleasure to attack her. My face was burning with it.

The damned little brat must be protected against her own idiocy, one says to one's self at such times. Others must be protected against her. It is a social necessity. And all these things are true. But a blind fury, a feeling of adult shame, bred of a longing for muscular release are the operatives. One goes on to the end.

In a final unreasoning assault I overpowered the child's neck and jaws. I forced the heavy silver spoon back of her teeth and down her throat till she gagged. And there it was – both tonsils covered with membrane. She had fought valiantly to keep me from knowing her secret. She had been hiding that sore throat for three days at least and lying to her parents in order to escape just such an outcome as this.

Now truly she *was* furious. She had been on the defensive before but now she attacked. Tried to get off her father's lap and fly at me while tears of defeat blinded her eyes.

Calling all patients
from A Case of Jerepigo *by H.C. Bosman*

The other day I took ill – a slight twinge in my right leg, a twinge going up and down, sort of. I sent for a doctor. This reminded me of that 'short prose narrative' of O. Henry's, which begins 'So I went to see a doctor'. Now, that story is one of my O. Henry favourites, and I have often wondered what did happen in that New York medical practitioner's consulting-room about half a century ago. I have also thought that the story would be very interesting told the other way around – i.e., bearing the title 'So I Went to See O. Henry,' and related by the doctor.

But that was not to be. For O. Henry could still walk, and so he walked into where the doctor was, and got examined, and after that walked out again. And so I expect that the only official record of the visit to the doctor by the then still unknown man of genius consisted of a number of unimaginative entries in the doctor's notebook. In the column headed, 'Name of Patient,' there would probably be nothing more than. 'Mr W.S. Porter,' and under 'Diagnosis' just that familiar annotation that has such time-honoured links with the science of healing: 'Drunk.'

Here is something to reflect on, now. You never hear of a case in which the patient enters the doctor's consulting-room and after a brief interview with the doctor – who has stood in the middle of the floor, swaying – the patient walks out and, before stepping into the lift, makes this entry in his own notebook: 'Diagnosis of Doctor's condition – Drunk.'

Oh, no, that sort of thing never happens. It is always the poor patient that gets unflattering remarks about himself written down in a well-bound appointment book for thoughtless people to get mirthful over in after years. Remarks like 'Gen. N. Bonaparte' – 'Fallen Arches,' or 'Sir Walter Raleigh' – 'Ye Mange,' or 'P.B. Shelley' – 'Bog Spavined,' or 'Miss C. Bronte' – 'Blue-Tongue.' Small wonder, therefore, that the patient has begun to break down under the weight of opprobrium and ridicule with which during the centuries his lot has been burdened – in fact, ever since Hippocrates first wrote (in BC 420) behind a sick man's name, in good Greek, 'Alcibiades, Esq., – Goofball Addict.'

But it is quite different with doctors, of course. I mean, for one thing, it has been proved that doctors are never addicted to drugs. The reason is quite obvious. Because he has constant access to every kind of dope there is, a doctor is not tempted to become a drug fiend. A couple of lungfuls of opium out of the old bamboo pipe just before breakfast does the average doctor until lunchtime. The early forenoon cocaine habit is not nearly as widespread among the members of the medical fraternity as the lay public imagines. Similarly, a whiff or two of Indian hemp, supplemented by a shot of morphia or codeine, sees the medical man through the particularly trying period which mid-afternoon is to most workers. And when he goes off duty he is quite content with a heroin injection, or with a few grains of fly agaric or Banisteria caapi. All of which goes to prove that while the patient is every kind of moron and disease-carrier and sot, the doctor is none of these things.

So that when a doctor looks at you with a fixed, glassy stare, you *know* (because it has been proved) that he is not drugged. He has got that dazed expression of a man listening to enchanting harmonies – and as if the bonds of time and space are broken – just through overwork. And when he acts queer, as though suffering from sensorial illusions – well, he's just thinking, that's all. Sensorial illusions, my foot. It's not the patient we're dealing with now.

Anyway, as a result of my having got that aforementioned twinge, I was suddenly able to see life from what was to me a novel angle. I realised that with all this medical progress business, and all this eulogising of people like Pasteur and Lister and Jennings, there was one person in grave danger of being overlooked – namely, the patient. Where would medical science be without the patient – lying in bed on his back, with one leg raised in the air, or just lying on his back? Or being wheeled on a trolley with the blankets pulled over his head after an operation? Or having the screens drawn around his bed at a solemn nod from the doctor, also after an operation? ... The person at the very core of every situation concerned with the treatment of disease or injury is none other than the patient.

Calling Dr Kildare. That's quite all right. But of what earthly use is Dr Kildare, unless there's Patient Willemse first? You could go on calling Dr Kildare until you were blue in the face, else. What the world has hitherto overlooked is the fact that the backbone of medical science and the Hollywood film industry is the hospital patient.

This is an injustice that I hope to see righted still within my own lifetime – a period not likely to be unduly extended in view of the fact that I am receiving daily treatment at the General Hospital, although it be only as an out-patient.

What is needed is a series of medical films on the lines of *Pasteur, The Story of Dr Erlich, Calling Dr Kildare, Dr Jekyll and Mr Hyde, Men in White* and the rest of them, but with this difference, that the accent is shifted slightly, so that the hero-surgeon is replaced by the hero-patient. A few titles of this newer sort of film that I can think of just off-hand are *Hospital Patient O'Higgins, Calling Patient O'Higgins, Patient O'Higgins's Last Op, Curtains for Patient O'H.*

For *Men in White* we could substitute *Men in Bed*, or *Men in Pyjamas* or – for a period film – *Men in Long Nightshirts* (in Technicolor perhaps). Another film in this series would be *Men in Dressing-Gowns*, meaning the convalescents sitting on the stoep in wheelchairs – survivors of spectacular major operations. . . . But, naturally, there are not so many in this class – c.f., *Patient O'Higgins's Last Op.* (And also *Curtains for Patient O'H.*) So *Men in Dressing-Gowns* could possibly just be made into an educational short.

Some day, when I have time to do a spot of research work, I would like to compile a volume on *Great Hospital Patients of the World*. Typical passages, dealing with typical pioneer patients, would read something after this style:

'There was no incentive for Heinrich B. Zoss (1857–1887) to leave his own country, Germany, to become a patient in new hospitals across the seas. The patients of those days had no hope of becoming famous men. . . . His arguments were denounced by all the eminent patients of his native land. . . . In despair he fled to Vienna, where he achieved his life's ambition of being acupunctured and moxibustioned within the same week, which was, strangely enough, also destined to be his last week. . . .'

Or again: 'Switzerland's pioneer hospital patient showed no unusual gifts as a boy for that brilliant career which, but for the jealousy of certain famous contemporaries, would have terminated in his being elected a Fellow of the Board of International Patients . . . Born in a charcoal-burner's hut, like many another patient of humble origin, he rose to be one of the leading patients at the Zurich hospital, where, in the course of a brief but memorable career, he (just) lived to see his intestines divided into etc., etc. . . .'

Or this one: 'Before closing the chapter on American patients, the name of Oswald Sauerbach must not be forgotten . . . Known as "the stormy petrel of American hospital wards," Sauerbach early in life advanced the startling theory that etc., etc. . . . The doctor who eventually performed this operation on Oswald Sauerbach lived to become a world-famous Professor of Surgery. Oswald did not.'

Calling Patient Willemse. Calling Patient Willemse. Calling Patient Willemse. No reply. Patient Willemse has had his chips (Cf., *Patient O'Higgins's Last Op*).

~

The doctor knows best
from Written in Sickness *by Damon Runyon*

A man has a pain in a certain spot.

It isn't a severe pain. It isn't an incapacitating pain. But it is none the less a pain.

The man goes to a doctor.

'Doc,' he says, 'I've got a kind of a pain.'

So the doctor examines him. He takes the man's temperature, feels his pulse. He looks down the man's throat. He listens to the man's chest. He tests his reflexes.

The doctor finds nothing. He gives the man some simple remedy and tells him that ought to do the trick.

The man is back in a few days. 'Doc,' he says, 'that pain is still there. I don't feel so good.'

The doctor makes another examination. He has the man go to an X-ray fellow for a few takes of his teeth and his interior. The doctor puts the exposures on a rack and gazes at them intently. He sees nothing. He lets the man look at them. The man does not see anything, either.

Then the doctor gives the man diathermic treatments. He gives him vitamin pills and vitamin hypodermics. The needles hurt the man like hell.

'How are you today?' the doctor asks the man on the man's next visit. The doctor is not taking the needles himself, so he has no call to cut himself in on the man's suffering with that 'we'.

'Doc,' the man says, 'that pain is still there. I don't feel so good.'

Now the doctor puts the man on a strict diet. He tells him to stop smoking and drinking and cease doing all the other things the man enjoys.

'Doc,' the man says, 'that pain is still there.'

The doctor commences to resent the man's attitude. He commences to hate the very sight of the man's kisser. So do his office attendants.

They look at one another knowingly when he appears for his treatments.

When the man's friends ask the doctor what's the matter with the man, the doctor shrugs his shoulders. He purses his lips. He smiles slightly. He as much as says there is nothing the matter with the man.

The man is observed taking one of the pills the doctor ordered.

'He's always taking pills,' the observer remarks. 'He's a hypochondriac. His doctor can't find a thing wrong with him.'

Now if the man has had a good break from life and remains a bachelor, he is not in such bad shape, but if he has the misfortune to be married he is in an awful fix because his wife and family are more difficult to convince that he has a pain than the doctor. They resent his attitude even more than the doctor.

'I've still got that pain,' he says to his wife.

'It's just your imagination,' she says. 'You never looked better in your life. You mustn't give way to every little ache that comes along. Think of all the suffering in the world. I'm really the one that ought to be in bed.'

'I don't feel so good,' the man says.

'Nonsense,' his wife says.

So the man finally hauls off and gives up the ghost. He ups and dies. His wife and family are astonished, and indignant.

'Well,' the man's friends say. 'He wasn't looking any too well the last time he was around and he was complaining about a pain, too. Must have been something radically wrong with the old boy, at that.'

The doctor is in a bit of a huff about the man dying that way.

~

Alf Garnett and Dr Becker
from In Sickness and in Health *by Johnny Speight*

INTERIOR OF DOCTOR'S WAITING-ROOM.

ALF IS SITTING WITH SOME OTHER PEOPLE WAITING. ALF THROWS MAGAZINE DOWN HE WAS LOOKING AT AND PICKS UP ANOTHER, SCOWLS AT IT, AND THROWS THAT DOWN.

ALF: (To receptionist)
Is he gonna be much longer?

RECEPTIONIST:
Which doctor are you waiting for?

ALF:
Becker.

RECEPTIONIST:
Doctor Becker?

ALF:
If he expects people to sit about waiting for him all day, he wants to get some comfortable, decent chairs in here!

RECEPTIONIST:
I'm sorry, but Doctor Becker has a full surgery this morning . . .

ALF:
He wouldn't have if we could afford to go somewhere else!

RECEPTIONIST:
He won't keep you much longer.

ALF GETS HIS PIPE OUT AND STARTS TO FILL IT.

RECEPTIONIST:
You can't smoke in here.

ALF:
I'm not smoking. I'm just putting tobacco in it. Getting it ready for when I can smoke it . . . when I get out of here, so I can fumigate me lungs . . . kill some of the germs I've had to breathe sitting here.

RECEPTIONIST:
Smoking's bad for you. It could kill you.

ALF:
What, at my age? If that don't kill me something else will. And if I gotta choice . . . (brandishing his pipe) . . . I'd sooner it was this. My problem is affording to smoke it, not worrying what it might do to me. Listen, Missis, at my age, on my bloody pension, I'm lucky I've got enough strength left in me hands to fill me pipe, an' enough money to buy tobacco to fill it with, an' enough power left in me lungs still to puff it with'

ALF ENTERS THE DOCTOR'S SURGERY AND SITS DOWN.

ALF:
Doctor Becker?

DOCTOR:
Yes. And you are . . .?

ALF:
Never mind who I am. I've gotta bone to pick with you. What's the idea, telling Mrs Hollingbery to sit back, put her feet up, an' take it easy?

DOCTOR:
Mrs Hollingbery? Oh yes . . . She's got a very painful leg . . .

ALF:
I've gotta a very painful leg. I've gotta very painful bum too, from sitting out there on a hard chair waiting to see you.

DOCTOR:
Who are you?

ALF:
I live with Mrs Hollingbery, an' I've had no breakfast over you, no dinner, an' I won't get no supper either . . .

DOCTOR:
Just a moment . . .

ALF:
No, you just a moment. How would you like it if I come round your house an' told your wife to sit back, put her feet up, an' take it easy? Eh? An you got no breakfast, an' no dinner or supper because of it? Eh?

DOCTOR:
Mrs Hollingbery is a patient of mine, and it's my duty to prescribe recuperative treatment that I believe will benefit her. She has a very painful leg, and . . .

ALF:
I've gotta very painful leg . . .

DOCTOR:
That maybe so . . . but . . .

ALF:
I had to have a new hip put in, but I don't complain about it. I'm in terrible pain with it, but I don't keep on about it.

DOCTOR:
You've had a hip replacement, have you?

ALF:
Yer an' I wouldn't mind another one.

DOCTOR:
Another one?

ALF:
I'd like 'em to replace the one they put in with one that fits properly.

DOCTOR:
You're having trouble with your leg are you?

ALF:
I've had trouble with that leg ever since they put in the new hip. But the leg I'm complaining about now ain't my leg, its Mrs Hollingbery's leg. All right, you've gotta prescribe for her as you say, but what about me? Who's gonna prescribe for me? I've not had any dinner today.

DOCTOR:
Hasn't Mrs Hollingbery eaten today either?

ALF:
Well, of course she ain't. You told her she's gotta rest.

DOCTOR:
Well, yes, but you live with her, couldn't you have provided a meal for her?

ALF:
Oh yer, an' what am I supposed to be, the unpaid social worker again, am I? It's all right for you sitting here, putting people on the sick list, telling 'em to put their feet up, an' rest ... But who d'you think's gonna look after 'em while you're prescribing recuperative treatments for 'em? Muggins, ain't it, eh? Muggins again. It was just the same when you put my wife in a wheelchair, God rest her ...

DOCTOR:
I didn't put your wife in a wheelchair ...

92

ALF:

One of your lot did. But you didn't provide anyone to push her. I mean, I didn't begrudge a thing I done for that woman, God rest her. It was pushing that wheelchair done my hip in, but I don't complain. I'm only grateful I was here to help her in her last days. It's left me a cripple, but I don't go round whining about it. That's the trouble. You willingly shoulder a burden for a loved one, an' you get put on.

DOCTOR:

Leave it with me, I'll pop round and take a look at Mrs Hollingbery tomorrow, and see what I can fix up . . .

ALF:

What, a social worker, you mean?

DOCTOR:

Something like that.

ALF: (rising)

Well, make sure you get someone a bit decent. Someone who don't mind a bit of work, an' who ain't got too much old lip. One who can cook an' don't mind doing a bit of hard work. The trouble with yer social workers, they wanna be too social. All most of 'em wanna do is sit there jawing with a cup of tea . . . Another thing you can do doctor, is prescribe a bit of nourishment for Mrs Hollingbery, and me if I'm gonna have to push her about in a chair . . . Write a note to the DSS, I know the procedure if you want any help . . . It's no good you prescribing people to spend their winters in a warmer climate 'cos the cold affects their limbs without the old werewithall . . . (rubbing his fingers together)

DOCTOR:

I haven't prescribed a warmer climate . . .

ALF:

That would help us. That an' plenty more food.

FADE

~

93

Malingering
from If Symptoms Persist *by Theodore Dalrymple*

It was about three years ago that I first noticed an unmistakable portent of the imminent downfall of Western civilisation: spelling errors, committed by junior doctors, began to appear in hospital notes. In my day, not after all so very long ago, such errors were unthinkable. I have even seen *necessary* spelt *neccesary*. Can the rot go further?

There has been another lamentable change observable in medical notes in the past couple of years: a loss of frankness. Ever since the Government, trying cravenly to pretend that it believed in human rights, in the open society etc., gave to patients the right to read their own notes (a retrograde step if ever there was one), doctors have been afraid to put in writing what they really think of their patients. Truth has given way yet again to silence.

Now as the practitioners of holistic medicine tell us *ad nauseam*, doctors should treat not just the disease or pathological process, but the whole person, since character and personality play such a large part in the healing process. It is therefore of vital clinical importance for a doctor to know that his patient is a snivelling rat, an untrustworthy toad or a verminous creep without any redeeming features whatsoever when he undertakes treatment. It can, for example, be dangerous to take a liar's word seriously, and doctors should therefore surely be allowed to pass comment in the notes on a patient's unattachment to truth, so that other doctors who come after him may know of it.

Alas, as the national character continues to disintegrate, or rather disappear, leaving only a kind of scowl behind, medical notes become blander and blander. The literary flourish and the written *cri de coeur*, which must once have relieved the doctor's feelings considerably, are now forbidden; no catharsis whatever is allowed. You can't even write any more that a patient is fat.

I was recently consulted by two men whose previous medical records I wished to read before coming to a conclusion about them. The first I suspected of malingering; the second claimed to have undergone a change of character in the past two months, something which he averred was indicative of illness and which I did not fully believe. Suffice it to say that he had a forensic motive for maintaining that he had undergone such a change in character.

By coincidence, their medical records from 20 years ago arrived on my desk the same day. By coincidence also, they had both consulted a doctor, now retired, who was famed locally for the uninhibited nature of his letters: he wrote his mind. Doctors in idle moments used to search out his notes for amusement.

Of my suspected malingerer, he wrote all those years ago:

Two conditions must be fulfilled to make the diagnosis of malingering: i) the absence of disease and ii) unequivocal evidence of gain brought about by malingering. The first condition is fulfilled in this man's case. As to the second condition, I should have thought that his continuing to draw sickness benefit while surreptitiously working constitutes sufficient evidence. He is a practised, unscrupulous and cunning malingerer.

His typed report about my second patient began with the following words:

This miserable creature . . .

I punched the air with my fist. 'Right on!' I exclaimed.

Hospitals

Hospital visit
from Writings from the New Yorker 1927–1976
by E.B. White

Modern medicine is a wonderful thing, but we doubt whether it ever catches up with modern man, who is way out in front and running strong. One morning at the hospital, *The Times* was delivered to our breakfast table (by a woman tall enough to reach to that dizzy height) and we turned idly to an article on tranquillizers, headed 'WARNS OF HEALTH PERIL.' Clinicians, the article said, have found some of the effects of the drugs to be Parkinsonism, allergic dermatitis, constipation, diarrhea, jaundice, and depression. We finished our frozen juice and turned to face an entering nurse, who presented us with a tiny paper cup containing a white pill. 'Take this,' she said, smiling a knowing smile. We bowed and she left. We picked up the pill, examined it closely, and there, sure enough, was the familiar monogram of Miltown. Dutifully we swallowed it, and immediately felt the first symptoms of Parkinson's disease, the first faint flush of yellow jaundice. Then we looked back at the tray and noticed that our morning milk had arrived in a wax-paper carton – the same sort of carton that was in the news some months ago, suspected by scientists of being carcinogenic. Recklessly we poured the milk and raised the glass to our image in the mirror. 'Cheers!' we croaked, and fell back onto the pillows, in the last stages of allergic dermatitis.

The curative value of a hospital, for us, is that it keeps us busy. In our normal life in the outside world, we seldom have anything to do from morning till night and we simply wander about, a writer who rarely writes, lonely and at peace, getting through the day cunningly, the way an alcoholic works his way along from drink to drink, cleverly spaced. But once we're in a hospital, the nights and days are crowded with events and accomplishment. Supper is at six, breakfast at nine, which means that for about fifteen hours we subsist in a semistarved condition, like a man in a lifeboat; and when our stomach is empty our mind and heart are full, and we are up and about, doing housework, catching up on correspondence, outwitting the air-conditioning system, taking sleeping pills, reading names on nurses' badges, arranging flowers, picking up after the last tenant, fighting the roller shade that has lost its spring, making plans for death, inventing dodges to circumvent therapy, attaching a string to the bed table to render it accessible to the immobilized patient, flushing undesirable medication down the toilet, prying into the private affairs of the floor nurse, gazing out at the wheeling planets and the lovely arabesques of the Jersey shore. Dawn comes, and an early nurse, to test with her little fingers whether our heart still beats. And then we shave and practice counting to fifteen, so that when they jab us with Sodium Pentothal and ask us to count, we can race them to the knockout. Busyness is really the solution to a man's life, in this cold sunless clime. And a hospital is the place.

~

Within limits
from Low Life *by Jeffrey Bernard*

The Middlesex Hospital,
Mortimer Street,
London W1

H.M. Prison,
Stanford Hill,
Sheerness, Kent

Dear Ken: Isn't it just typical that both you and I should be in open prisons during Royal Ascot week? Perhaps we should confine our sinning to the winter months, although, as far as you're concerned, conditions would be a little sharper than they would be for me. Eva told me she'd been to see you and that you *seemed* to be bearing up. I take my hat off to you. I'm here for just a few days and already gloom descends only to be lifted by trifling entertainments like eating fairly awful food, ticking off items on the following day's menu and chasing the newspaper man down the corridor as he tries to escape without making a sale. A sadist, I shouldn't wonder. But I shouldn't moan to you of all people, banged up as you are in a dormitory full of what might be a very dodgy lot. My cell, as it were, consists of four and my three companions are dead ringers for any and all the other trios I've ever served time with in hospitals. It's a bit like being in rep.

Mr James is the paisley dressing-gown sort and the paisley dressing-gown has usually seen better days. He has silver hair, a clipped military moustache and Tiptree jam on top of his locker and not the cheap stuff. He does *The Daily Telegraph* crossword, usually has trouble with the 'waterworks' and has a rather genteel sort of visitor. He often thinks he's dying but he's as tough as leather. On my left we have Mr Croft who has a pituitary gland disorder which seems to fascinate him as much as it does the medical staff. He's fat, farts a fair amount and is an extremely useful dustbin and waste disposal unit when my friends and visitors bring me excessive amounts of fruit. He's a *Daily Mirror* crossword man and, unlike most tabloid addicts, he's delightfully unsycophantic towards the Middlesex staff. Not a forelock-tugger, this one. He drinks vast quantities of orangeade and has a strangely musical snore. Last night he changed key at least four times. Very fond of telling the nurses that they're the light of his life.

On my immediate right my fellow sufferer is Mr Jones who absolutely laps up tests of any kind, blood-lettings, X-rays and inquisitions from students. The Joneses of the hospital world would be nothing without their illnesses. Diabetes to Jones is what eggs are to bacon. It's just as well for him that the condition is incurable. But he's not daft. He can read a paper, urinate, smoke a cigarette and listen to Radio 2 on his earphones all at the same time and that makes some professional jugglers look a trifle green. Last night he fell asleep with the earphones in and I was tempted to wake him up with a sharp switch over to Radio 3. The funny thing about a lot of Joneses is the way their wives seem proud of them being ill: 'Ooh yes, George has been terribly ill. He nearly died last year, didn't you George? Eight hours they said he had but he's still here, aren't you George?'

As you may imagine, my visitors are slightly different. Norman came to see me yesterday and brought me a vast amount of fruit and cheese. He said I'd been missed that lunch-hour session in the Coach and I said how could I be missed, I'd only been in the Middlesex for a few hours. 'Business is business,' he said. And I thought I'd never be loved for my money.

By the way, I gather from your letter to our mutual friend that you are incarcerated with some fairly childish nuts and that there was a fracas in your hut over a Mars bar recently. It's pretty much the same here and we have a daily drama in the day room over what we'll watch on television. Normally and quite rightly it should go by a majority vote, but last night an Irishman flipped when we opted for the news and not an epic about some stolen emeralds dumped in a lake by a villain and safeguarded by piranha fish. The Irishman went quite berserk and called me and Mr Jones some horrible names. Unfortunately for him he's on a drip and it's quite difficult to hit yours truly – slow on his feet this week thanks to various drugs – when you're attached to a stand supporting a bottle of saline solution. Anyway, I had a word with him this morning – a captive audience, you might say – and he's been told that we're watching Royal Ascot today come what may, otherwise he'll be in need of medical care. I hope the atmosphere is better in the nick and I hope to see you in time for the Manchester November Handicap.

Yours, Jeff.

IN SICKNESS AND IN HEALTH

Health

'He had had much experience of physicians, and said, "The only way to keep your health is to eat what you don't want, drink what you don't like, and do what not."'

Mark Twain

Longevity
from Endotoxin *by Lewis Thomas*

Dr Oliver Wendell Holmes once laid out the dictum that the key to longevity was to have a chronic incurable disease and take good care of it. Even now, 150 years later, this works. If you have chronic arthritis you are likely to take a certain amount of aspirin most days of your life, and this may reduce your chances of dropping dead from coronary thrombosis. When you are chronically ill, you are also, I suppose, less likely to drive an automobile, or climb ladders, or fall down the cellar stairs carrying books needing storage, or smoke too much, or drink a lot.

~

No life
from Written in Sickness *by Damon Runyon*

You have been noticing an uneasy sensation in region of the Darby Kelly and the croaker says it looks to him like it might be –

'Well, nothing serious, if you are careful about what you eat and take these here powders'.

'All right, Doc. Careful is the word from now on. Thanks.'

'Wait a minute. No orange juice.'

'What, no orange juice, Doc? Always have orange juice for break-fast.'

'No, no orange juice.'

'Okay, Doc. That's gonna be tough, but grapefruit is just as good.'

'No grapefruit, either. No acids.'

'No grapefruit? Say, what does a guy do for breakfast, Doc?'

'Cereals.'

'Don't like cereals, Doc.'

'No syrup.'

'You don't mean a little sorghum on wheat cakes, do you, Doc?'

'No sorghum. No wheat cakes. No sugar.'

'You don't mean no sugar in the coffee, Doc? Just a couple of spoons a cup?'

'Yes, and no coffee.'

'Now look, Doc. You don't mean no coffee at all?'

'No coffee.'

'Say, Doc, that's all right about no sugar, but you must be kidding about no coffee at all.'

'No coffee.'

'Not even a coupla cups a meal, Doc? Why, that's just a taste.'

'No coffee.'

'Doc, that ain't human.'

'No candy.'

'Not even a little bitsy box of peppermints at the movies, Doc?'

'No, no peppermints. No ice.'

'Yo ain't talking about a tiny dab of banana ice cream, are you, Doc? The kind that goes down so slick?'

'Yes, no sweets at all. No highly spiced stuff. No herring.'

'What kind, Doc?'

'Any kind. No herring.'

'But you don't mean a little of that chef's special, Doc? The kind with the white sauce on it?'

'No herring.'

'Not even matjes, Doc?'

'No herring.'

'Well, all right, Doc. No herring. Gefüllte fish will have to do.'

'No gefüllte fish. No goulash.'

'What kind of goulash, Doc? Hungarian?'

'Any kind. No salami. No highly seasoned Italian food:'

'I never eat that more than a couple times a week, anyway; I'll take a lobster Fra Diavolo now and then.'

'None of that.'

'Are you sure about the herring, Doc? There must be some kind that're all right.'

'No herring.'

'It's a conspiracy. Whoever heard of a little herring hurting anybody? Why, Doc, people have been eating herring for years and it never bothered them.'

'No herring.'

'Well, all right, no herring after tonight and tomorrow. What's this list, Doc?'

'It's your diet. Follow it closely.'

'But there ain't anything on it a guy can eat, Doc. It's terrible. You were just kidding about the coffee, weren't you, Doc? No coffee? Can you imagine a guy trying to live without coffee – what? You can't!'

'And no cigarettes.'

'Doc, a guy might as well be dead, hey?'

~

How to live to be 200
from Literary Lapses *by Stephen Leacock*

Twenty years ago I knew a man called Jiggins, who had the Health Habit.

He used to take a cold plunge every morning. He said it opened his pores. After it he took a hot sponge. He said it closed the pores. He got so that he could open and shut his pores at will.

Jiggins used to stand and breathe at an open window for half an hour before dressing. He said it expanded his lungs. He might, of course, have had it done in a shoe store with a boot-stretcher, but after all it cost him nothing this way, and what is half an hour?

After he had got his undershirt on, Jiggins used to hitch himself up like a dog in harness and do Sandow exercises. He did them forwards, backwards, and hind-side up.

He could have got a job as a dog anywhere. He spent all his time at this kind of thing. In his spare time at the office, he used to lie on his stomach on the floor and see if he could lift himself up with his knuckles. If he could, then he tried some other way until he found one that he couldn't do. Then he would spend the rest of his lunch hour on his stomach, perfectly happy.

In the evenings in his room he used to lift iron bars, cannon-balls, heave dumb-bells, and haul himself up to the ceiling with his teeth. You could hear the thumps half a mile.

He liked it.

He spent half the night slinging himself around his room. He said it made his brain clear. When he got his brain perfectly clear, he went to bed and slept. As soon as he woke, he began clearing it again.

Jiggins is dead. He was, of course, a pioneer, but the fact that he dumb-belled himself to death at an early age does not prevent a whole generation of young men from following in his path.

They are ridden by the Health Mania.

They make themselves a nuisance.

They get up at impossible hours. They go out in silly little suits and run Marathon heats before breakfast. They chase around barefoot to get the dew on their feet. They hunt for ozone. They bother about pepsin. They won't eat meat because it has too much nitrogen. They won't eat fruit because it hasn't any. They prefer albumen and starch and nitrogen to huckleberry pie and doughnuts. They won't drink water out of a tap. They won't eat sardines out of a can. They won't use oysters out of a pail. They won't drink milk out of a glass. They are afraid of alcohol in any shape. Yes, sir, afraid. 'Cowards.'

And after all their fuss they presently incur some simple old-fashioned illness and die like anybody else.

Now people of this sort have no chance to attain any great age. They are on the wrong track.

Listen. Do you want to live to be really old, to enjoy a grand, green, exuberant, boastful old age and to make yourself a nuisance to your whole neighbourhood with your reminiscences?

Then cut out all this nonsense. Cut it out. Get up in the morning at a sensible hour. The time to get up is when you have to, not before. If your office opens at eleven, get up at ten-thirty. Take your chance on ozone. There isn't any such thing anyway. Or, if there is, you can buy a Thermos bottle full for five cents, and put it on a shelf in your cupboard. If your work begins at seven in the morning, get up at ten minutes to, but don't be liar enough to say that you like it. It isn't exhilarating and you know it.

Also, drop all that cold-bath business. You never did it when you were a boy. Don't be a fool now. If you must take a bath (you don't really need to), take it warm. The pleasure of getting out of a cold bed and creeping into a hot bath beats a cold plunge to death. In any case, stop gassing about your tub and your 'shower,' as if you were the only man who ever washed.

So much for that point.

Next, take the question of germs and bacilli. Don't be scared of them. That's all. That's the whole thing, and if you once get on to that you never need to worry again.

If you see a bacilli, walk right up to it, and look it in the eye. If one flies into your room, strike at it with your hat or with a towel. Hit it as hard as you can between the neck and the thorax. It will soon get sick of that.

But, as a matter of fact, a bacilli is perfectly quiet and harmless if you are not afraid of it. Speak to it. Call out to it to 'lie down.' It will understand. I had a bacilli once, called Fido, that would come and lie at my feet while I was working. I never knew a more affectionate companion, and when it was run over by an automobile, I buried it in the garden with genuine sorrow.

(I admit this is an exaggeration. I don't really remember its name; it may have been Robert.)

Understand that it is only a fad of modern medicine to say that cholera and typhoid and diphtheria are caused by bacilli and germs; nonsense. Cholera is caused by a frightful pain in the stomach, and diphtheria is caused by trying to cure a sore throat.

Now take the question of food.

Eat what you want. Eat lots of it. Yes, eat too much of it. Eat till you can just stagger across the room with it and prop it up against a sofa cushion. Eat everything that you like until you can't eat any more. The only test is, can you pay for it? If you can't pay for it, don't eat it. And listen – don't worry as to whether your food contains starch, or albumen, or gluten, or nitrogen. If you are a damn fool enough to want these things, go and buy them and eat all you want of them. Go to a laundry and get a bag of starch, and eat your fill of it. Eat it, and take a good long drink of glue after it, and a spoonful of Portland cement. That will gluten you, good and solid.

If you like nitrogen, go and get a druggist to give you a canful of it at the soda counter, and let you sip it with a straw. Only don't think that you can mix all these things up with your food. There isn't any nitrogen or phosphorus or albumen in ordinary things to eat. In any decent household all that sort of stuff is washed out in the kitchen sink before the food is put on the table.

And just one word about fresh air and exercise. Don't bother with either of them. Get your room full of good air, then shut up the windows and keep it. It will keep for years. Anyway, don't keep using your lungs all the time. Let them rest. As for exercise, if you have to take it, take it and put up with it. But as long as you have the price of a hack and can hire other people to play baseball for you and run races and do gymnastics when you sit in the shade and smoke and watch them – great heavens, what more do you want?

~

Caution: living may be dangerous to your health
From An Almanac of Words at Play *by Willard Espy*

After counting my pulse and reading Stephen Leacock, I conclude that this may be a risky year.

'Just think of it,' wrote Leacock [see page 21], 'a hundred years ago there were no bacilli, no ptomaine poisoning, no diphtheria and no appendicitis. Rabies were little known and imperfectly developed. All of these we owe to medical science. Even such things as psoriasis and peritonitis and trypanosomiasis, which are now household names, were known only to the few and were quite beyond the reach of the great mass of the people.'

Medical science has stridden since Leacock's time. Nowadays life's risks include glue on postage stamps, hormones in chicken, antibiotics in beef, dyes in lipstick, plastic falsies, mercury in fish, radiation from TV, cranberries, cyclamates, the mist from lubricating oil, and the lining of tin cans.

Jogging causes heart attacks in the elderly, and slipped disks in the young; bed rest encourages blood clots; eat horse meat, my sister Dale says, and you will get the trots; the drinker is headed for cirrhosis, and the nondrinker for a nervous breakdown; coffee leads to gout; tea is constipating; eggs clog the arteries. If you bib wine, expect cancer of the larynx. If you sleep, you dream, and an exciting dream may wind up in a coronary occlusion.

To cap the climax, as advocates of birth control might put it, semen has been charged with responsibility for cancer of the cervix. ('This is carcinogenic, dear,' ejaculated Tom anticlimactically.)

Wilbur Cross understood. 'Caution!' he cried. 'Living may be dangerous to your health!'

Sickness

Illness
from The Youngest Science *by Lewis Thomas*

One of the hard things to learn in medicine, even harder to teach, is what it feels like to be a patient. In the old days, when serious illness was a more commonplace experience, shared round by everyone, the doctor had usually been through at least a few personal episodes on his own and had a pretty good idea of what it was like for his patient. A good many of the specialists in pulmonary disease who were brought up in the early years of this century had first acquired their interest in the field from having had tuberculosis themselves. Some of the leading figures in rehabilitation medicine had been crippled by poliomyelitis. And all physicians of those generations knew about pneumonia and typhoid at first hand, or at least once removed, in themselves or their immediate families.

It is very different today. The killing or near-killing illnesses are largely reserved for one's advancing years. No one goes through the six or eight perilous weeks of typhoid anymore, coming within sight of dying every day, getting through at the end with a stronger character perhaps, certainly with a different way of looking at life. The high technologies which are turned on to cope with serious disease – the electronic monitors in intensive care units, the chemotherapy drugs for cancer, the *tour de force* accomplishments of contemporary surgery, and the mobilization of increasingly complex procedures for diagnosis in medicine – are matters to be mastered only from lecture notes and books, and then by actual practice on patients, but very few doctors have more than an inkling of what it is actually like to go through such experiences. Even the childhood contagions are mostly gone, thanks to vaccines for measles, whooping cough, chicken pox, and the like, thanks especially to the easy control of streptococcal infections. Today's young doctors do not know what it is to have an earache, much less what it means to have an eardrum punctured.

The nearest thing to a personal education in illness is the grippe. It is almost all we have left in the way of on-the-job training, and I hope that somehow it can be spared as we proceed to eliminate so many other human diseases. Indeed, I would favor hanging on to grippe, and its cousin the common cold, for as long as possible. A case could be made, I think, for viewing the various viruses involved in these minor but impressive illnesses as a set of endangered species, essentially *good* for the human environment, something like snail darters.

Most people afflicted with grippe complain about it, and that is one of its virtues. It is a good thing for people to have, from time to time, something real to complain about, a genuine demon. It is also a good thing to be laid up once in a while, compelled by nature to stop doing whatever else and to take to bed. It is an especially good thing to have a fever and the malaise that goes along with fever, when you know that it will be gone in three or four days but meanwhile entitles you to all the privileges of the sick: bed rest, ice water on the bed table, aspirin, maybe an ice bag on the head or behind the neck, and the attentions of one's solicitous family. Sympathy: how many other opportunities turn up in a lifetime to engage the sympathy and concern of others for something that is not your fault and will surely be gone in a few days? Preserve the grippe, I say, and find some way to insert it into the practical curriculum of all medical students. Twice a year, say, the lecture hall in molecular biochemistry should be exposed to a silent aerosol of adenovirus, so that the whole class comes down at once. Schedules being what they are in medical school, this will assure that a good many students will be obliged to stay on their feet, working through the next days and nights with their muscle pains and fever, and learning what it is like *not* to be cared for. Good for them, and in a minor way good for their future as doctors.

The real problem is the shock of severe, dangerous illness, its unexpectedness and surprise. Most of us, patients and doctors alike, can ride almost all the way through life with no experience of real peril, and when it does come, it seems an outrage, a piece of unfairness. We are not used to disease as we used to be, and we are not at all used to being incorporated into a high technology.

I have learned something about this, but only recently, too late to do much for my skill at the bedside. On several occasions, starting around age sixty-four, I have had a close look from the bed itself at medicine and surgery and, as I shall relate, an even closer look at myself. On balance, I have very much liked what I have seen, but only

111

in retrospect, once out of bed and home free. While there, I discovered that being a patient is hard work.

It is often said that people who have been precariously ill, especially those who have gone through surgical operations, love to talk about their trials and will do so at length to anyone ready to listen. I rather doubt this. Being ill is a peculiarly private experience, and most of the people I know who have gone through something serious tend to be reserved about it, changing the subject when it comes up. But here I am, about to talk about my times on the line and the things I learned. I only do so, I must say in advance, out of professional interest.

The first, and most surprising of all, was an obscure kind of pneumonia, chills, fever, prostration, and all, occurring suddenly on a Tuesday afternoon. I took to bed at home in good cheer, anticipating several days of warm soup, cold drinks, fluffed-up pillows, and ample family ministrations. But a week went by and I kept on with the chills and fever, so my wife called the doctor, a friend of mine and a real, house-calling doctor. He did the usual things, including taking samples of blood, murmured something about a virus 'going around', and predicted that the fever would be gone in another day or two. But the next day I was in a hospital bed having more blood tests, being examined by platoons of interns and residents, and in and out of the X-ray department having pictures taken of all sites including bones. The laboratory tests had revealed a hemoglobin level of just under 8 grams percent, half the normal value, and it had become an urgent matter to discover where the blood had gone, or was going.

Within the next few days the pneumonia vanished, along with the chills and fever, and I had become a new sort of diagnostic problem.

To be worked up for anemia of unknown origin is strenuous exercise. The likeliest cause was blood loss, and the likeliest source was the intestinal tract – what is known, ominously, as silent bleeding. I received two transfusions, and then plunged headlong into technology. A bone marrow biopsy was, as I recall, the first piece of work, done neatly and quickly on a pelvic bone with rapid-fire explanations by the hematologist as he went along, telling me what I would feel and when it would hurt, but despite his reassurances I could not avoid the strong sense that having one's bone marrow sucked into a syringe was an unnatural act, no way for a human being to be treated. It did not in fact hurt much, but the small crunching of bone by the trocar followed by the peculiar and unfamiliar pain in the marrow itself were strange sensations, not at all nice.

I have performed bone marrow biopsies myself, long ago as an intern and from time to time since, and have always regarded the procedure as a minor one, almost painless, but it had never crossed my mind that it was, painless or not, so fundamentally unpleasant.

The rest of the workup was easy going, and at times engrossing. The walls of my stomach and upper intestinal tract were marvelously revealed by a barium meal, and those of my bowel by a similar enema, and all was well. But I continued to bleed, somewhere in that long channel, and more transfusions were needed.

It is not an easy task for doctors to look after doctors, and especially difficult when the doctor-patient is a colleague and close friend. It requires walking a fine line, making sure not to offend professional pride by talking down to the doctor-patient, but also making sure that the patient does what he is told to do. I was treated with great tact and firmness. The colleagues and friends who had me as a responsibility remained my good friends, but there was never a question as to my status: I was a patient and they expected me to behave like one. I was not to try making decisions about my own diagnosis and treatment. I was not allowed to go home for a few days, which I wanted very much to do at several times during what turned out to be a long period of hospitalisation; it was explained very gently that the source of bleeding was still unknown and I might have a more massive hemorrhage at any time, rather less gently that if it happened I might suffer a lot of brain damage and I'd better not be doing that at home.

With negative X-rays, my intestinal tract needed a different kind of look. On the possibility that I might have a polyp somewhere, bleeding freely but too small to show up by X-ray, I was wheeled off to the endoscopy service for examination by the colonoscope, an incredibly long and flexible quartz fiberoptic tube through which all parts of the large intestine can be viewed under direct illumination by light sent in from outside. As a nice gesture of professional courtesy, the doctor stopped at frequent intervals during this procedure and passed the viewing end of the instrument over my shoulder and in front of my left eye. 'Care to take a look?' he asked. I had never looked through this wonderful instrument before, although I had seen many photographs of the views to be had. It would have been interesting in any case, I suppose, but since it was the deep interior of my own intestine that I was looking at, I became totally absorbed. 'What's that?' I cried, as something red moved into view. He took a look and said, 'That's just you. Normal mucosa.'

A few days after this fascinating but negative excursion, I had another episode of bleeding, my hemoglobin dropped to a disturbing level, more transfusions were given, and it was decided that I would probably need surgery in order to remove the part that was presumably bleeding. But without knowing the exact source, this could mean taking out a lot of intestine and, even then, missing it. The gastroenterologist who had me in charge, Dr Paul Sherlock, knew of one obscure possibility not yet excluded, one that I had never heard about – a condition produced by an abnormal connection between an artery and vein in the intestinal wall – which had recently been reported as a cause of intestinal hemorrhage.

This was not, as it seemed to me at the time, a guess in the dark. The X-rays and colonoscope had ruled out cancer of the colon (which is what I was pretty sure I had, at the outset), and diverticulosis (little cracks in the intestinal wall), and polyps had been excluded as well. The new syndrome of arteriovenous anomaly was about all that was left.

Finding out required close collaboration between the gastroenterologists and radiologists. A catheter was inserted in the femoral artery, high up in the right leg, and pushed up into the aorta until its tip reached the level of the main arteries branching off to supply the large intestine. At this point, an opaque dye was injected, to fill all those arteries. Just before pressing the syringe, Dr Robin Watson, the X-ray chief, warned me that I would feel a sense of heat, not to worry. It was a brand new sensory impression, perhaps never experienced except by patients undergoing this kind of arteriography: for about thirty seconds I felt as if the lower half of my body had suddenly caught fire, then the feeling was gone. Meanwhile, movies were being taken of the entire vascular bed reached by the dye, and the diagnosis was solidly confirmed. Dr Watson came into the room a few minutes later with sample pictures displaying the lesion. 'Care to take a look?' he asked. I was enchanted: there, in just one spot somewhere on the right side of my colon, was a spilled blur of dye, and the issue was settled. It struck me as a masterpiece of technological precision, also as a picture with a certain aesthetic quality, nice to look at. I could hear in the distance the voices of other doctors, quietly celebratory as doctors are when a difficult diagnosis is finally nailed down.

That evening I was visited by the anaesthesiologist for the brief but always reassuring explanation of the next day's events, and in the morning I rolled down the hall, into the elevator, and down to the operating room, pleasantly stoned from Valium. The next things I saw were the clock on the wall of the recovery room and the agreeable face of my friend the nurse in charge, who told me that it had gone very well. I have no memory of the operating room at all, only the sound of the wall switch and the hissing of the automatic doors as my litter entered the place.

That was my first personal experience with the kind of illness requiring hospital technology. Thinking back, I cannot find anything about it that I would want to change or try to improve, although it was indeed, parts of it anyway, like being launched personless on the assembly line of a great (but quiet) factory. I was indeed handled as an object needing close scrutiny and intricate fixing, procedure after procedure, test after test, carted from one part of the hospital to another day after day until the thing was settled. While it was going on I felt less like a human in trouble and more like a scientific problem to be solved as quickly as possible. What made it work, and kept such notions as 'depersonalization' and 'dehumanization' from even popping into my mind, was the absolute confidence I felt in the skill and intelligence of the people who had hold of me. In part this came from my own knowledge, beforehand, of their skill, but in larger part my confidence resulted from observing, as they went about their work, their own total confidence in themselves.

The next two course offerings were trauma. I'd never had real trauma before in all my life – or only once, when as a small boy in grammar school I'd been hit on the head by a pitched baseball and knocked out for a moment. The next day my head began to itch, and I went around the house and back and forth to school, scratching my head incessantly and complaining to everyone that the baseball had injured the nerves. My mother was skeptical of this, as she was about most self-diagnosis, and took a close look at my scalp. I was infested by dense families of head lice, caught perhaps from somebody's cap at school. In no time, but with a great deal of anguish caused by neat kerosene and larkspur shampoos, endless rakings with a fine-tooth comb, and finally a very short haircut, I was cured, although I'm not sure my mother ever thought of me again as quite the same boy. Anyway, that was all my trauma until I was sixty-six years old.

I was in the surf at Amagansett, floating in a high leisurely wave, and turned to catch it for a clean ride to the beach, when suddenly something went wrong with my right knee. After some floundering and swallowing a lot of water, I made the trip in under breakers and tried to stand. I couldn't, and had to wave for help. I was hoisted out and horsed along by friends, unable to place my weight on my right leg. On the way up the beach I was met by Dr Herbert Chasis, a Bellevue colleague, and his wife, Barbara. Herbert knows more about kidney disease and hypertension that anyone I know, and Barbara had served as chief of the psychomedical wards during my years at Bellevue. They were sympathetic of course, but also to my surprise highly knowledgeable about knees and, like all good Bellevue people, ready to help. Indeed, Chasis had in his beach bag a proper knee brace, which he helped me put on, and explained to me that I had undoubtedly torn a knee cartilage (which he had done some years earlier; hence the equipment). Presently, crutches were provided as well, and off I went, home to get dressed and into Manhattan for a visit to the Hospital for Special Surgery. X-rays again, and to my astonishment, another fiberoptics instrument, this time an arthroscope for looking into the interior of joints. In it went, moved around this part and that of the knee, and then it stopped. 'Care to take a look?' asked the surgeon, handing me the eyepiece. I stared, transfixed, at the neat geometry of cartilage lining the joint, gray and glistening in the light, and then I saw what he had seen, a sizable piece of cartilage broken and dislodged. 'Thank you,' I thought to say, 'what now?' 'Out,' he replied. So, Valium again, the unremembered operating room, and a long elliptical incision stitched with countless neat threads which I saw directly the next morning when the dressing was changed and I was commanded to get out of bed and stand on the leg, pain or no pain. Good for it, I was told, but I forget why. Teach it a lesson, maybe. Then on crutches for a few weeks, a single crutch for a few more, exercises thrice daily – lifting heavy weights by my foot (which I did for a few days and then began telling lies about) – and finally full recovery except for the odd pain now and then. Another triumph. I began to feel almost ready to write a textbook.

One more, and then I've finished, I trust. I was invited to give an evening lecture at the Cosmopolitan Club in New York, a place filled with dignity and intellectual women, including my wife. I prepared a talk on symbiosis, with a few lantern slides to illustrate one of my favorite models of insect behavior, the mimosa girdler. Halfway through the talk I called for the slides, the lights went out, I approached the screen to point to the location of the mandible-work of the beetle – and fell off the platform into the dark. Hauled to my feet, I found myself unable to move my left arm because of pain in the shoulder. I felt for the shoulder with my right hand and found an empty cavity. Someone brought a chair and sat me down while I caught my breath, and several sympathetic voices suggested that I cancel the evening. I wanted to finish the girdler story, however, and hunched back to the podium. It must have been a painful talk for the audience. I thought no one would notice the shoulder, and I droned on to finish the lecture, sweating into my eyeglasses and onto my manuscript, bracing my elbow against the podium, thinking that I was getting away with it nicely. Then I noticed that Dr André Cournand, the great cardiologist from Bellevue, had moved from his seat in the front row and taken a chair alongside the podium, watching me carefully. I remembered the old anecdotes about that hospital, the car crash, the exploded street, and the figure of authority thrusting through the crowd: 'Stand aside, I am a Bellevue man.' If I topple, André will catch me, I thought.

Anyway, I finished it, although I'm not sure anyone was listening. An ambulance had been summoned, and I was carted off once more, on a litter, to Memorial. An X-ray showed the shoulder dislocated and fractured ('Care to take a look?'), and my friends set about trying to get it back in place, me lying on my stomach buzzing with morphine, with the left arm hanging down, Ted Beattie (chief of surgery at Memorial) on the floor pulling down on my arm, but it wouldn't slip back in place. Finally, after a half hour of tugging, it was decided that I would have to be fixed under a general anaesthetic, and a call went out for the head of the anaesthesia department, Paul Goldiner. It was now 10 p.m., and Paul was at home in Westchester County. He hurried to his car and started the drive along the parkway to New York. Five minutes from home he passed the scene of a car crash and noticed a man lying prone on the grass. He stopped, went over to the man, found him pulseless and not breathing, and set about resuscitation. Anaesthesiologists are the best of all professionals at this skill, and shortly he had the man breathing again and conscious. He ran back to his car and set off again for New York. By this time, Beattie's maneuvers had snapped my humerus back into its joint, but it was too late to call Goldiner and tell him to stay home. He arrived at the door to be informed that his trip had been unnecessary, then told his own jubilant story; the trip had been the best he'd ever made. It is not often given to chiefs of anaesthesiology to save a life on the open highway, and Goldiner was a happy man. I have often wished I could locate his patient someday and have him take Paul Goldiner and me out to lunch.

That was the last of my trial runs as patient, up to now anyway. I know a lot more than I used to know about hospitals, medicine, nurses, and doctors, and I am more than ever a believer in the usefulness of technology, the higher the better. But I wish there were some easier way to come by this level of comprehension for medical students and interns, maybe a way of setting up electronic models like the simulated aircraft coming in for crash landings used for pilot training. Every young doctor should know exactly what it is like to have things go catastrophically wrong, and to be personally mortal. It makes for a better practice.

I have seen a lot of my inner self, more than most people, and you'd think I would have gained some new insight, even some sense of illumination, but I am as much in the dark as ever. I do not feel connected to myself in any new way. Indeed, if anything, the distance seems to have increased, and I am personally more a dualism than ever, made up of structure after structure over which I have no say at all. I have the feeling now that if I were to keep at it, looking everywhere with lenses and bright lights, even into the ventricles of my brain (which is a technical feasibility if I wanted to try it), or inside the arteries of the heart (another easy technique these days), I would be brought no closer to myself. I exist, I'm sure of that, but not in the midst of all that soft machinery. If I am, as I suppose is the case at bottom, an assemblage of electromagnetic particles, I now doubt that there is any center, any passenger compartment, any private green room where I am to be found in residence. I conclude that the arrangement runs itself, beyond my management, needing repairs by experts from time to time, but by and large running well, and I am glad I don't have to worry about the details. If I were really at the controls, in full charge, keeping track of everything, there would be a major train wreck within seconds.

And I do not at all resent any of the parts for going wrong. On the contrary, having seen what they are up against, I have more respect for them than I had before. I tip my hat to all of them, and I'm glad I'm here outside, wherever that is.

~

Illness is good for you

from A Dustbin of Milligan *by Spike Milligan*

One good appendicitis –
Or a cure for St Vitus dance
Pays for a Harley Street surgeon's
Vacation in the South of France.

ALCOHOL AND TOBACCO

Alcohol

'One swallow does not make a summer. Perhaps not. But there are ever so many occasions when one swallow – just one single swallow – is better than nothing to drink at all. And if you get enough of them they do *make a summer.'*

Stephen Leacock

'Dr Rice's friend . . . came home drunk and explained it to his wife, and his wife said to him, "John, when you have drunk all the whiskey you want, you ought to ask for a sarsaparilla." He said, "Yes, but when I have drunk all the whiskey I want I can't say sarsaparilla." '

Mark Twain

Alcoholism and alcohol
from Fit To Lead? *by Hugh L'Etang*

Predisposition to alcoholism is one of the great mysteries of medicine, as great perhaps as the causes of cancer. We owe a great debt to those alcoholics who have the gift of expressing their thoughts, feelings and theories about this ubiquitous illness. They ring up the curtain on a problem play and, by revealing glimpses of their inner selves, provide a fleeting opportunity to penetrate the depths of the mystery. Too often it is only our lack of sensitivity which prevents us from receiving the signals sent out by those in distress and from deciphering the clues which could help to solve the enigma. Although writers are conspicuous in the alcoholic ranks they are probably no more self-indulgent in this respect than their social or professional equals. Indeed the apparent liability of writers to alcoholism may be exaggerated because their words and letters, their thoughts and feelings, are often preserved for posterity whilst the more commonplace alcoholic, less articulate or even illiterate, remains anonymous. Ernest Hemingway once remarked on the irresponsibility that follows the awful responsibility of writing to say nothing of the depression and the lassitude, symptoms that are all too easily relieved by alcohol. This view is supported by Negley Farson who maintained that drinking is an occupational disease of Journalists due to the constant strain and tension involved in working against the clock and beating deadlines. Writing is certainly not unique in causing strain and tension, but it is also a lonely trail and writers are only too well aware of that feeling of emotional emptiness and flatness when for the moment they have exhausted their powers of imagination and creativity. Then they may resort to alcohol as a quick and easy method of finding convivial company, relaxation and amusement. Even more important, as they wind down, fresh thoughts and ideas can be fed into, and dredged from, the subconscious. Farson makes the novel suggestion that the boredom and emptiness of uninteresting lives make men drown the sorrows of the present rather than those of the past. Loneliness, or possibly an increased difficulty in associating with others, is not confined to creative writers and may be an unavoidable penalty for any leader who has scaled the highest peaks. Allowance must also be made for the demanding routine and inevitable familiarity associated with so many occupations, turning what once was of absorbing interest into unutterable boredom. This may explain in part some of James Joyce's alcoholic sprees for one biographer has written: 'No one was in fact quicker to find life tedious, or more eager to shun equilibrium, whether by drinking or moving. Joyce throve on flurry'.

It is possible that the intense and solitary creativity of writers in particular leads to some biochemical deficit, unmeasurable by any current laboratory tests, and which alcohol can quickly and conveniently relieve. It has also been claimed that certain inborn abnormalities of carbohydrate metabolism predispose an individual to alcoholism. When the blood sugar is lowered the resultant symptoms of faintness, anxiety, hunger and nervousness may be accompanied by a craving for alcohol. Alcohol itself has the capacity to lower the level of blood sugar, and the apparently stimulant effect of two large gins before lunch may be succeeded by drowsiness and ineptitude which is painfully apparent in the late afternoon. It is also possible that certain alcoholics are unduly sensitive to changes in blood sugar rather than blood alcohol which may explain why the two American writers, Sinclair Lewis and Scott Fitzgerald, were adversely affected by relatively small amounts of alcohol. It is more than a coincidence that, when they stopped drinking alcohol, they both had a craving for carbohydrate in the form of chocolate. But the biochemistry of alcoholism must not obscure the psychological causes and effects so vividly described by Sinclair Lewis' second wife, Dorothy Thompson:

> This restless, dynamic, overcharged, demanding personality, which is you, becomes intensified to the point of madness. It is energy completely explosive and completely off the track.

Another American writer, William Faulkner, drank for a number of reasons which provided a variety of excuses. Alcohol eased the anticipatory fears of shyness and was (or did it become?) a cure for pain, fever, backache, anxiety, unhappiness or depression. Faced with an unacceptable decision or unavoidable obligation 'he might make himself incapable of fulfilling it' or, when trapped inescapably, 'he'd give in to what he called the chemistry of craving and go overboard'. Physiological and psychological satisfaction from alcohol may be learned and imprinted early and, as with many potential alcoholics, drinking was a habit in Faulkner's family and an important aspect of a man's life. There was an even more compelling reason. Later in his life he sustained a severe burn while lying on a steam pipe in a drunken stupor. 'Why do you do this?' he was asked; 'Because I like to' was his reply, and unhappily it is an answer that many alcoholics could give.

Even to those who conform to the socially accepted or at times socially demanded patterns of drinking, many alcoholic beverages are admittedly pleasant to take. It is difficult to mention the ubiquitous liability to alcoholism without seeming to preach, or to warn of its dangers without appearing unmanly. Paradoxically the manifestations of acute alcoholism, entertaining, terrifying or disgusting as they can be, are by no means the most serious effects of this disease although they are the aspects which are most obvious in public or private life. Indeed dramatic episodes of acute alcoholism in a newsworthy personality, which arouse curiosity, condemnation or smug feelings of superiority, can divert attention from the decline of the furtive, chronic alcoholic whose activities may not make newspaper headlines but who is more than likely to harm his country, his family and himself. Alcoholism is a physical and psychological dependence on one specific drug of addiction and on the basis of this definition there are around 400,000 alcoholics in the United Kingdom alone. When the incidence of cirrhosis of the liver (scarring and shrinking due to cell destruction) is taken as a crude measure of alcohol intake the oft-maligned publican takes a second place to the 'company director' whilst in this particular league table the medical practitioner is placed embarrassingly high. One unfortunate conclusion is that diagnosis, arising as it so often does from a medical or domestic crisis, may come too late. Acceptance of the existence of alcoholism, to say nothing of the recognition of its ravages, are made difficult by what at times amounts to a conspiracy of silence on the part of professional or political colleagues. But there are clues which should alert the inquiring layman or the suspicious doctor despite the tendency of the victim to avoid any interrogation or examination. It should not be too difficult for intimates to be aware of the pervading smell of alcohol (even if partly masked by peppermint), loss of appetite, diarrhoea, nose bleeding, premature obesity, frequent accidents, loss of memory, sleeplessness and impotence.

Because alcohol can invade and damage so many parts of the body its toxic effects, like that of a widespread infection such as syphilis, cause alcoholism to be a deceptive imitator of many other diseases and make a precise diagnosis more difficult. The acute manifestations of alcoholism are all too readily portrayed on stage and screen but the insidious and more damaging effects on the heart, central nervous system and liver are often missed for far too long. Shakiness, nausea, retching and sweating due to sudden withdrawal of alcohol, or the later stage of delirium tremens signified by confusion, disorientation in time and space, restlessness, fear, suspicion and terrifying hallucinations, are but the outward and more easily recognized signs. Less obvious are those effects which, without diligent enquiry about the intake of alcohol, can mistakenly be attributed to other causes. Shortness of breath, irregular or rapid pulse and enlargement of the heart occur in many types of heart disease although, in that caused by drinking (alcoholic cardiomyopathy), excessive sweating, particularly at night, is more common than in other forms of heart failure. Incoordination and a staggering gait (even when sober), tingling, numbness, wasting or weakness in the arms and legs and muscular weakness or wasting, because they can occur in so many other diseases of the nervous system, clearly create diagnostic difficulty. The florid complexion together with the facial and bodily obesity, and even certain changes in the blood chemistry, found in some alcoholics

126

have much in common with a glandular disorder called Cushing's disease. Alcohol also influences human biochemistry in other ways and the comatose drunkard should never be ignored for tomorrow he may be dead rather than sober. Dangerously low levels of blood sugar, at times tragically irreversible, may be caused by excess of alcohol in normal drinkers as well as in poorly-controlled diabetic patients on insulin.

Could alcoholic cardiomyopathy account for Scott Fitzgerald's death at the early age of 44 years? In November 1940, after he had almost collapsed in a drug-store, an electrocardiogram revealed evidence of heart disease. On 20 December he stumbled on leaving a theatre and nearly fainted again. Next day he died of unspecified heart disease. William Faulkner was rather more fortunate. Although his drinking caused the equivalent of one or two serious illnesses a year for 30 years his mind and body withstood the ravages surprisingly well. It was not until 1953, in his 56th year, that he had periods of amnesia which he called spells of complete forgetting. Blackouts after bouts of heavy drinking in February and March led to medical investigations; the liver function tests were normal and the electroencephalogram revealed no organic disease but merely 'some hypersensitivity of the brain waves'. In March 1959 his liver 'seemed enlarged' but was apparently normal in 1961. Early in 1962 his heart was not enlarged and the electrocardiogram which showed a 'steady rhythm', was 'a very good tracing for a man of sixty-four'. Readmitted to hospital in July, because of back pain and the early warning signs of an impending drinking spree, the pain spread to the front of his chest and he died, presumably of a myocardial infarction, on the 6th.

~

Rum and the Navy
from a speech made in Cardiff, Wales, 1970
by Sir Dick Caldwell

The sailor and alcohol attracted attention before the 13th century BC, when it is said that the abuse of wine complicated the voyage of Ulysses, and as early as 1194 laws were introduced in the Navy, one of which was that a ship's master was not bound to provide for the care of any seaman who was injured through drunkenness but might turn him out of his ship.

Alcohol first appears to have been regularly distributed with Naval victuals in an atmosphere of filth, verminous infestation and acute shortage of men, late in the 16th century, when beer supplied by the Deputy Director of Victuals was blamed as a source of gross morbidity and mortality both prior to and during the repulse of the Spanish *Armada*. Five years later Captain Hawkins, while sailing off the Cape Verde Islands gave beer or diluted wine to men suffering from both beri-beri and scurvy and from about that time a daily ration of a gallon of beer per man, which contained enough alcohol to stop it deteriorating as quickly as water, was authorised.

About this time the Navy was almost continuously present in the West Indies and from 1731 half a pint of neat rum was provided daily to every man on board, as an alternative to beer or wine.

In 1740 Admiral Vernon lost 395 of 1,700 men he put ashore at Jamaica, and was appalled at 'the swinish vice of drunkenness which was so visibly increasing in the Navy'; he accordingly ordered that the Rum should be diluted with 4 parts of water, and should be served twice daily. Interestingly enough it was here that the name 'grog' was born and has persisted amongst mariners ever since. Admiral Vernon, they say, invariably wore a coat of Grosgrain material, and was nicknamed 'Old Grog' as a consequence. This name was applied subsequently, in a slightly derisory manner, to the watered-down rum ration which he had brought about.

*

It is obvious that apart from being used as a substitute for the vile and often stinking drinking water carried on board in these days, rum was also used to drown the sailors' woes, and deaden the impact of the really appalling conditions in which they served. Today we must find it hard to believe that such conditions existed.

*

Men were constantly flogged for drunkenness, theft, insolence, laziness, sometimes for smiling, and sometimes for failing to smile. The normal minimum punishment was 12 lashes; 3 dozen was usual; 6 dozen was frequent; 500 was about as many as most men could take and live. 1,000 was a death sentence, and intended to be so. Generally the last few hundred strokes were inflicted on a corpse. Throughout the ordeal a drummer beat out the Rogues March, and whenever a man collapsed into insensibility, he was forcibly fed with rum so that he would come round and miss nothing of the pain. The art was to keep the man alive until all the lashes had been given.

*

Again and again it is borne in upon us that the men regarded their rum ration as an anodyne, and antidote against the poison of everyday life, a solace against the filth, the misery and the squalor of their existence. Authority would not, and did not change the squalor, and no-one dared to lay a sacrilegious hand-upon the seaman's daily half pint of rum, even though Lord Keith addressed their Lordships in 1812 saying: 'It is observable and deeply to be lamented that almost every crime originates in drunkenness, and that a large proportion of the men who are maimed and disabled are reduced to that situation by accidents that happen from the same abominable vice; it is an evil of great magnitude and one which it will be impossible to prevent so long as the present excessive quantity of spirits is issued in The Royal Navy.' Thus spoke Lord Keith, but to little avail.

*

A few months ago, after prolonged deliberations, Their Lordships decided to abolish the rum ration for good, after 300 years of its issue. The wisdom and benefit of this action was not clearly apparent to 'Jolly Jack' and on the last day of issue, a rum barrel was sadly and ceremoniously buried at sea with full Naval Honours.

～

Beer
by John Timbs

About 1730, Pulteney, afterwards the Earl of Bath, lay for a long time at Lord Chetwynd's house of Ingestre, in Staffordshire, sick, very dangerously, of a pleuritic fever. This illness cost him an expense of 740 guineas for physicians and after all, his cure was accomplished merely by a draught of small beer. Dr Hope, Dr Swynsen, and other physicians from Stafford, Lichfield, and Derby were called in, and carried off about 250 guineas of the patient's money, leaving the malady just where they found it. Dr Freind went down post from London, with

Mrs Pulteney and received 300 guineas, for the journey. Dr Broxholm went from Oxford, and received 200 guineas. When these two physicians who were Pulteney's particular friends, arrived, they found his case to be quite desperate, and gave him over, saying that everything had been done, that could be done. They prescribed some few medicines, but without the least effect. He was still alive, and was heard to mutter, in a low voice, 'small beer, small beer.' They said, 'Give him small beer, or anything.' Accordingly, a great silver cup was brought, which held two quarts of small beer; they ordered an orange to be squeezed into it, and gave it to him. Pulteney drank off the whole at a draught, and demanded another. Another cupful was administered to him; and soon after that he fell into a profuse perspiration, and a profound slumber for nearly twenty-four hours. In his case the saying was eminently verified, 'If he sleep he shall do well.' From that time forth, he recovered wonderfully, insomuch that in a few days the physicians took their leave. The joy over his recovery was diffused over the whole country; for he was then in the height of that popularity which, after his elevation to the peerage, he completely forfeited.

~

In a pickle
from Low Life *by Jeffrey Bernard*

I read that a member of the General Medical Council has called on his colleagues for quicker identification and treatment for alcoholic doctors. The article, in *The Times*, was headed 'Alcoholic Doctor Tells How He Fought Back'. There are two things that interest me here: first the business of identifying an alcoholic, and secondly the matter of fighting back. How on earth they can have trouble in not identifying an alcoholic immediately, heaven alone knows. I can spot one a mile away. But could they spot my friend Keith, I wonder? They must be blind as bats. Anyway, Keith woke up one day sitting in pitch darkness. He groped around for a while and realised slowly that he was in a cinema. Further groping got him to an exit door and he eventually got out on to the street. He didn't know what town he was in but made his way to a pub where, with great embarrassment, he asked the barman where he was. 'Dover,' he was told. Then it all came back to him. 'Christ Almighty,' he said, 'I got married yesterday.' I can put the

General Medical Council in touch with several Keiths, but I suppose only the 3,000 out of 81,000 alcoholic doctors in this country would be able to identify them quickly.

But we must help the medical profession and give them some clues. A man I know once went to a literary booze-up and walked over to a glass-fronted bookcase to see what sort of stuff his host had to read. To his amazement there were no books in the case, only John Raymond standing there in a stupor. I myself once woke up in Cowes of all places and I have even woken up in a drawer at the bottom of a wardrobe. That was fairly frightening. Trying to open a drawer from the inside. It's quite tricky. Then we have our hero on the *Mirror*. I've mentioned him before but, for the benefit of doctors, he is worth recalling. He broke into a pickle factory one night with his girlfriend with the purpose of laying her and fell into a vat of chutney. Then we have the doctors themselves. There were two of them, patients like myself in 1972 in Max Glatt's ward in St Bernard's Hospital. One of them was addicted to barbiturates. He didn't interest me, no drug addicts do, but I asked the alcoholic doctor how did he first know he was an alcoholic and he told me, 'When I sprayed vaginal deodorant on a man's face.'

But the business of the doctor telling how he 'fought back' gets me. I fought back, too. I fought back from two and a half years of the most boring, depressing desolation of sobriety you can imagine. I wouldn't go on the wagon again for all the tea in China.* For two and a half years I felt apart from the human race. The day I cracked in 1976 I called round to my friend Eva and we cracked a bottle of scotch. Then we went round to the Dover Castle – always full of doctors – and we met up eventually with Frank Norman and drank more scotch. After all those years a bottle of the stuff is damn nigh a killer. Of course it is poison. Frank took me to the Connaught for breakfast the next day and I thought I was going to die. The fact that I'm here now and that Eva and Frank are dead seems unfair.

To go back to the doctors: they apparently consider heavy drinking to be more than four pints of beer a day, or four doubles or a bottle of wine a day. I should have thought that to be the national average lunchtime consumption. But just listen to this. 'I do not remember ever making a mistake, but one of the worst aspects of alcoholism is that you black out. One day I had to ring up the surgery to make sure I had done one of my visits the night before.'

Well, surprise, surprise. What I want to know is, if he blacked out how the hell does he *know* he never ever made a mistake? The wrong leg off? I know I've had the wrong leg *over* because I too have had to ring up the surgery to find out where and if I had done one of my visits the night before. I just don't understand how doctors can be so naive. Well, I do. It's the old business of all the time at school and then in hospital of not seeing anything much of life itself. The Middlesex ought to send their students along to the Coach. They'd find ample opportunity to practise spotting and identifying alcoholics. They're the ones smiling.

*(Since writing this piece, Jeffrey Bernard has had his right leg off and gone back on the wagon.)

~

A cure for drinking
from Selected Stories *by Anton Chekhov*

The well-known reader and comedian, Mr Feniksov-Dikobrazov II, had been engaged to appear as a guest artist, and was arriving at the city of D—— in a first-class coach. Everyone who had come to the station to meet him knew that the celebrated actor had bought his first-class ticket only two stations back, for show, and that up to that point he had traveled third; they also observed that in spite of the chilly autumn weather he wore only a summer cape and a worn seal-skin cap; nevertheless, when the sleepy, bluish face of Dikobrazov II appeared, everyone felt a quiver of excitement and an eagerness to meet him. The manager of the theater. Pochechuev, kissed him three times, in the Russian manner, and carried him off to his own apartment.

The celebrity was to have begun his engagement two days later, but fate decided otherwise; the day before the performance a pale, distraught manager rushed into the box office of the theater and announced that Dikobrazov II would be unable to play.

'He can't go on!' declared Pochechuev, tearing his hair. 'How do you like that? For a month – one whole month – it's been advertised in letters three feet high that we'd have Dikobrazov: we've built it up, we've gone all out, sold subscriptions, and now this low trick! Hanging's too good for him!'

'But what's the matter? What happened?'

'He's on a binge, damn him!'

'What of it? He'll sleep it off.'

'He'll croak before he sleeps it off! I know him from Moscow; when he starts lapping up vodka, it's a couple of months before he comes out of it. This is a binge – a real binge! No, it's just my luck! And why am I so unfortunate? Whom do I take after to be cursed with such luck? All my life this dark cloud has been hanging over my head – why? Why?' (Pochechuev was a tragedian by nature as well as by profession; strong expressions, accompanied by beating his breast with his fists, were very becoming to him.) 'What a vile, infamous, despicable slave am I to place my head beneath the blows of fate! Would it not be more worthy to give up this role of the eternal victim of a hostile fate, and simply put a bullet through my head? What am I waiting for? Oh, God, what am I waiting for?' Pochechuev covered his face with his hands and turned to the window.

Besides the cashier there were many actors and play-goers present in the box office, everyone offering advice, consolation, and encouragement, and the occasion bore a sententious and oracular quality; no one went beyond 'vanity of vanities,' 'think nothing of it,' and 'maybe it'll turn out all right.' Only the cashier, a fat dropsical man, said anything to the point.

'But, Prokl Lvovich,' he said, 'you should try curing him.'

'Nobody in the world can cure a binge!'

'Don't say that. Our hairdresser cures them completely. He treats the whole town.'

Pochechuev, by now ready to snatch at a straw, was overjoyed at this possibility, and within five minutes the theatrical hairdresser, Fyodor Grebeshkov, stood before him. If you will visualize a tall, bony, hollow-eyed man with a long sparse beard and brown hands, who bears a striking resemblance to a skeleton activated by means of screws and springs, and if you dress this figure in an incredibly threadbare black suit, you will have a portrait of Grebeshkov.

'Hello, Fedya!' said Pochechuev. 'I hear, my friend, that you have the cure for a drinking bout. Do me a favor – not as an employee, but as a friend – cure Dikobrazov! You see, he's on a binge.'

'God be with him!' Grebeshkov pronounced in a doleful bass voice. 'Indeed, I do treat actors of the commoner sort, and merchants, and officials; but this is a celebrity, known throughout Russia!'

'Well, what of it?'

'In order to knock it out of him, it is necessary to produce a revolution in all the organs and members of the body. I will produce this revolution in him; he will get well; and then he will get on his high horse with me. 'You dog,' he will say, 'how dare you touch my person.' We know these celebrities!'

'No, no, don't shirk it, brother. One must take the thorns with the roses. Put on your hat and let's go.'

When Grebeshkov entered Dikobrazov's room a quarter of an hour later, he found the famous man lying in bed, glaring malevolently at a hanging lamp. The lamp was motionless, but Dikobrazov did not take his eyes from it. 'You'd better quit spinning,' he muttered. 'I'll show you how to spin, you devil! I smashed the decanter and I'll smash you, too. You'll see! A-a-a-h . . . now the ceiling's going round. I know – it's a conspiracy! But the lamp – the lamp! It's the smallest, but it turns the most . . . Just wait . . .'

The comedian got up, dragging the sheet after him and knocking glasses off the little table as he staggered toward the lamp; halfway there he stumbled against something tall and bony.

'What's that?' he roared, lifting his haggard eyes. 'Who are you? Where'd you come from, hah?'

'I'll show you who I am – get into bed!' And not even waiting for Dikobrazov to follow his instructions, Grebeshkov swung his arm and brought his fist down on the back of the actor's head with such force that he fell head over heels onto the bed. In all probability he had never been struck before, because in spite of his drunkenness, he gazed up at Grebeshkov with wonder and even curiosity.

'You . . . you hit me? But, wait . . . you hit me?'

'I hit you'. Do you want more?' This time the hairdresser struck him in the teeth. Either the strength of the blow or the novelty of the situation had an effect; the comedian's eyes ceased wandering and a glimmer of reason appeared in them. He jumped up, and with more curiosity than anger, began to examine Grebeshkov's pale face and filthy coat.

'You . . . you use your fists? You dare?' he mumbled.

'Shut up!' Again a blow in the face.

'Easy! Easy!' Pochechuev's voice was heard from the next room. 'Easy, Fedyenka!'

'That's nothing, Prokl Lvovich. He himself will thank me for it in the end.'

'Even so, take it easy!' exclaimed Pochechuev tearfully, as he glanced into the room. 'It may be nothing to you, but it sends a chill down my spine. Think of it: in broad daylight, to beat an intelligent, celebrated man, who's in his right mind – and in his own apartment, too! Ach!'

'It's not him that I'm beating, Prokl Lvovich, but the devil that's inside him. Go away now, please, and don't upset yourself . . . Lie down, devil!' Fedya fell upon the comedian. 'Don't move! Wha-at?'

Dikobrazov was seized with horror. It seemed to him that all the whirling objects he had smashed had entered into a conspiracy, and now, with one accord, were flying at his head.

'Help!' he cried. 'Save me! Help!'

'Cry! Cry out, you devil, you! The worst is yet to come! Now listen: if you say one more word, or make the slightest movement, I'm going to kill you! I shall kill you without a regret. There is no one, brother, to intercede for you; even if you were to fire a cannon, nobody would come. But if you are quiet and submissive, I'll give you a little vodka. Here's your vodka!'

Grebeshkov took a pint of vodka out of his pocket and flashed it before the comedian's eyes. At the sight of the object of his passion, the drunken man forgot all about his beating and whinnied with delight. The hairdresser then took a dirty little piece of soap from his vest pocket and stuck it into the bottle. When the vodka became cloudy and soapy he set about adding all sorts of junk to it: saltpeter, ammonium chloride, alum, sodium sulphate, sulphur, resin, and various other 'ingredients' that are sold in a chandlery. The comedian peered at Grebeshkov, avidly following the movements of the bottle. In conclusion the hairdresser burned a scrap of rag, poured the ashes into the vodka, shook it, and approached the bed.

'Drink!' he said, half filling a glass with the mixture. 'At once!'

The comedian gulped it down with delight, gasped, and was immediately goggle-eyed. His face went white, and perspiration stood out on his forehead.

'Drink some more,' suggested Grebeshkov.

'No, I don't want to! But, wait –'

'Drink, so you'll – Drink! I'll kill you!'

Dikobrazov drank, then fell onto the pillow with a moan. A moment later he raised himself slightly, and Fyodor was able to satisfy himself that the mixture had worked.

'Drink some more! Let your guts turn inside out, it's good for you. Drink!'

And then the torture commenced: the actor's guts were literally turned inside out. He jumped up, then tossed on the bed, following with horror the slow movements of his merciless and indefatigable enemy. Grebeshkov did not leave his side for a moment, and sedulously pummeled him when he refused the mixture; a beating was followed by the mixture, the mixture by a beating. Never in all his life had the poor body of Feniksov–Dikobrazov II endured such outrage and humiliation; and never had the famous artist been so weak and helpless as he was now. At first he cried out and struggled, then he grew silent, and finally, convinced that the protests only led to further beatings, he began to weep. At length Pochechuev, who was standing behind the door listening, could bear it no longer, and ran into the room.

'Damn it all!' he cried, waving his arms. 'It would be better to lose the subscription money, and let him have his vodka – only stop torturing him, please! He'll die on us, damn you! Look at him, you can see, he's absolutely dead! I should have known better than to get mixed up with you!'

'That's nothing. He'll be grateful for it, you'll see. Hey, you – what's going on there! Grebeshkov turned to the comedian. 'You'll get it in the neck!'

The hairdresser was busy with Dikobrazov till evening; he himself was tired, worn out. At last the comedian was too weak even to moan, and seemed to have petrified, with an expression of horror on his face. This state was followed by something resembling sleep.

The next day, to the great surprise of Pochechuev, the comedian awoke; it seems he was not dead! On awakening he examined the room with dull, wandering eyes, and then began to recall what had happened.

'Why do I ache all over?' he wondered. 'I feel exactly as though a train had run over me. Shall I have a drink of vodka? Hey! Who's there? Vodka!'

Pochechuev and Grebeshkov were standing behind the door.

'He's asking for vodka!' Pochechuev was horrified. 'That means you didn't cure him!'

'What are you talking about, Prokl Lvovich?' Grebeshkov was surprised. 'Do you think you can cure anyone in a day? I'd be thankful if he were cured in a week – and here you are talking of a day! You might even cure one of those weak fellows in five days, but this one has the constitution of a merchant. He's tough!'

'Why didn't you tell me this before, you devil?' roared Pochechuev.

'Whom do I take after to have this luck? Cursed as I am, what more can I expect from fate? Wouldn't it be more sensible to end it all – to put a bullet through my head right now?'

Despite the gloomy view that Pochechuev took of his fate, Dikobrazov II was playing within a week, and the subscribers' money did not have to be returned.

Grebeshkov put on the comedian's make-up, handling his head with such deference that no one would have suspected his former treatment of the man.

'What vitality!' marveled Pochechuev. 'I nearly died just watching that torture, but he, as if nothing had happened, not only thanks that devil Fedka, but wants to take him to Moscow with him! It's a miracle, that's what it is!'

~

The effect of alcohol on the learning abilities of the goldfish
from Drunken Goldfish and other Irrelevant Scientific Research
by William Hartston

Goldfish immersed in 3.1% alcohol will overturn (lose the righting reflex) within six to eight minutes. Because of this tendency to fall over when drunk, the goldfish is a good model for research on the effects of alcohol. When preliminary studies in 1968 and 1969 indicated that goldfish tended to forget things when drunk, and that Siamese Fighting Fish became more aggressive after a little drink or two, their attraction as experimental animals became irresistible. (It should also be mentioned that you can cut out a great deal of the goldfish brain without impairing its memory. This is a useful option to have in memory research.) Finally, leaving a goldfish stewing in alcoholic water is one way to ensure that its blood alcohol level is maintained at a known concentration.

The first important result concerns the effect of alcoholic blackouts. R.S. Ryback, in his classic 1969 paper 'The Use of Goldfish as a Model for Alcohol Amnesia in Man' (*Quarterly J. Studies on Alcohol*, 30, 877–82), gave the fish a simple learning task. In a mildly alcoholic solution, they were taught to turn in a particular direction (left or right) in a Y-shaped maze. Once training was successfully completed, some of the fish were removed to a high-alcohol solution where they stayed for an hour. The fish soon looked sluggish and some turned over on their sides within the hour.

Three days later, all the fish were tested again in the same mildly alcoholic water of the training sessions. Those who had never tasted strong drink remembered their learning task excellently. Those who had blacked out forgot it, while those who had sampled the heavy liquor without collapsing also retained most of their learning.

So a mildly inebriated goldfish will remember what you teach it, unless it continues drinking until it is paralytic.

Further experiments by Ryback demonstrated that goldfish memory is state-dependent, i.e., its ability to recall something depends on the state of the water being the same as that in which it was first trained. So if you teach a goldfish something sober, it may well forget it when drunk; but if you teach it something when it is intoxicated, it will forget it when it has sobered up. Amazingly, the same result has been shown to hold for humans, whose ability to recall lists of words or nonsense-syllables depends in the same manner upon their alcoholic states at time of recall and memorization being the same.

Tobacco

'A custome lothsome to the eye, hateful to the nose, harmefull to the brain, dangerous to the lungs, and the blacke stinking fume thereof, neerest resembling the horrible Stigian Smoke of the pit that is bottomless.'

King James I

Chain smokers respiration
from Lancet: In England Now

Cheyne-Stokes breathing, first described in 1818, is periodic respiration associated with severe heart disease.

We were doing a ward-round when we came by an unconscious man with heavily nicotine-stained fingers, who was breathing in a curious grunting fashion, and whilst unconscious making singular repetitive movements as though he was taking his right hand to his mouth. He smoked eighty cigarettes per day and the actions suggested that he was continuing to smoke imaginary cigarettes. The registrar queried the type of respiration that the patient exhibited. Without hesitation the physician replied, 'This is obviously a case of Chain Smokers respiration.'

~

Giving it up
from Lancet: In England Now

I have stopped smoking cigarettes. How smug I am. Nobody dislikes me more than me too. There are no compensations. My singing voice has improved, but then I could not sing a note in key before, so the only effect is that my bathroom voice penetrates more piercingly into the privacy of my musically minded family. My breathing also is freer.

Great lumps of lovely fresh air sweep down into alveoli that have been smoke filled for years. So, also, do large dollops of the metropolitan atmospheric cocktail of diesel oil and smog. My squash rackets has improved of course, but in any case I am too old to be playing the game at all, and the extra effort that I can now put into it must be taxing my coronaries to the limit.

Appreciation of good food and wine is a long-forgotten and now renewed delight; particularly to my tailor, who has done all that safety and decency permits in the way of letting out, and now with undisguised enthusiasm embarks upon a new sartorial building programme.

Actually, this stopping of cigarettes has not been too bad – I have taken the edge off the misery by an occasional cigar. Being inexperienced, I have not always been inspired in my selection of cigars, and if during one of the inevitable attacks of vertigo which accompany an unfortunate choice I should fall under a bus I do hope I live long enough to laugh at the clever way in which I have avoided a lung tumour.

~

The shattered health of Mr Podge
from Moonbeams from the Larger Lunacy
by Stephen Leacock

'How are you, Podge?' I said, as I sat down in a leather armchair beside him.

I only meant 'How-do-you-do?' but he rolled his big eyes sideways at me in his flabby face (it was easier than moving his face) and he answered:

'I'm not as well to day as I was yesterday afternoon. Last week I was feeling pretty good part of the time, but yesterday about four o'clock the air turned humid, and I don't feel so well.'

'Have a cigarette?' I said.

'No, thanks; I find they affect the bronchial toobes.'

'Whose?' I asked.

'Mine,' he answered.

'Oh, yes,' I said, and I lighted one. 'So you find the weather trying,' I continued cheerfully.

'Yes, it's too humid. It's up to a saturation of sixty-six. I'm all right till it passes sixty-four. Yesterday afternoon it was only about sixty-one, and I felt fine. But after that it went up. I guess it must be a contraction of the epidermis pressing on some of the sebaceous glands, don't you?'

'I'm sure it is,' I said. 'But why don't you just sleep it off till it's over?'

'I don't like to sleep too much,' he answered. 'I'm afraid of it developing into hypersomnia. There are cases where it's been known to grow into a sort of lethargy that pretty well stops all brain action altogether –'

'That would be too bad,' I murmured. 'What do you do to prevent it?'

'I generally drink from half to three-quarters of a cup of black coffee, or nearly black, every morning at from eleven to five minutes past, so as to keep off hypersomnia. It's the best thing, the doctor says.'

'Aren't you afraid,' I said, 'of its keeping you awake?'

'I am,' answered Podge, and a spasm passed over his big yellow face. 'I'm always afraid of insomnia. That's the worst thing of all. The other night I went to bed about half-past ten, or twenty-five minutes after – I forget which – and I simply couldn't sleep. I couldn't. I read a magazine story, and I still couldn't; and I read another, and still I couldn't sleep. It scared me bad.'

'Oh, pshaw,' I said; 'I don't think sleep matters as long as one eats properly and has a good appetite.'

He shook his head very dubiously. 'I ate a plate of soup at lunch,' he said, 'and I feel it still.'

'You *feel* it!'

'Yes,' repeated Podge, rolling his eyes sideways in a pathetic fashion that he had, 'I still feel it. I oughtn't to have eaten it. It was some sort of a bean soup, and of course it was full of nitrogen. I oughtn't to touch nitrogen,' he added, shaking his head.

'Not take any nitrogen?' I repeated.

'No, the doctor – both doctors – have told me that. I can eat starches, and albumens, all right, but I have to keep right away from all carbons and nitrogens. I've been dieting that way for two years, except that now and again I take a little glucose or phosphates.'

'That must be a nice change,' I said, cheerfully.

'It is,' he answered in a grateful sort of tone.

141

There was a pause. I looked at his big twitching face, and listened to the heavy wheezing of his breath, and I felt sorry for him.

'See here, Podge,' I said, 'I want to give you some good advice.'

'About what?'

'About your health.'

'Yes, yes, do,' he said. Advice about his health was right in his line. He lived on it.

'Well, then, cut out all this fool business of diet and drugs and nitrogen. Don't bother about anything of the sort. Forget it. Eat everything you want to, just when you want it. Drink all you like. Smoke all you can – and you'll feel a new man in a week.'

'Say, do you think so!' he panted, his eyes filled with a new light.

'I know it,' I answered. And as I left him I shook hands with a warm feeling about my heart of being a benefactor to the human race.

Next day, sure enough, Podge's usual chair at the club was empty.

'Out getting some decent exercise,' I thought. 'Thank Heaven!'

Nor did he come the next day, nor the next, nor for a week.

'Leading a rational life at last,' I thought. 'Out in the open getting a little air and sunlight, instead of sitting here howling about his stomach.'

The day after that I saw Dr Slyder in black clothes glide into the club in that peculiar manner of his, like an amateur undertaker.

'Hullo, Slyder,' I called to him, 'you look as solemn as if you had been to a funeral.'

'I have,' he said very quietly, and then added, 'poor Podge!'

'What about him?' I asked with sudden apprehension.

'Why, he died on Tuesday,' answered the doctor. 'Hadn't you heard? Strangest case I've known in years. Came home suddenly one day, pitched all his medicines down the kitchen sink, ordered a couple of cases of champagne and two hundred havanas, and had his house-keeper cook a dinner like a Roman banquet! After being under treatment for two years! Lived, you know, on the narrowest margin conceivable. I told him and Silk told him – we all told him – his only chance was to keep away from every form of nitrogenous ultra-stim-ulants. I said to him often, "Podge, if you touch heavy carbonized food, you're lost."'

'Dear me,' I thought to myself, 'there *are* such things after all!'

'It was a marvel,' continued Slyder, 'that we kept him alive at all. And, of course' – here the doctor paused to ring the bell to order

142

two Manhattan cocktails – 'as soon as he touched alcohol he was done.'

So that was the end of the valetudinarianism of Mr Podge.

I have always considered that I killed him.

But anyway, he was a nuisance at the club.

COUGHS AND SNEEZES AND OTHER DISEASES

Coughs

Of coughs and sneezes
from A Book of Learned Nonsense *by Edward Lear*

O! Mimber for the County Louth
   Residing at Ardee!
Whom I, before I wander South
   Partik'lar wish to see: –

I send you this. – That you may know
   I've left the Sussex shore,
And coming here two days ago
   Do cough for evermore.

Or gasping hard for breath do sit
   Upon a brutal chair,
For to lie down in Asthma fit
   Is what I cannot bear.

Or sometimes sneeze: and always blow
   My well-develloped nose.
And altogether never know
   No comfort nor repose.

~

Cough
by Celcus

Cough generally arises from excoriation of the fauces, which is contracted in many ways. Hence when their healthy condition has been restored, the cough itself is brought to an end. Sometimes, however, it is a distinct affection, and when inveterate, is got rid of with difficulty. Sometimes it is dry, sometimes excites a discharge of rheum. It is requisite to drink hyssop every second day; to run with the breath held in, but by no means in the dust; to read aloud, which at first is impeded by the cough, but afterwards gets the better of it: then to walk: afterwards to be exercised also by the hands, and to rub the chest for a long time: after these, to eat three ounces of the richest figs, boiled over a brasier. Besides, if the cough be moist, strong frictions with certain of the calefacients are serviceable, in such a manner that the head may also be well rubbed at the same time: also dry cupping the chest; mustard applied to the external fauces until it slightly excoriate; a drink made of mint, sweet almonds, and starch; and taking at first bread and afterwards any mild food. But if the cough be dry, and that be exceedingly troublesome, the taking of a cyath of austere wine assists it, provided that be done at intervals, and not oftener than three or four times: it is requisite also to eat a small portion of the very best assafœtida; to take the juice of leek or of horehound; squills as a linctus; to sip vinegar of squills, or certainly acrid vinegar, or two cyaths of wine with a clove of bruised garlic.

A cough is benefited by travelling, long voyaging, residence at the sea-side, swimmings; by sometimes taking bland food, as mallows and nettle; sometimes that which is acrid, as garlic boiled in milk; by gruels, to which assafœtida has been added, or in which onions have been boiled to wasting; by fresh eggs with sulphur; and by first giving water to drink, and then this and wine, in their turns, varying them every other day.

~

The experience of the McWilliamses with membranous croup
from The Complete Short Stories *by Mark Twain*

(As related to the author of this book by Mr McWilliams, a pleasant New York gentleman whom the said author met by chance on a journey.)

Well, to go back to where I was before I digressed to explain to you how that frightful and incurable disease, membranous croup, was ravaging the town and driving all mothers mad with terror, I called Mrs McWilliams's attention to little Penelope and said:

'Darling, I wouldn't let that child be chewing that pine stick if I were you.'

'Precious, where is the harm in it?' said she, but at the same time preparing to take away the stick – for some women cannot receive even the most palpably judicious suggestion without arguing it; that is, married women.

I replied:

'Love, it is notorious that pine is the least nutritious wood that a child can eat.'

My wife's hand paused, in the act of taking the stick, and returned itself to her lap. She bridled perceptibly, and said:

'Hubby, you know better than that. You know you do. Doctors *all* say that the turpentine in pine wood is good for weak back and the kidneys.'

'Ah – I was under a misapprehension. I did not know that the child's kidneys and spine were affected, and that the family physician had recommended –'

'Who said the child's spine and kidneys were affected?'

'My love, you intimated it.'

'The idea! I never intimated anything of the kind.'

'Why my dear, it hasn't been two minutes since you said –'

'Bother what I said! I don't care what I did say. There isn't any harm in the child's chewing a bit of pine stick if she wants to, and you know it perfectly well. And she *shall* chew it, too. So there, now!'

'Say no more, my dear. I now see the force of your reasoning, and I will go and order two or three cords of the best pine wood today. No child of mine shall want while I –'

'O *please* go along to your office and let me have some peace. A body can never make the simplest remark but you must take it up and go to arguing and arguing and arguing till you don't know what you are talking about, and you *never* do.'

'Very well, it shall be as you say. But there is a want of logic in your last remark which –'

However, she was gone with a flourish before I could finish, and had taken the child with her. That night at dinner she confronted me with a face as white as a sheet:

'O, Mortimer, there's another! Little Georgie Gordon is taken.'

'Membranous croup?'

'Membranous croup.'

'Is there any hope for him?'

'None in the wide world. O, what is to become of us!'

By and by a nurse brought in our Penelope to say goodnight and offer the customary prayer at the mother's knee. In the midst of 'Now I lay me down to sleep,' she gave a slight cough! My wife fell back like one stricken with death. But the next moment she was up and brimming with the activities which terror inspires.

She commanded that the child's crib be removed from the nursery to our bedroom; and she went along to see the order executed. She took me with her, of course. We got matters arranged with speed. A cot bed was put up in my wife's dressing room for the nurse. But now Mrs McWilliams said we were too far away from the other baby, and what if *he* were to have the symptoms in the night – and she blanched again, poor thing.

We then restored the crib and the nurse to the nursery and put up a bed for ourselves in a room adjoining.

Presently, however, Mrs McWilliams said suppose the baby should catch it from Penelope? This thought struck a new panic to her heart, and the tribe of us could not get the crib out of the nursery again fast enough to satisfy my wife, though she assisted in her own person and well nigh pulled the crib to pieces in her frantic hurry.

We moved down stairs; but there was no place there to stow the nurse, and Mrs McWilliams said the nurse's experience would be an inestimable help. So we returned, bag and baggage, to our own bedroom once more, and felt a great gladness, like storm-buffeted birds that have found their nest again.

Mrs McWilliams sped to the nursery to see how things were going on there. She was back in a moment with a new dread. She said:

'What *can* make Baby sleep so?'

I said:

'Why, my darling, Baby *always* sleeps like a graven image.'

'I know. I know; but there's something peculiar about his sleep, now. He seems to – to – he seems to breathe so *regularly*. O, this is dreadful.'

'But my dear he always breathes regularly.'

'Oh, I know it, but there's something frightful about it now. His nurse is too young and inexperienced. Maria shall stay there with her, and be on hand if anything happens.'

'That is a good idea, but who will help *you*?'

'You can help me all I want. I wouldn't allow anybody to do anything but myself, any how, at such a time as this.'

I said I would feel mean to lie abed and sleep, and leave her to watch and toil over our little patient all the weary night – but she reconciled me to it. So old Maria departed and took up her ancient quarters in the nursery.

Penelope coughed twice in her sleep.

'Oh, why *don't* that doctor come! Mortimer, this room is too warm. This room is certainly too warm. Turn off the register – quick!'

I shut it off, glancing at the thermometer at the same time, and wondering to myself if 70 *was* too warm for a sick child.

The coachman arrived from down town, now, with the news that our physician was ill and confined to his bed. Mrs McWilliams turned a dead eye upon me, and said in a dead voice:

'There is a Providence in it. It is foreordained. He never was sick before. Never. We have not been living as we ought to live, Mortimer. Time and time again I have told you so. Now you see the result. Our child will never get well. Be thankful if you can forgive yourself; I never can forgive *myself*.'

I said, without intent to hurt, but with heedless choice of words, that I could not see that we had been living such an abandoned life.

'*Mortimer!* Do you want to bring the judgment upon Baby, too!'

Then she began to cry, but suddenly exclaimed:

'The doctor must have sent medicines!'

I said:

'Certainly. They are here. I was only waiting for you to give me a chance.'

'Well, do give them to me! Don't you know that every moment is precious now? But what was the use in sending medicines, when he *knows* that the disease is incurable?'

I said that while there was life there was hope.

'Hope! Mortimer, you know no more what you are talking about than the child unborn. If you would –. As I live, the directions say give one teaspoonful once an hour! Once an hour! – as if we had a whole year before us to save the child in! Mortimer, please hurry. Give the poor perishing thing a tablespoonful, and *try* to be quick!'

'Why, my dear, a tablespoonful might –'

'*Don't* drive me frantic! . . . There, there, there, my precious, my own; it's nasty bitter stuff, but it's good for Nelly – good for Mother's precious darling; and it will make her well. There, there, there, put the little head on Mamma's breast and go to sleep, and pretty soon – Oh, I know she can't live till morning! Mortimer, a tablespoonful every half hour will –. Oh, the child needs belladonna too; I know she does

151

– and aconite. Get them, Mortimer. Now do let me have my way. You know nothing about these things.'

We now went to bed, placing the crib close to my wife's pillow. All this turmoil had worn upon me, and within two minutes I was something more than half asleep. Mrs McWilliams roused me:

'Darling, is that register turned on?'

'No.'

'I thought as much. Please turn it on at once. This room is cold.'

I turned it on, and presently fell asleep again. I was aroused once more:

'Dearie, would you mind moving the crib to your side of the bed? It is nearer the register.'

I moved it, but had a collision with the rug and woke up the child. I dozed off once more, while my wife quieted the sufferer. But in a little while these words came murmuring remotely through the fog of my drowsiness:

'Mortimer, if we only had some goose-grease – will you ring?'

I climbed dreamily out, and stepped on a cat, which responded with a protest and would have got a convincing kick for it if a chair had not got it instead.

'Now, Mortimer, why do you want to turn up the gas and wake up the child again?'

'Because I want to see how much I am hurt, Caroline.'

'Well look at the chair, too – I have no doubt it is ruined. Poor cat, suppose you had –'

'Now I am not going to suppose anything about the cat. It never would have occurred if Maria had been allowed to remain here and attend to these duties, which are in her line and are not in mine.'

'Now Mortimer, I should think you would be ashamed to make a remark like that. It is a pity if you cannot do the few little things I ask of you at such an awful time as this when our child –'

'There, there, I will do anything you want. But I can't raise anybody with this bell. They're all gone to bed. Where is the goose-grease?'

'On the mantel-piece in the nursery. If you'll step there and speak to Maria –'

I fetched the goose-grease and went to sleep again. Once more I was called:

'Mortimer, I so hate to disturb you, but the room is still too cold for me to try to apply this stuff. Would you mind lighting the fire? It is all ready to touch a match to.'

I dragged myself out and lit the fire, and then sat down disconsolate.

'Mortimer, don't sit there and catch your death of cold. Come to bed.'

As I was stepping in, she said:

'But wait a moment. Please give the child some more of the medicine.'

Which I did. It was a medicine which made a child more or less lively; so my wife made use of its waking interval to strip it and grease it all over with the goose-oil. I was soon asleep once more, but once more I had to get up.

'Mortimer, I feel a draft. I feel it distinctly. There is nothing so bad for this disease as a draft. Please move the crib in front of the fire.'

I did it; and collided with the rug again, which I threw in the fire. Mrs McWilliams sprang out of bed and rescued it and we had some words. I had another trifling interval of sleep, and then got up, by request, and constructed a flax-seed poultice. This was placed upon the child's breast and left there to do its healing work.

A wood fire is not a permanent thing. I got up every twenty minutes and renewed ours, and this gave Mrs McWilliams the opportunity to shorten the times of giving the medicines by ten minutes, which was a great satisfaction to her. Now and then, between times, I reorganized the flax-seed poultices, and applied sinapisms and other sorts of blisters where unoccupied places could be found upon the child. Well, toward morning the wood gave out and my wife wanted me to go down cellar and get some more. I said:

'My dear, it is a laborious job, and the child must be nearly warm enough, with her extra clothing. Now mightn't we put on another layer of poultices and –'.

I did not finish, because I was interrupted. I lugged wood up from below for some little time, and then turned in and fell to snoring as only a man can whose strength is all gone and whose soul is worn out. Just at broad daylight I felt a grip on my shoulder that brought me to my senses suddenly. My wife was glaring down upon me and gasping. As soon as she could command her tongue she said:

'It is all over! All over! The child's perspiring! What *shall* we do?'

'Mercy, how you terrify me! *I* don't know what we ought to do. Maybe if we scraped her and put her in the draft again –'

'O, idiot! There is not a moment to lose! Go for the doctor. Go yourself. Tell him he *must* come, dead or alive.'

I dragged that poor sick man from his bed and brought him. He looked at the child and said she was not dying. This was joy unspeakable to me, but it made my wife as mad as if he had offered her a personal affront. Then he said the child's cough was only caused by some trifling irritation or other in the throat. At this I thought my wife had a mind to show him the door. Now the doctor said he would make the child cough harder and dislodge the trouble. So he gave her something that sent her into a spasm of coughing, and presently up came a little wood splinter or so.

'This child has no membranous croup,' said he. 'She has been chewing a bit of pine shingle or something of the kind, and got some little slivers in her throat. They won't do her any hurt.'

'No,' said I, 'I can well believe that. Indeed the turpentine that is in them is very good for certain sorts of diseases that are peculiar to children. My wife will tell you so.'

But she did not. She turned away in disdain and left the room; and since that time there is one episode in our life which we never refer to. Hence the tide of our days flows by in deep and untroubled serenity.

[Very few married men have such an experience as McWilliams's, and so the author of this book thought that maybe the novelty of it would give it a passing interest to the reader.]

~

Just the one
from Low Life *by Jeffrey Bernard*

Last Tuesday was as nasty a day as I can remember. I had a bronchoscopy at the Brompton Chest Hospital and it made my eyes water, I can tell you. I was woken up by apprehension at 5 a.m. – the sickening sort I used to feel waiting for the 10.15 from Newbury wondering if they'd taken the buffet car off – and wandered slowly all the way to the hospital, pausing at a bench in Hyde Park to smoke some cigarettes, indulge in some self-pity, and attempt an estimate of the number of my days. Wiping the tears from my red, white and blue eyes I strode purposefully on, thinking England Expects and Once more into the breach. I got to the hospital two hours early and sat on the steps smoking more cigarettes.

While I waited in the ward for my pre-med injection a couple of nurses and a young doctor told me so many times that I had nothing to worry about that I knew I had. Above their reassuring smiles their eyes were screaming at the thought of themselves having a bronchoscopy. So they wheeled me off and the pre-med had relieved me of very, very little anxiety. Now this is what happens and doctors need read no further. You're put in a semi-reclining position and the man squirts some anaesthetic jelly up each nostril which really does make your eyes water. Then he sprays your throat with something to dry it up a little, and then it's sprayed with anaesthetic which induced more coughing. Then it's crunchtime. The amazing, reptilian tube with its light at the end is inserted into your hooter. My man had a little difficulty getting through and around the top and a Welsh nurse patted me and said, 'It'll be all right. You've such a small nose, you see. But pretty it is too.' I attempted some facetious jocularity to the effect that small noses didn't mean small everything but, too late, the snake was in my throat. My man, its charmer, now began to take great interest and he repeatedly said to his colleague, 'Come and have a look at this', as they stared intently through the other end. Quite obviously there are more navigational problems getting into the lung than I realised. But they were two good men and they told me what was happening all the time. I got one fright. Before getting to the voice box, the one that produced such old immortals as 'I'll Have Just the One', he said, 'I think you've got thrush.' Jesus, that's all I need, I thought, having just discovered Miss Right again. But it was a false alarm.

Then a rather alarming thing happened. He attached a syringe on his end of the line and squirted anaesthetic down. My end didn't like it and tried to reject it. I thought I'd throw up and choke. This he did three times in rapid succession. Then he had trouble in getting into the lung itself – small again, no doubt, in the nurse's opinion – and probably difficult to enter owing to the pub ashtray that's been lodged there for some time. Once in the lung the snake spewed more anaesthetic and I retched and coughed and shook.

The lads were fascinated, though, and really enjoying themselves. 'See this.' 'What about that?' 'Look at this.' One of them even held my hand, seeing my discomfort. I was rather touched in spite of being busy coughing. Well, they spent what seemed an age looking around the old bellow. More anaesthetic squirts and then something like a thin wire was put down to 'brush' the lung and get a sample of whatever it is that lives on that dreadful, stalagmite-encrusted surface.

Then a bit more looking around and chatting and then it was suddenly whipped out of me.

'There we are, all over. It seems to me that you've got a perfectly average lung with maybe some scarring.' Of course, I demanded my money back. What a bloody horrible experience. Then it was almost like handshaking time. 'Well done.' 'You were very good, dear. Behaved very well, you did.' 'Yes, jolly good.' It was rather like being debriefed in an old Ealing film. Perhaps it was the pre-med and all the anaesthetic. I felt like saying, 'I'd like to claim one Me 109 and a possible, sir.' 'Jolly good show, chaps.'

Back in my empty ward I dozed. After three hours or so I thought I'd try a cigarette. Leaning out of the window to avoid detection and still weaker than I realised, I nearly fell out. Now that's a thought. I've never been in traction or an orthopaedic hospital. I might give it a whirl next year.

Colds

'Never be afraid of open windows. People don't catch cold in bed. This is a popular fallacy. With proper bed clothes and hot bottles you can always keep a patient warm in bed and well ventilated at the same time ... I know an intelligent humane house surgeon who makes a practice of keeping the ward windows open. The physicians and surgeons invariably close them while going their rounds; and the house surgeon very properly as invariably opens them whenever the doctors have turned their backs.'

Florence Nightingale

'If you want a cure for a cold, put on two pullovers, take up a baton, poker or pencil, tune the radio to a symphony concert, stand on a chair, and conduct like mad for an hour or so and the cold will have vanished. It never fails. You know why conductors live so long? Because we perspire so much.'

Sir John Barbirolli

The cold
from Writings from the New Yorker 1927–1976
by E.B. White

We are at this writing in bed, entertaining our first cold of the 1951–52 virus season. It would greatly satisfy our curiosity to know at precisely what moment the virus gained entrance and took hold – for there must have been such a moment, such a division point. Prior to that moment, we were a whole man; subsequent to it, and until the symptoms appeared, we were the unwitting host to evil and corrup-

157

tion. One wonders about all such tremendous turning points: the moment when a child is conceived, the moment when the tide stops flooding and starts ebbing. We have often wondered at precisely what moment in life our defenses were successfully breached by another, deadlier virus – the point that marked the exact end of youth's high innocence and purity of design, the beginning of compromise, acquiescence, conformity, and the general lassitude of maturity. There must in every person's life (except a few rare ones) have been such a moment. In the case of the cold, the lag between the penetration of the disease and the appearance of the symptoms is a matter of hours; in the case of the other virus, a matter of years.

Statisticians have computed the very great interruptive strength of the common cold in our society, have shown how it slows the wheels of industry. That is only one side to the virus, however. We are such docile creatures, normally, that it takes a virus to jolt us out of life's routine. A couple of days in a fever bed are, in a sense, health-giving; the change in body temperature, the change in pulse rate, and the change of scene have a restorative effect on the system equal to the hell they raise. We heard once of a man who went to bed with a cold one day and never got up again. The seizure was soon over and his health restored, but the adventure of being in bed impressed him deeply and he felt that he had discovered his niche at last.

Medical science understands this paradox of the virus, and virus diseases are now the white hope of cancer research. (It has already been shown that they tend to congregate in cancer cells.) Thermometer in mouth, we await the day of victory, when the common cold, which has long been the butt of our anger, will emerge as the knight that slew the dragon.

~

Curing a cold
from The Complete Short Stories *by Mark Twain*

It is a good thing, perhaps, to write for the amusement of the public, but it is a far higher and nobler thing to write for their instruction, their profit, their actual and tangible benefit. The latter is the sole object of this article. If it prove the means of restoring to health one solitary sufferer among my race, of lighting up once more the fire of hope and joy in his faded eyes, of bringing back to his dead heart again the quick, generous impulses of other days, I shall be amply rewarded for my labor; my soul will be permeated with the sacred delight a Christian feels when he has done a good, unselfish deed.

Having led a pure and blameless life, I am justified in believing that no man who knows me will reject the suggestions I am about to make, out of fear that I am trying to deceive him. Let the public do itself the honor to read my experience in doctoring a cold, as herein set forth, and then follow in my footsteps.

When the White House was burned in Virginia City, I lost my home, my happiness, my constitution, and my trunk. The loss of the two first-named articles was a matter of no great consequence, since a home without a mother or a sister, or a distant young female relative in it, to remind you, by putting your soiled linen out of sight and taking your boots down off the mantel-piece, that there are those who think about you and care for you, is easily obtained. And I cared nothing for the loss of my happiness, because not being a poet, it could not be possible that melancholy would abide with me long. But to lose a good constitution and a better trunk were serious misfortunes. On the day of the fire my constitution succumbed to a severe cold, caused by undue exertion in getting ready to do something. I suffered to no purpose, too, because the plan I was figuring at for the extinguishing of the fire was so elaborate that I never got it completed until the middle of the following week.

The first time I began to sneeze, a friend told me to go and bathe my feet in hot water and go to bed. I did so. Shortly afterwards, another friend advised me to get up and take a cold shower-bath. I did that also. Within the hour, another friend, assured me that it was policy to 'feed a cold and starve a fever'. I had both. So I thought it best to fill myself up for the cold, and then I sat back and let the fever starve awhile.

In a case of this kind, I seldom do things by halves; I ate pretty heartily; I conferred my custom upon a stranger who had just opened his restaurant that morning: he waited near me in respectful silence until I had finished feeding my cold, when he inquired if the people about Virginia City were much afflicted with colds? I told him I thought they were. He then went out and took in his sign.

I started down toward the office, and on the way encountered another bosom friend, who told me that a quart of salt water, taken warm, would come as near curing a cold as anything in the world. I hardly thought I had room for it, but I tried it anyhow. The result was surprising. I believed I had thrown up my immortal soul.

Now, as I am giving my experience only for the benefit of those who are troubled with the distemper I am writing about, I feel that they will see the propriety of my cautioning them against following such portions of it as proved inefficient with me, and acting upon this conviction, I warn them against warm salt water. It may be a good enough remedy, but I think it is too severe. If I had another cold in the head, and there were no course left me but to take either an earthquake or a quart of warm salt water, I would take my chances on the earthquake.

After the storm which had been raging in my stomach had subsided, and no more good Samaritans happening along, I went on borrowing handkerchiefs again and blowing them to atoms, as had been my custom in the early stages of my cold, until I came across a lady who had just arrived from over the plains, and who said she had lived in a part of the country where doctors were scarce, and had from necessity acquired considerable skill in the treatment of simple 'family complaints'. I knew she must have had much experience, for she appeared to be a hundred and fifty years old.

She mixed a decoction composed of molasses, aquafortis, turpentine, and various other drugs, and instructed me to take a wine-glass full of it every fifteen minutes. I never took but one dose; that was enough; it robbed me of all moral principle, and awoke every unworthy impulse of my nature. Under its malign influence my brain conceived miracles of meanness, but my hands were too feeble to execute them; at that time, had it not been that my strength had surrendered to a succession of assaults from infallible remedies for my cold, I am satisfied that I would have tried to rob the graveyard. Like most other people, I often feel mean, and act accordingly; but until I took that medicine I had never revelled in such supernatural depravity, and felt proud of it. At the end of two days I was ready to go to doctoring again. I took a few more unfailing remedies, and finally drove my cold from my head to my lungs.

I got to coughing incessantly, and my voice fell below zero; I conversed in a thundering base (*sic*), two octaves below my natural tone; I could only compass my regular nightly repose by coughing myself down to a state of utter exhaustion, and then the moment I began to talk in my sleep, my discordant voice woke me up again.

My case grew more and more serious every day. Plain gin was

recommended; I took it. Then gin and molasses; I took that also. Then gin and onions; I added the onions, and took all three. I detected no particular result, however, except that I had acquired a breath like a buzzard's.

I found I had to travel for my health. I went to Lake Bigler with my reportorial comrade, Wilson. It is gratifying to me to reflect that we traveled in considerable style; we went in the Pioneer coach, and my friend took all his baggage with him, consisting of two excellent silk handkerchiefs and a daguerreotype of his grandmother. We sailed and hunted and fished and danced all day, and I doctored my cough all night. By managing in this way, I made out to improve every hour in the twenty-four. But my disease continued to grow worse.

A sheet-bath was recommended. I had never refused a remedy yet, and it seemed poor policy to commence then; therefore I determined to take a sheet-bath, notwithstanding I had no idea what sort of arrangement it was. It was administered at midnight, and the weather was very frosty. My breast and back were bared, and a sheet (there appeared to be a thousand yards of it) soaked in ice-water, and wound around me until I resembled a swab for a Columbiad.

It is a cruel expedient. When the chilly rag touches one's warm flesh, it makes him start with sudden violence, and gasp for breath just as men do in the death agony. It froze the marrow in my bones, and stopped the beating of my heart. I thought my time had come.

Young Wilson said the circumstance reminded him of an anecdote about a negro who was being baptized, and who slipped from the parson's grasp, and came near being drowned. He floundered around, though, and finally rose up out of the water considerably strangled, and furiously angry, and started ashore at once, spouting water like a whale, and remarking, with great asperity, that 'one o' dese days some gent'l'man's nigger gwyne to get killed wid jis' such dam foolishness as dis!'

Never take a sheet-bath – never. Next to meeting a lady acquaintance, who, for reasons best known to herself, don't see you when she looks at you, and don't know you when she does see you, it is the most uncomfortable thing in the world.

But, as I was saying, when the sheet-bath failed to cure my cough, a lady friend recommended the application of a mustard plaster to my breast. I believe that would have cured me effectually, if it had not been for young Wilson. When I went to bed, I put my mustard plaster – which was a very gorgeous one, eighteen inches square – where I could reach it when I was ready for it. But young Wilson got hungry in the night and – here is food for the imagination.

After sojourning a week at Lake Bigler, I went to Steamboat Springs, and beside the steam baths, I took a lot of the vilest medicines that were ever concocted. They would have cured me, but I had to go back to Virginia City, where, notwithstanding the variety of new remedies I absorbed every day, I managed to aggravate my disease by carelessness and undue exposure.

I finally concluded to visit San Francisco, and the first day I got there, a lady at the hotel told me to drink a quart of whisky every twenty-four hours, and a friend up town recommended precisely the same course. Each advised me to take a quart; that made half a gallon. I did it, and still live.

Now, with the kindest motives in the world, I offer for the consideration of consumptive patients the variegated course of treatment I have lately gone through. Let them try it: if it don't cure, it can't more than kill them.

~

The common cold
by Johnny Speight

With medical science at the cutting edge of the high technology syndrome people are saying, 'Why can't they cure the common cold?'

They're performing miracles of surgery. They're so far advanced in genetics they can now determine a baby's characteristics in the womb and change them. If a child shows signs of homosexuality, they can alter it and make them heterosexual. This is pleasing for all those sex bigots out there, though why it should be I don't understand. They should welcome homosexuality as one of the most innovative steps we have taken this century . . .

The common cold isn't *common* in the accepted sense at all as it afflicts the high and mighty as much as it affects the poor and lowly.

Germs are not particular who they infect or make their home on. They are true democrats and egalitarians. A fly or any other germ-carrying pest will bite a filthy dirty tramp, and for his next bite will move onto the filthy rich owner of a Rolls Royce. They're both the same to the fly. They're both fresh meat. A wasp will sting anyone anywhere it fancies. Theres no protocol. Germs will infect a royal palace as quickly and readily as they will infect a slum. A strong wind will blow them there so fast, the first sneeze in the slum will be echoed in the palace.

Admitted, they're not too keen on places that are too hygienic – it puts them off their food a bit. (They're a bit like the aristocracy, I suppose; they like their food to be running alive – with their own kind. Eating with their mates. Its the community spirit. Like us, we prefer to eat in crowded restaurants ourselves. If its popular it must be good – well, that's another argument.)

There's a story. Two germs eating.

One of them said to his mate, 'Hey, you been next door? It's so hygienic in there.'

And his mate said, 'D'you mind? I'm eating.'

So why don't they wage war on these germs and cure us all of the common cold?

Well, take a look around any chemist. You'll see the shelves piled high with thousands upon thousands of common cold remedies. Giant corporates all over the world manufacture billions of bottles of these remedies every day. Every bathroom medicine cabinet in almost every house in the world contains several bottles of them. And these are replenished or newly recommended ones given a try. Even the distillers are in on the game, saying a drop of scotch helps a cold, and a few more drops will make you feel better about it anyway – a good excuse for getting pissed if one is needed; and the tobacco industry claims their snuff will clear your head and help you with your sneezing. (Remember every time you sneeze you make a million germs homeless – sod'em!)

So can you imagine what would happen if some nutty scientist came up with a cure for it?

'What's the prick trying to do, ruin a four billion dollar industry?'

They'd shoot him first and bury his cure with him.

Next week: Are One Arm People A Threat To The Glove Industry?

Wind

The wind
by Walter Harris

The theory of Flatus's flying through the body seems as hidden and
unknown to us, as the nature of stormy winds, when they war sometimes in the sky with a great noise and thundering, is a hard and difficult philosophical speculation. And indeed, as winds sometimes
raise storms and tossing of the waves from the bottom of the sea up
to heaven, as they sometimes cause tremblings and earthquakes when
they are enclosed in the bowels of the earth; so do Flatus's, being bred
and shut up in human bodies, cause gripings, racking pains, and con-
vulsions.

~

Diary, 6 & 7 October 1663
from The Diary by Samuel Pepys

6 *October*. Finding myself beginning to be troubled with wind, as I
used to be, and with pain in making water, I took a couple of pills that
I had by me of Mr Hollyards.

7 *October*. They wrought in the morning and I did keep my bed; and
my pain continued on me mightily, that I keeped within all day in

great pain, and could break no wind nor have any stool after my physic had done working. So in the evening I took coach and to Mr Hollyards, but he was not at home; and so home again. And whether the coach did me good or no I know not, but having a good fire in my chamber, I begun to break six or seven small and great farts; and so to bed and lay in good ease all night, and pissed pretty well in the morning.

~

The illest of winds
from The Sunday Telegraph *(8 August 1993)*
by James Le Fanu

Few of my columns have elicited so vigorous a response as the one in which, at the beginning of the year, I wrote about Irritable Bowel Syndrome (IBS). From the Isle of Skye to the Isle of Wight the letters poured in. Because of the enigmatic nature of the disorder virtually everyone had a different story to tell.

The symptoms were highly variable both in type and intensity: colicky pain, a bloated tummy, explosive diarrhoea, constipation and (socially very embarrassing) the passing of prodigious quantities of flatus. And then, most important of all, were the 'cures' for virtually all, found by a process of trial and error. Many had identified certain foods as precipitating their symptoms, and excluding them from the diet were dramatically effective; while others had found that one type of food made them better. Some suspected that too much acid was the culprit and found relief with antacids, others praised the virtues of charcoal tablets. 'Stress', that ubiquitous phenomenon, was frequently indicted, and a variety of ways of coping with the help of deep breathing or 'visualisation' were advocated. One reader was cured instantly by acupuncture.

No other medical condition encompasses such diversity of causation, symptomatology and treatment, and therein lies the problem. The standard medical model of a disease is that even if a cause is not precisely known, it is characterised by a predictable cluster of symptoms and responds to specific treatment. Where, as with IBS, this is clearly not the case, doctors tend to be frustrated and respond in one of a variety of ways.

The first is outright denial. IBS, I have been assured by a gastroenterologist knighted for his distinguished services to medical research, does not exist. The second is a dismissive approach where, having 'excluded serious pathology' – that is after tests for colitis or cancer turn out to be normal – doctors leave their patients to get on with their lives as best they can. The next is to offer some spurious explanation of which 'stress' and a 'bad diet' are commonest, along with the latest fashionable advice about healthy eating, which nowadays means a high fibre diet. This is particularly unfortunate, as many sufferers attest it often makes their symptoms a lot worse.

Little wonder, then, that people with IBS take themselves off in droves to 'alternative' medical practitioners, though I doubt their treatments are any more effective than those of the orthodox camp.

Warts

Warts are common enough in the Ozarks
from Ozark Superstitions *by Vance Randolph*

(Mrs May Kennedy McCord. Springfield, Missouri has collected and written down 125 wart cures).

An old man in Pineville, Missouri, told me as a great secret that he could cure any wart by squeezing a drop of blood out of it on a grain of corn and feeding the corn to a red rooster. According to another version of this story, it is best to rub the wart with two grains of corn, feed one to the rooster, and carry the other in your pocket. When you lose the grain from your pocket, the wart will be gone. The losing must be accidental, but that is not difficult; most cabins are full of rodents, and a grain of corn in the pocket of one's overalls will soon 'turn up missin'.

Another 'sleight' for getting rid of a wart is merely to prick it with a thorn until it bleeds, then throw the thorn over the left shoulder and walk away without looking back.

*

Or you may just rub the wart with a piece of onion, then throw the onion backward over your right shoulder and walk away without looking back. Another school contends that it is best to touch your wart with a whole red onion; then you cut the onion in two, eat half of it and bury the other half; when the buried part decays, the wart will disappear.

*

A group of old-timers in Phelps county, Missouri, contend that the best way to dispose of warts is to carry a black cat, freshly killed, into

167

a graveyard at night. Some say that the dead cat must be placed on the grave of a person buried the same day, and if this person has led a wicked life, so much the better.

There is a widespread belief that warts can be 'charmed off' by touching them with the hand of a corpse. I have seen this tried several times. The warts disappeared after a while, just as they generally do under any other treatment, or with no treatment at all. On the other side of the balance, I have met an undertaker who handles many bodies every year, and both his hands are covered with warts!

~

On warts
from The Medusa and the Snail *by Lewis Thomas*

Warts are wonderful structures. They can appear overnight on any part of the skin, like mushrooms on a damp lawn, full grown and splendid in the complexity of their architecture. Viewed in stained sections under a microscope, they are the most specialized of cellular arrangements, constructed as though for a purpose. They sit there like turreted mounds of dense, impenetrable horn, impregnable, designed for defense against the world outside.

In a certain sense, warts are both useful and essential, but not for us. As it turns out, the exuberant cells of a wart are the elaborate reproductive apparatus of a virus.

You might have thought from the looks of it that the cells infected by the wart virus were using this response as a ponderous way of defending themselves against the virus, maybe even a way of becoming more distasteful, but it is not so. The wart is what the virus truly wants; it can flourish only in cells undergoing precisely this kind of overgrowth. It is not a defense at all; it is an overwhelming welcome, an enthusiastic accommodation meeting the needs of more and more virus.

The strangest thing about warts is that they tend to go away. Fully grown, nothing in the body has so much the look of toughness and permanence as a wart, and yet, inexplicably and often very abruptly, they come to the end of their lives and vanish without a trace.

And they can be made to go away by something that can only be called thinking, or something like thinking. This is a special property of warts which is absolutely astonishing, more of a surprise than cloning or recombinant DNA or endorphin or acupuncture or anything else currently attracting attention in the press. It is one of the great mystifications of science: warts can be ordered off the skin by hypnotic suggestion.

Not everyone believes this, but the evidence goes back a long way and is persuasive. Generations of internists and dermatologists, and their grandmothers for that matter, have been convinced of the phenomenon. I was once told by a distinguished old professor of medicine, one of Sir William Osler's original bright young men, that it was his practice to paint gentian violet over a wart and then assure the patient firmly that it would be gone in a week, and he never saw it fail. There have been several meticulous studies by good clinical investigators, with proper controls. In one of these, fourteen patients with seemingly intractable generalized warts on both sides of the body were hypnotized, and the suggestion was made that all the warts on one side of the body would begin to go away. Within several weeks the results were indisputably positive; in nine patients, all or nearly all of the warts on the suggested side had vanished, while the control side had just as many as ever.

It is interesting that most of the warts vanished precisely as they were instructed, but it is even more fascinating that mistakes were made. Just as you might expect in other affairs requiring a clear understanding of which is the right and which the left side, one of the subjects got mixed up and destroyed the warts on the wrong side. In a later study by a group at the Massachusetts General Hospital, the warts on both sides were rejected even though the instructions were to pay attention to just one side.

I have been trying to figure out the nature of the instructions issued by the unconscious mind, whatever that is, under hypnosis. It seems to me hardly enough for the mind to say, simply, get off, eliminate yourselves, without providing something in the way of specifications as to how to go about it.

I used to believe, thinking about this experiment when it was just published, that the instructions might be quite simple. Perhaps nothing more detailed than a command to shut down the flow through all the precapillary arterioles in and around the warts to the point of strangulation. Exactly how the mind would accomplish this with precision, cutting off the blood supply to one wart while leaving others intact, I couldn't figure out, but I was satisfied to leave it there anyhow. And I was glad to think that my unconscious mind would have to take the responsibility for this, for if I had been one of the subjects I would never have been able to do it myself.

But now the problem seems much more complicated by the information concerning the viral etiology of warts, and even more so by the currently plausible notion that immunologic mechanisms are very likely implicated in the rejection of warts.

If my unconscious can figure out how to manipulate the mechanisms needed for getting around that virus, and for deploying all the various cells in the correct order for tissue rejection, then all I have to say is that my unconscious is a lot further along than I am. I wish I had a wart right now, just to see if I am that talented.

There ought to be a better word than 'Unconscious', even capitalized, for what I have, so to speak, in mind. I was brought up to regard this aspect of thinking as a sort of private sanitarium, walled off somewhere in a suburb of my brain, capable only of producing such garbled information as to keep my mind, my proper Mind, always a little off balance.

But any mental apparatus that can reject a wart is something else again. This is not the sort of confused, disordered process you'd expect at the hands of the kind of Unconscious you read about in books, out at the edge of things making up dreams or getting mixed up on words or having hysterics. Whatever, or whoever, is responsible for this has the accuracy and precision of a surgeon. There almost has to be a Person in charge, running matters of meticulous detail beyond anyone's comprehension, a skilled engineer and manager, a chief executive officer, the head of the whole place. I never thought before that I possessed such a tenant. Or perhaps more accurately, such a landlord, since I would be, if this is in fact the situation, nothing more than a lodger.

Among other accomplishments, he must be a cell biologist of world class, capable of sorting through the various classes of one's lymphocytes, all with quite different functions which I do not understand, in order to mobilize the right ones and exclude the wrong ones for the task of tissue rejection. If it were left to me, and I were somehow empowered to call up lymphocytes and direct them to the vicinity of my wart (assuming that I could learn to do such a thing), mine would come tumbling in all unsorted, B cells and T cells, suppressor cells and killer cells, and no doubt other cells whose names I have not learned, incapable of getting anything useful done.

Even if immunology is not involved, and all that needs doing is to shut off the blood supply locally, I haven't the faintest notion how to set that up. I assume that the selective turning off of arterioles can be done by one or another chemical mediator, and I know the names of some of them, but I wouldn't dare let things like these loose even if I knew how to do it.

Well, then, who does supervise this kind of operation? Someone's got to, you know. You can't sit there under hypnosis, taking suggestions in and having them acted on with such accuracy and precision, without assuming the existence of something very like a controller. It wouldn't do to fob off the whole intricate business on lower centers without sending along a quite detailed set of specifications, way over my head.

Some intelligence or other knows how to get rid of warts, and this is a disquieting thought.

It is also a wonderful problem, in need of solving. Just think what we would know, if we had anything like a clear understanding of what goes on when a wart is hypnotized away. We would know the identity of the cellular and chemical participants in tissue rejection, conceivably with some added information about the ways that viruses create foreignness in cells. We would know how the traffic of these reactants is directed, and perhaps then be able to understand the nature of certain diseases in which the traffic is being conducted in wrong directions, aimed at the wrong cells. Best of all, we would be finding out about a kind of superintelligence that exists in each of us, infinitely smarter and possessed of technical know-how far beyond our present understanding. It would be worth a War on Warts, a Conquest of Warts, a National Institute of Warts and All.

Cancer

Curtailing the tobacco pandemic
by Alan Blum from In Cancer: Principles and Practice of Oncology

By all rights, lung cancer should have been included along with small-pox as one of the diseases that was eradicated in the 20th century. Instead, to the undying shame of the health professions – and due to the untiring energy of the transnational tobacco conglomerates – the production, distribution, marketing, and use of tobacco continue to grow in every corner of the world. Deaths from lung cancer are expected to exceed 3 million a year by the turn of the century.

Since US Surgeon General Leroy E. Burney issued a policy statement in 1957 that accepted the cause-effect relation between cigarette smoking and lung cancer, each succeeding Surgeon General has been committed to curbing the use of tobacco. In 1964 the Report of the Advisory Committee to the Surgeon General on Smoking and Health reviewed and summarized the devastating scientific case against smoking. This document and an analysis produced in the United Kingdom in 1962 by the Royal College of Physicians galvanized the medical community and the public alike. The Surgeon General's report was written by ten eminent biomedical scientists who had been selected by Surgeon General Luther Terry from a list of 150 people (none of whom had taken a public position on the subject of smoking and health) approved by major health organizations and the tobacco industry.

Concerns about smoking had long been raised in the scientific community. In 1928 Lombard and Doering reported a higher incidence of smoking among patients with cancer than among controls. Ten years later Pearl reported that persons who smoked heavily had a shorter life expectancy than those who did not smoke. In 1939 Ochsner and DeBakey began reporting their observations on the relation between smoking and lung cancer. They and other outspoken opponents of smoking, such as Dwight Harkin and William Overholt, were met with derision by the medical profession, more than two thirds of whom smoked.

Not until the epidemiologic work in the 1950s of Doll and Hill in the United Kingdom and Hammond and Horn in the United States did the medical profession begin to take the problem seriously. Cigarette advertisements continued to appear in the *Journal of the American Medical Association* and other medical journals until the mid-1950s. A Viceroy cigarette advertisement published in medical journals in 1954 thanked the 64,985 doctors who visited Viceroy exhibits at medical conventions that year. Such scientific displays existed at various state medical society meetings until the 1980s. In 1978 the American Medical Association (AMA) issued a report, 'Tobacco and Health,' which summarized research projects that confirm the findings of the 1964 Surgeon General's report and cemented the association between smoking and heart disease. This report was entirely underwritten by the tobacco industry, which in effect had succeeded in muting any official action-oriented stance on the part of the AMA for 14 years.

Nonetheless, since 1985 when it first called for a ban on tobacco advertising, the AMA and its publications have become increasingly outspoken in the effort to curtail the use and promotion of tobacco. The AMA has funded two national conferences on tobacco and has made the subject of smoking and health one of its four top priorities. Pressure by the AMA led the Joint Commission on Accreditation of Healthcare Organizations to institute a policy mandating that accredited health facilities be smoke-free environments as of 1992.

Considering its $350 million annual income, the American Cancer Society (ACS) has been cautious and conservative in challenging the tobacco industry. Not until 1983 did the organization begin to address the subject of cigarette advertising. On the other hand, the ACS *has* made several major contributions, including the adoption of the annual stop-smoking day known as the Great American Smokeout, the sponsorship of world conferences on smoking and health (which currently draw 1000 people and are held every 3 years), and the creation of Globalink (a worldwide electronic communication network to aid the sharing of antitobacco strategies). The American Academy of Family Physicians has led medical specialty organizations in confronting tobacco problems by means of training for physicians in smoking cessation and financial support for antitobacco advocacy groups such as Doctors Ought to Care (DOC).

Various chapters of the American Lung Association have done substantive lobbying and taken aggressive public stances in accelerating the passage of local clean indoor air legislation.

Governmental agencies, public health organizations, and academic institutions have not exerted much leadership on this issue. A remarkable grassroots antismoking movement that arose in the 1970s with the goal to create smoke-free public places impelled more traditional organizations to action. These groups – Action on Smoking and Health, Group Against Smoking Pollution, and Americans for Nonsmokers' Rights – paved the way for measures such as the federal ban on smoking in aircrafts and local laws that restrict smoking, remove cigarette vending machines, and ban the distribution of free tobacco samples.

Although numerous prospective studies conducted over the past 40 years have documented multifarious disease risks associated with smoking, cancer has been linked to tobacco use for more than two centuries. In 1761, John Hill, a London physician, reported an association between the use of snuff and cancer of the nose. The first US Surgeon General's Report on Smoking and Health in 1964 concluded that cigarette smoking was the major cause of lung cancer in men and was causally related to laryngeal cancer and oral cancer in men. More than 57,000 subsequent studies and 20 additional reports of the Surgeon General have documented the impact of tobacco use on morbidity and mortality in the United States and abroad. It is now understood that approximately 40% of all cancer deaths are attributable to cigarette smoking; smoking is thus responsible for more than 434,000 deaths per year in the United States, or 18% of all deaths.

Smoking is the major cause of cancers of the lung, larynx, oral cavity, and esophagus and is a contributory factor in cancers of the pancreas, bladder, kidney, stomach, and uterine cervix. Overall, cigarette smoking has been identified as the chief preventable cause of deaths due to cancer in the United States.

~

Cancer ward
from Cancer Ward *by Aleksandr Solzhenitsyn*

On top of it all, the cancer wing was 'number thirteen'. Pavel Nikolayevich Rusanov had never been and could never be a superstitious person but his heart sank when they wrote 'Wing 13' down on his admission card. They should have had the ingenuity to give number thirteen to some kind of prosthetic or obstetric department.

But this clinic was the only place where they could help him in the whole republic.

'It isn't, it isn't cancer, is it, Doctor? I haven't got cancer?' Pavel Nikolayevich asked hopefully, lightly touching the malevolent tumour on the right side of his neck. It seemed to grow almost daily, and yet the tight skin on the outside was as white and inoffensive as ever.

'Good heavens no, of course not.' Dr Dontsova soothed him, for the tenth time, as she filled in the pages of his case history in her bold handwriting. Whenever she wrote, she put on her glasses with rectangular frames rounded at the edges, and she would whisk them off as soon as she had finished. She was no longer a young woman; her face looked pale and utterly tired.

It had happened at the outpatients' reception a few days ago. Patients assigned to a cancer department, even as outpatients, found they could not sleep the next night. And Dontsova had ordered Pavel Nikolayevich to bed *immediately*.

Unforeseen and unprepared for, the disease had come upon him, a happy man with few cares, like a gale in the space of two weeks. But Pavel Nikolayevich was tormented, no less than by the disease itself, by having to enter the clinic as an ordinary patient, just like anyone else. He could hardly remember when last he had been in a public hospital, it was so long ago. Telephone calls had been made, to Evgeny Semenovich, Shendyapin, and Ulmasbaev, and they rang other people to find out if there were not any 'VIP wards' in the clinic, or whether some small room could not be converted, just for a short time, into a special ward. But the clinic was so cramped for space that nothing could be done.

The only success that he had managed to achieve through the head doctor was to bypass the waiting-room, the public bath and change of clothing.

Yuri drove his mother and father in their little blue Moskvich right up to the steps of Ward 13.

In spite of the slight frost, two women in heavily laundered cotton dressing-gowns were standing outside on the open stone porch. The cold made them shudder, but they stood their ground.

Beginning with these slovenly dressing-gowns, Pavel Nikolayevich found everything in the place unpleasant: the path worn by countless pairs of feet on the cement floor of the porch; the dull door-handles, all messed about by the patients' hands; the waiting-room, paint peeling off its floor, its high olive-coloured walls (olive seemed somehow such a dirty colour), and its large slatted wooden benches with not enough room for all the patients. Many of them had come long distances and had to sit on the floor. There were Uzbeks in quilted, wadded coats, old Uzbek women in long white shawls and young women in lilac, red and green ones, and all wore high boots with galoshes. One Russian youth, thin as a rake but with a great bloated stomach, lay there in an unbuttoned coat which dangled to the floor, taking up a whole bench to himself. He screamed incessantly with pain. His screams deafened Pavel Nikolayevich and hurt him so much that it seemed the boy was screaming not with his own pain, but with Rusanov's.

Pavel Nikolayevich went white around the mouth, stopped dead and whispered to his wife, 'Kapa, I'll die here. I mustn't stay. Let's go back.'

Kapitolina Matveyevna took him firmly by the arm and said, 'Pashenka! Where could we go? And what would we do then?'

'Well, perhaps we might be able to arrange something in Moscow.'

Kapitolina Matveyevna turned to her husband. Her broad head was made even broader by its frame of thick, clipped coppery curls.

'Pashenka! If we went to Moscow we might have to wait another two weeks. Or we might not get there at all. How *can* we wait? It is bigger every morning!'

His wife took a firm grip of his arm, trying to pass her courage on to him. In his civic and official duties Pavel Nikolayevich was unshakable, and therefore it was simpler and all the more agreeable for him to be able to rely on his wife in family matters. She made all important decisions quickly and correctly.

The boy on the bench was still tearing himself apart with his screams.

'Perhaps the doctors would come to our house? We'd pay them,' Pavel Nikolayevich argued, unsure of himself.

'Pasik!' his wife chided him, suffering as much as her husband. 'You know I'd be the first to agree. Send for someone and pay the fee. But we've been into this before: these doctors don't treat at home, and they won't take money. And there's their equipment, too. It's impossible.'

Pavel Nikolayevich knew perfectly well it was impossible. He had only mentioned it because he felt he just had to say something.

According to the arrangement with the head doctor of the oncology clinic, the matron was supposed to wait for them at two o'clock in the afternoon, there at the foot of the stairs which a patient on crutches was carefully descending. But the matron was nowhere to be seen, of course, and her little room under the stairs had a padlock on the door.

'They're all so unreliable!' fumed Kapitolina Matveyevna. 'What do they get paid for?'

Just as she was, two silver-fox furs hugging her shoulders, she set off down the corridor past a notice which read: 'No entry to persons in outdoor clothes.'

Pavel Nikolayevich remained standing in the waiting-room. Timidly he tilted his head slightly to the right and felt the tumour that jutted out between his collar-bone and his jaw. He had the impression that in the half-hour since he had last looked at it in the mirror as he wrapped it up in a muffler, in that one half-hour it seemed to have grown even bigger. Pavel Nikolayevich felt weak and wanted to sit down. But the benches looked dirty and besides he would have to ask some peasant woman in a scarf with a greasy sack between her feet to move up. Somehow the foul stench of that sack seemed to reach him even from a distance.

When will our people learn to travel with clean, tidy suitcases! (Still, now that he had this tumour it didn't matter any longer.)

Suffering miserably from the young man's cries and from everything that met his eyes and entered his nostrils, Rusanov stood, half-leaning on a projection in the wall. A peasant came in carrying in front of him a half-litre jar with a label on it, almost full of yellow liquid. He made no attempt to conceal the jar but held it aloft triumphantly, as if it were a mug of beer he had spent some time queuing up for. He stopped in front of Pavel Nikolayevich, almost handing him the jar, made as if to ask him something but looked at his sealskin hat and turned away. He looked around and addressed himself to a patient on crutches:

'Who do I give this to, brother?'

The legless man pointed to the door of the laboratory.

Pavel Nikolayevich felt quite sick.

Again the outer door opened and the matron came in, dressed only in a white coat. Her face was too long and she was not at all pretty.

She spotted Pavel Nikolayevich immediately, guessed who he was and went up to him.

'I'm sorry,' she said breathlessly. In her haste her cheeks had flushed the colour of her lipstick. 'Please forgive me. Have you been waiting long? They were bringing some medicine, I had to go and sign for it.'

Pavel Nikolayevich felt like making an acid reply, but he restrained himself. He was glad the wait was over. Yuri came forward, in just his suit with no coat or hat, the same clothes he had worn for driving, carrying the suitcase and a bag of provisions. A blond forelock was dancing about on his forehead. He was very calm. 'Come with me,' said the matron, leading the way to her little store-room-like office under the stairs. 'Nizamutdin Bahramovich said you'd bring your own underwear and pyjamas. They haven't been worn, have they?'

'Straight from the shop.'

'That's absolutely obligatory, otherwise they'd have to be disinfected, you understand? Here, you can change in there.'

She opened the plywood door and put on the light. In the little office with its sloping ceiling there was no window, only a number of coloured-pencil diagrams hanging from the walls.

Yuri brought in the suitcase silently, then left the room. Pavel Nikolayevich went in to get changed. The matron had meanwhile dashed off somewhere, but Kapitolina Matveyevna caught her up.

'Nurse!' she said. 'I see you're in a hurry.'

'Yes, I am rather.'

'What's your name?'

'Mita.'

'That's a strange name. You're not Russian, are you?'

'No, German . . .'

'You kept us waiting.'

'Yes, I'm sorry. I had to sign for those . . .'

'Now listen to me, Mita. I want you to know something. My husband is an important man who does extremely valuable work. His name is Pavel Nikolayevich.'

'I see. Pavel Nikolayevich, I'll remember that.'

'He's used to being well looked after, you see, and now he's seriously ill. Couldn't he have a nurse permanently on duty with him?'

Mita's troubled face grew even more worried. She shook her head.

'Apart from the theatre nurses we have three day nurses to deal with sixty patients. And two night nurses.'

'You see! A man could be dying and screaming his head off and no one would come!'

'Why do you think that? Everyone gets proper attention.'

('Everyone' – what is there to say to her if she talks about 'everyone'?)

'Do the nurses work in shifts?'

'That's right. They change every twelve hours.'

'This impersonal treatment, it's terrible. My daughter and I would be delighted to take turns sitting up with him. Or I'd be ready to pay for a permanent nurse out of my own pocket. But they tell me that's not allowed either.'

'I'm afraid not. It's never been done before. Anyway, there's nowhere in the ward to put a chair.'

'God, I can just imagine what this ward's like! I'd like to have a good look round it! How many beds are there?'

'Nine. Your husband's lucky to get straight into a ward. Some new patients have to lie in the corridors or on the stairs!'

'I'm still going to ask you to arrange with a nurse or an orderly for Pavel Nikolayevich to have *private* attention. You know the people here, it would be easier for you to organize it.' She had already clicked open her big black bag and taken out three fifty-rouble notes.

Her son, who was standing nearby, turned his head away silently.

Mita put both hands behind her back.

'No, no! I have no right . . .'

'I'm not giving them to you!' Kapitolina Matveyevna pushed the fan of notes into the front of the matron's overall. 'But if it can't be done legally and above board . . . All I'm doing is paying for services rendered! I'm only asking you to be kind enough to pass the money on to the right person!'

'No, no.' The matron felt cold all over. 'We don't do that sort of thing here.'

The door creaked and Pavel Nikolayevich came out of the matron's den in his new green-and-brown pyjamas and warm, fur-trimmed bedroom slippers. On his almost hairless head he wore a new raspberry-coloured Uzbek skull-cap. Now that he had removed his winter overcoat, collar and muffler, the tumour on the side of his neck, the size of a clenched fist, looked strikingly ominous. He could not even hold his head straight any longer, he had to tilt it slightly to one side.

His son went in to collect the discarded clothing and put it away in the suitcase. Kapitolina Matveyevna had returned the money to her handbag. She looked anxiously at her husband.

'Won't you freeze like that? You should have brought a nice warm dressing-gown with you. I'll bring one when I come. Look, here's a scarf.' She took a scarf out of her pocket. 'Wrap it round your throat, so you won't catch cold.' In her silver foxes and her fur coat, she looked three times as strong as her husband. 'Now go into the ward and get yourself settled in. Unpack your food and think what else you need. I'll sit here and wait. Come down and tell me what you want and I'll bring everything this evening.'

She never lost her head, she always knew what to do next. In their life together she had been her husband's true comrade. Pavel Nikolayevich looked at her with a mixture of gratitude and suffering and then glanced at his son.

'Well, are you off then, Yuri?'

'I'll take the evening train, Father.' He came towards them. He always behaved respectfully in his father's presence. He was not by nature an emotional man, and his good-bye to his father now was as unemotional as ever. His reactions to life all ran at low-voltage.

'That's right, son. Well, this is your first important official trip. Be sure and set the right tone from the start. And don't be too soft, mind. Your softness could be your downfall. Always remember you're not Yuri Rusanov, you're not a private individual. You're a representative of the law, do you understand?'

Whether or not Yuri understood, it would have been hard at that moment for Pavel Nikolayevich to find more appropriate words. Mita was fussing about and anxious to be going.

'I'll wait here with Mother,' said Yuri, with a smile. 'Don't say good-bye, Dad, just go.'

'Will you be all right on your own?' Mita asked.

'Can't you see the man can hardly stand up? Can't you at least take him to his bed, and carry his bag for him?'

Orphan-like, Pavel Nikolayevich looked back at his family, refused the supporting arm Mita offered and, grasping the bannister firmly, started to walk upstairs. His heart was beating violently, not at all, so far, because of the climb. He went up the stairs as people mount – what do they call it? – a sort of platform where men have their heads cut off.

The matron ran on upstairs in front of him carrying his bag, shouted something from the top to someone called Maria, and before Pavel Nikolayevich had finished the first flight was already running past him down the other side of the staircase and out of the building, thereby showing Kapitolina Matveyevna what sort of solicitude her husband could expect in this place.

*

Within a few hours, that first evening in the ward, Pavel Nikolayevich became haunted with fear.

The hard lump of his tumour – unexpected, meaningless and quite without use – had dragged him in like a fish on a hook and flung him on to this iron bed – a narrow, mean bed, with creaking springs and an apology for a mattress.

*

But Pavel Nikolayevich was different. The lump of his tumour was pressing his head to one side, made it difficult for him to turn over, and was increasing in size every hour. Only here the doctors did not count the hours. All the time from lunch to supper no one had examined Rusanov and he had had no treatment. And it was with this very bait that Dr Dontsova had lured him here – immediate treatment. Well, in that case she must be a thoroughly irresponsible and criminally negligent woman. Rusanov had trusted her, and had lost valuable time in this cramped, musty, dirty ward when he might have been telephoning and flying to Moscow.

Resentment at the delay and the realization of having made a mistake, on top of the misery of his tumour, so stabbed at Pavel Nikolayevich's heart that he could not bear *anything*, from the noise of plates scraped by spoons, to the iron bedsteads, the rough blankets, the walls, the lights, the people. He felt that he was in a trap, and that until the next morning any decisive step was impossible.

*

Weren't some girls lovely! Pavel Nikolayevich gazed with pleasure at her (Zoya's) generous, tightly-laced figure and her wide, almost staring eyes. He gazed at her with detached admiration, and felt himself soften. She held the thermometer out to him with a smile. She was standing right next to the tumour but gave no sign, not even by a raised eyebrow, that she was horrified by the thing or that she had never seen one like it before.

'Hasn't any treatment been prescribed for me?' asked Rusanov.

'Not yet.' She smiled apologetically.

'But why not? Where are the doctors?'

'They've finished work for the day.'

There was no point in being angry with Zoya, but it must be someone's fault that he was not being treated! He had to do something! Rusanov despised inactivity and ineffectual characters. When Zoya came back to read his temperature he asked her, 'Where's your outside telephone? How can I find it?'

After all, he could make up his mind right now and telephone Comrade Ostapenko!

*

Already that morning he had taken certain resolute steps. As soon as the registrar's office was open he had telephoned home and told his wife what he had decided during the night: applications were to be made through all possible channels; he must be transferred to Moscow; he would not risk staying and dying in this place. Kapa knew how to get things done, she must already have set to work. Of course, it was sheer weakness – he shouldn't have been afraid of a tumour and stooped to taking a bed in a place like this. Nobody would ever believe it, but it was a fact that since three o'clock yesterday afternoon no one had even come to feel whether the tumour had grown bigger. Nobody had given him any medicine. Assassins in white coats – that was well said. They'd just hung up a temperature chart for idiots to look at. The orderly hadn't even come in to make his bed. He had had to do it himself! My word, our medical institutions still need a great deal of smartening up!

At last the doctors appeared, but they still wouldn't enter the room.

Finally, though, they came into the ward: Dr Dontsova. Dr Gangart and a portly, grey-haired nurse with a note-book in her hand and a towel over her arm. The entry of several white coats all at once always brings with it a wave of attention, fear and hope; and the strength of these feelings grows with the whiteness of the gowns and caps and the sternness of the faces. The sternest and most solemn of all has that of the nurse Olympiada Vladislavovna.

*

Sitting up sternly in bed, bald, in his skull-cap and glasses, Pavel Nikolayevich looked rather like a school-teacher, not any old school-teacher but a distinguished one who had brought up hundreds of pupils. He waited until Ludmila Afanasyevna was quite close to his bed, then he adjusted his glasses and declared, 'Comrade Dontsova, I shall be forced to inform the Ministry of Health of the way things are conducted in this clinic. And I shall have to telephone Comrade Ostapenko.'

She did not tremble or go pale, but perhaps her complexion became a little more pasty. She made a strange movement with her shoulders, a circular movement as though her shoulders were tired and longed to be rid of the harness which held them.

'If you have good contacts in the Ministry of Health,' she agreed with him at once, 'and if you're in a position to telephone Comrade Ostapenko, I can think of several more things you might add. Shall I tell you what they are?'

'There is nothing that needs to be added. Your display of indifference is quite enough as it is. I have been in here for *eighteen* hours, and nobody is giving me treatment. And I am a . . .' (There was nothing more he could say to her. Surely she could supply the rest herself!)

Everyone in the room was silent, staring at Rusanov. It was Gangart who was shocked, not Dontsova. Her lips tightened into a thin line. She frowned and knit her brows, as if she had seen something irrevocable take place and been powerless to avert it.

Dontsova, her large frame towering over the seated Rusanov, did not even permit herself a frown. She made another circular movement of her shoulders and said in a quiet, conciliatory tone, 'That's why I'm here – to give you treatment.'

'No. It's too late now.' Pavel Nikolayevich cut her short. 'I've seen quite enough of the way things are done here, and I'm leaving. No one shows the slightest interest, nobody bothers to make a diagnosis!' There was an unintended tremble in his voice: he was really offended.

'You've had your diagnosis,' Dontsova said slowly, both hands gripping the foot of his bed, 'and there's nowhere else for you to go. No other hospital in the Republic will take patients with your particular illness.'

'But you told me I don't have cancer! . . . What is the diagnosis?'

'Generally speaking, we don't have to tell our patients what's wrong with them, but if it will make you feel any better, very well – it's lymphoma.'

183

'You mean it's not cancer?'

'Of course it's not.' Her face and voice bore no trace of the bitterness that naturally comes from a quarrel, for she could see clearly enough the fist-sized tumour under his jaw. Who could she feel bitter against? The tumour? 'Nobody forced you to come here. You can discharge yourself whenever you like. But remember ...' She hesitated. 'People don't only die of cancer.' It was a friendly warning.

'What's this? Are you trying to frighten me?' Pavel Nikolayevich exclaimed. 'Why are you doing it? That's against the rules of professional etiquette.' He was still rattling away as hard as he could, but at the word 'die' everything had suddenly frozen inside him. His voice was noticeably softer when he added, 'You ... you mean my condition is all that dangerous?'

'Of course it will be if you keep moving from one hospital to another. Take off your scarf. Stand up please.'

He took off his scarf and stood up on the floor. Gently Dontsova began to feel the tumour and then the healthy side of the neck, comparing the two. She asked him to move his head back as far as it would go. (It wouldn't go very far. The tumour immediately began to pull it back.) Next he had to bend it forward as far as possible, then twist it to the left and the right.

So that was it! His head had apparently already lost practically all its freedom of movement, that amazing effortless freedom which when we possess it goes completely unnoticed.

'Take off your jacket, please.'

His green-and-brown pyjama jacket had large buttons and was the right size. No one would have thought it could be difficult to take off. But when he stretched his arms it pulled at his neck, and Pavel Nikolayevich groaned. The situation *was* serious! The impressive, grey-haired nurse helped him untangle himself from the sleeves.

'Do your armpits hurt?' Dontsova asked. 'Does anything bother you?'

'Why, might it spread down there as well?' Rusanov's voice had now dropped and was even quieter than Ludmila Afanasyevna's.

'Stretch your arms out sideways.' Concentrating and pressing hard, she began to feel his armpits.

'What sort of treatment will it be?' Pavel Nikolayevich asked.

'Injections. I told you.'

'Where? Right into the tumour?'

'No. Intravenously.'

'How often?'

'Three times a week. You can get dressed now.'

'And an operation is . . . impossible?'

(Behind the question lay an overriding fear – of being stretched out on the operating table. Like all patients he preferred any other long-term treatment.)

'An operation would be pointless.' She was wiping her hands on the towel the nurse held out to her.

I'm very glad to hear it, Pavel Nikolayevich thought to himself. Nevertheless he would have to consult Kapa. Using personal influence in a roundabout way was never very easy. In reality the influence he had was not as much as he might have wished for, or as great as he was now pretending it was. It was not at all an easy thing to telephone Comrade Ostapenko.

'All right, I'll think about it. Then we'll decide tomorrow?'

'No,' said Dontsova mercilessly, 'you must decide today. We can't give any injections tomorrow, it's Saturday.'

More rules! Doesn't she realize rules are made to be broken? 'Why on earth can't I have injections on Saturday?'

'Because we have to follow your reactions very carefully, both on the day of the injection and the day after. And we can't do that on a Sunday.'

'So you mean . . . it's a serious injection?'

Ludmila Afanasyevna did not answer. She had already moved to Kostoglotov's bed.

'Couldn't we wait till Monday . . .?'

'Comrade Rusanov! You accused us of waiting eighteen hours before treating you. How can you now suggest waiting seventy-two?' (She had already won the battle. Her steamroller was crushing him; there was nothing he could do.) 'Either we take you in for treatment or we don't. If it's yes, you will have your first injection at eleven o'clock this morning. If it's no, then you must sign to the effect that you refuse to accept our treatment and I'll have you discharged today. But we certainly don't have the right to keep you here for three days without doing anything. While I'm finishing my rounds in this room, please think it over and tell me what you've decided.'

Rusanov buried his face in his hands.

Gangart, her white coat fitting tightly right up to her neck, walked silently past him. Olympiada Vladislavovna followed like a ship in full sail.

*

It was very quiet in the ward. Rusanov sighed, and raised his head from his hands. His words rang through the room. 'Doctor, I give in. Inject me.'

(Like Oleg Kostoglotov, the central character of this novel, and Solzhenitsyn himself, Pavel Nikolayevich Rusanov was cured of his tumour.)

~

Breast cancer
from The Healing Art *by A.N. Wilson*

For Dorothy and Pamela, the nightmare had happened. It was over. Nothing would ever be the same. The dreadful words had been spoken. The surgeon's knife had cut into their breasts. Neither woman used the word 'cancer'. It was not even that which scared them. The shock brought with it a sense of self-loathing and empti-ness which was more akin to shame than to fear; it was more like hav-ing suffered rape than being under sentence; not desexed, but mutilated. Dignity abandoned, they separately fell back on irrational faiths, awaiting what comfort these could yield.

Dorothy was a believer in modern medicine. Pamela was less sure. She trusted in luck, and the Virgin Mary and the power of prayer. But neither of them mentioned these things, as they sat in the day-room, waiting for Mr Tulloch to announce the results of their X-rays. The operations had happened six weeks before. Pamela had been dis-charged rather sooner than Dorothy, but now they found themselves together again for what was called 'the six-week check-up'.

'They say Swansea is very good,' said Dorothy; 'for philosophy, that is.'

She sat perched on one of the grey plastic stackable chairs, her perm gently resting against the glossy cream paintwork of the wall. Her face still had its reassuringly placid roundness, but her neck looked scraggier than Pamela remembered it, and her eyes were ringed with purplish shadows which made her seem still the invalid.

They gazed out at the room from time to time, weary and frightened, but for the most part she kept them focused on her shoes. She fiddled with a white plastic handbag as she spoke, fastening and unfastening it, taking out and putting back paper handkerchieves as she explained her son's academic aspirations.

'We'd hoped he'd do something a bit more practical. Well, like medicine. But I dare say we'd all be better off if we could be a bit more philosophical.' The corners of her mouth, defiantly turned up in a smile which suggested the adjective winsome, seemed to be making the point as bravely as they could. She added a little defensively, 'Look on the bright side, that's what I say. There's a lovely hall of residence, I think they call it, and we thought the man in charge sounded very nice from Barry's description.'

'I hope he will be very happy,' said Pamela. She was a tall, thin, good-looking woman fifteen years younger than Dorothy. Thick blonde tresses were piled up on an intelligent head in a somewhat fantastic pyramid.

'Had you heard it was good? Swansea? For philosophy, I mean. I told Barry I'd ask you if I saw you again.'

'I'm afraid I don't know.'

It was hard not to sound a little crushing in reply to Dorothy's very natural assumption that Pamela, because she taught in a university, would know everything about everywhere.

'They keep you waiting, though, don't they?' said Dorothy, momentarily allowing her mind to abandon Barry, and gazing rather desolately about the day-room. On the simulated teak table in front of them were some back numbers of *The Lady* and *Woman's Realm*. Beyond the intolerably jaunty curtains was a scrubby patch of lawn, parched by an unusually hot summer. It was the ninth week without rain. Beyond what had been the grass, were a row of prefabricated huts. Each of the huts was labelled with the lower-case which is now standard in every hospital: one door read 'Chest clinic', another 'Speech therapy'. Only one door remained unreformed. Directly on to the fading pinewood, an unskilled hand had some years before painted the single word 'BLOOD'.

'Mind you,' pursued Dorothy to catch and swallow up Pamela's melancholy silence, 'you mustn't grumble. I expect Mr Tulloch is very busy.'

Pamela had not thought about it. She did not feel inclined to agree, but she said that she did, and asked Dorothy about her garden.

Although they only had in common the experience of six weeks before, it had been so violent and appalling that they were inevitably drawn together by it, and felt a closeness for each other which neither could properly express. Dorothy's had been the first face that Pamela had seen when she had come round from the anaesthetic in that little ward in the previous month. Her smile had been truly sympathetic; an understanding which only a fellow-sufferer could have conveyed was contained in it. Neither of them had ever openly discussed their operations; for they were alike in their diffidence, and it had been a comfort to be in a small room, only two beds, and escape some of the unsparing confidences of the larger wards. But if discussion had been avoided, it would have been equally impossible not to allude in some way to their state; and Pamela had been moved, as well as terribly pained, by Dorothy saying one day, 'Shame, too. Worse for you, being so young and that.'

Since childhood, when churchgoing had become an obsessive occupation, Pamela had shuddered to contemplate St Agatha. *Emblem*, she remembered reading with horror in a book about saints in her father's library, *breasts on a dish*. Mr Tulloch had, in the event, been kinder than the virgin-martyr's tormentors, and only removed quite a small lump; though Dorothy had had a whole breast removed. Nevertheless, Pamela's fear and revulsion was, and remained, intense. Quite genuinely, and unlike Dorothy, she had no fear of death. But, months with a plastic bracelet reading *Pamela Cowper* on a wrist growing daily bonier and thinner, as the pain grew more intense and the nurses more jaunty and the doctors, when one saw them, more officious; while her lovely clothes hung in the wardrobe unworn, and her few friends gradually failed to keep up their regular visits; while her pretty house accumulated dust and damp and she stared and stared at the blank hospital walls, unable, eventually, to read, to pray, even to think because of the pain, and the ignominy of incontinence and bed-sores – these she dreaded, as she sat half-hearing about Dorothy's dahlias and waiting for her audience with Mr Tulloch. Her father, the Archdeacon, had died in that way. She knew that she did not have the moral stamina to face such a passing herself.

Mr Tulloch, a rat-faced Scot in a white coat, strutted about X-ray, only a few yards from where the women sat, shouting at nurses whom he always addressed in the third person plural.

'They are a disgrace,' he trilled, 'a bloody disgrace. What use to a man is *that*?'

The object to which he pointed was a decomposing foetus, only aborted the previous morning. The fluid in which it had been pre-served – a student nurse had actually placed it in the jar – had come from a bottle marked *formaldehyde*. A lab technician had blundered. The consultant would now be unable to conduct the tests he had hoped to do. The girl from whom the foetus had been removed would have to be lied to – like all the other patients with whom he was obliged to deal in a hurry. Her womb was in danger. Tulloch ran through the formulas in which this could be expressed – *further tests ... I'd feel happier maybe if we could whip you in and have a bit closer look at you ...*

He felt worn out. It was already three days since his wife had left for Argyllshire. By rights, he should have been with her now, a trout stream gurgling about his waders, the reassuring click of his reel being the only sound to disturb the natural peacefulness of the glen. But, with one colleague in the middle of a divorce, another off sick and three housemen recently left, what could a man do? At nine that morning, he had given a lecture about hysterectomy to some student midwives. He had been in the consulting room since seven minutes past ten.

'Take it away,' he said, pointing at the jar as he sipped his instant coffee from a plastic cup. 'Take the bloody thing away.'

'Where shall we put it, Mr Tulloch?'

'God! Haven't they any bloody common sense? Aren't there any bloody dustbins in this hospital? Burn it, throw it away, get rid of it.'

A curly-headed registrar, Richard Crawford if the rectangle of plastic on his lapel told the truth, came into the room with a buff envelope and said, 'Here are the negs of those women waiting outside.'

'What women?'

'The six-week check-ups. They've just come from X-ray. You said you wanted to have a look at them.'

'Course I do. They're my bloody patients, aren't they?'

Once the fit was on, he could not have stopped himself being angry, even if it had been suggested that he tried. He grabbed the envelopes in haste and emptied the negatives on to the surface of his desk. An electric screen, designed for the purpose, was lit up, and he held the filmy grey images up to it each in turn.

'All right,' he said, quickly, tossing one down; and with another, 'all right, all right. Looks clear. Now, let's see, what have we here? Oh, Christ!'

Crawford peered over Tulloch's shoulder. A nurse came into the room and said, 'Sister wants to know when you will be ready to go down to the theatre, Mr Tulloch.'

'When I'm ready and not when she bloody well says so is the answer to that! God! Do they think I can be in two places at once? Do they think I have four pairs of hands? Do they? Who do they think I am? Look at them! They burst in here . . .'

The nurse had hurried back to the theatre sister to say that Mr Tulloch would be ten minutes.

'Are you going to tell her?'

Rage abated slightly because Crawford's face looked so young and anxious.

'Tell her what?'

The registrar picked up Pamela's envelope and refreshed his memory of her particulars.

'She's only thirty-nine.'

'It's spread so rapidly.' Horror and scientific curiosity blended in the surgeon's voice as he consulted the negative once more. 'We can't operate on that. What's the woman called?'

'Pamela Cowper. She's a don.' Crawford was still at the stage of his career when he remembered who patients were. He recalled the serene, beautiful face of Miss Cowper as she smiled at him on his ward rounds. A shame to have the tits off someone like that. The other woman, in his recollection, was a bag.

As if reading his thoughts, Mr Tulloch said, 'There's no justice in life, Rick. I'll see these women. You go down and tell that Irish bitch that I'll be in the theatre in ten minutes.'

In the day-room, Dorothy and Pamela had abandoned gardens and were discussing travel.

'I felt so guilty this year – it quite ruined Barry and George's holiday. We had been going to France. Not Normandy, we've been there. It would have been nice for Barry to have a proper break after his As. Still, they were very good about it.'

'I'm sure they were.' Pamela more than mildly envied Dorothy her family. Nobody's holiday had been ruined by her own stay in the hospital.

'We generally go abroad most years now. Take all our own food and that, and sleep in the Dormobile. We've seen some lovely places. Italy, Spain, Florence. Did you manage to have a holiday?'

'I usually contrive to go away later in the summer,' said Pamela with a sigh, adding, and wishing she hadn't, 'after the school holidays are over, places are less crowded.'

'Well, we've had to go away in school holidays because of Barry.' She had not exactly taken offence, but there was a note of affront in her voice. 'Do you go abroad much?'

Pamela did not know of a way of saying that she disliked foreign travel – that it always ended in diarrhoea – without becoming still more offensive. She was glad – until she felt her heart leaping into her mouth – when a nurse came in at that moment and summoned Dorothy to the Presence.

It was comforting to be alone. Ever since the operation, she had felt this craving for solitude. There was no one with whom she felt on terms of sufficient intimacy to say, 'I have had a lump cut out of my breast.' In consequence, she preferred to keep the matter a secret. It had not been discovered until the beginning of the Long Vacation, so there had been no need to receive the sympathy of colleagues. She had informed the Principal by post and received a kind letter back saying that she must, if necessary, spend the next term on sick leave. There had been no need for the two of them to meet. Indeed, by the time Pamela read the reply, the Principal was on her way to Siberia to look for limestone.

So, throughout the hot summer, Pamela had guarded the secret. People at church knew that she had been in hospital with an unspecified illness. Sourpuss had visited her in hospital. He alone knew her condition and his austere, shy manner was soothing to her. There would be no danger of unseemly physical intimacies being discussed with him. Tall as a beanpole, grey, ascetic, disgruntled, he had been the perfect visitor. He had brought her the poems of George Herbert and *The Real Charlotte in* World's Classics, sensible little books that you could read in bed without your arms getting tired, and even slip into a dressing-gown pocket if you anticipated an abnormally long time on the loo. He had talked about pleasant neutral topics like botany and the Electoral Roll.

On the day she came home, he had brought her a framed watercolour sketch of a weeping ash. She had expressed gratitude, but it had given her less initial pleasure than the books, or the handkerchieves which he had presented on a later day. It seemed a vulgar extravagance to have bought a reproduction of an old painting at one of those glorified postcard shops which call themselves galleries. But looking at it again when he had gone she realized that she had been ungracious. He had meant it kindly. Who was it? Not Gainsborough; the trees in Gainsborough always had the hectic quality of cardboard about to collapse in amateur theatricals. It was too neat for Turner, and yet too mannered, not sufficiently innocent, for a Pre-Raphaelite. She wondered whether it was a reproduction of one of Ruskin's sketches, and as she peered at it through the glass, at the hand-made paper and delicate brush-strokes, she realized that it was not a reproduction at all, but the real thing.

Her displeasure when he first handed it over, had, however, registered, and he had created an atmosphere on subsequent occasions when reference to it was made which made inquiries about it difficult. She had hung it in pride of place over her chimney-piece, but talk about it was not yet forthcoming on either side.

Pamela did not exactly have men in her life. Sourpuss only touched its fringes. The only male friend in any way close to her was John Brocklehurst, whom people wrongly suspected of being her 'intended', but who was, in any case, on sabbatical leave in America until October. Normally, they had holidays in Wales together before the beginning of each term; but they had separate bedrooms. Once, at the beginning of their friendship, an alternative arrangement had presented itself. But perhaps it did not, strictly, appeal to either of them. She was glad that she had made nothing of his hint. Platonic friendships could, she had discovered, since breaking her heart and someone else's marriage over the other sort ten years earlier, be quite as adventurous, and ultimately less in danger of becoming dull. It was dullness in life that she sought to avoid, quite as much as heartbreak. It was, perhaps, above all the dullness of being ill which oppressed her and made her not want to communicate it in a letter to John. Their friendship was based on shared humour and mutual interests, and would have no place for injections and bedpans and X-rays.

Her reveries were interrupted by the return of Dorothy, whose wasted features were lit up now by a flush of pride.

'He says I'm coming on ever so well. The X-ray's quite clear.'

'Oh, my dear, I'm so glad.'

Pamela rose and for the first time in their lives the women kissed.

'I'd been so, well, frightened.'

'Of course you had.'

Dorothy was crying a little now.

'Silly, really. Mustn't grumble. It's just such a relief.'

As she held the quivering, bird-like form in her arms, Pamela felt suddenly cold, as if Dorothy's fear had communicated itself, been actually passed on to her. Over the older woman's shoulder, she saw a nurse at the door.

'Miss Cowper? Mr Tulloch will see you now, dear.'

'Shall I wait for you?' said Dorothy. 'I'm getting a taxi home. George said he'd take me, but he's funny about hospitals. Besides, he needed the car for work. You go off to work, I said. I'll be all right on my own. So it would be no trouble to wait.'

'It's very kind of you. But don't wait. I might be long, and someone is coming to collect me.'

This lie flew out rather desperately, and she hoped Dorothy's taxi would have come by the time she was slinking back to her Simca in the car park. She somehow could not face sharing a return home. She knew that, in her relief, and joy, a flood of anxiety which had hitherto been held in check was now bursting through Dorothy, but Pamela could not share it; not yet, not yet.

'Well, drop me a line and let me know how you are.' Dorothy's tone implied that she knew her place. They had exchanged addresses in the ward when Pamela was discharged, but neither of them had done anything about it. 'I'll . . .'

The nurse stood waiting impatiently.

'I'll be anxious,' Dorothy added. She sighed when Pamela left the room. For some reason she had come to love her.

Mr Tulloch looked up from his desk and smiled lugubriously at Pamela as she was admitted.

'Ah,' he said, 'Miss . . . er.'

'Cowper.'

'Miss Cowper. Come and sit down.'

She knew at once what he was going to say. She wished that she knew what she would say in return. It had only been such a small lump. He had said that there was a ninety per cent chance, whatever that meant, of it not spreading. But now his face told her everything.

'How am I?' she asked, to help him out.

'We've encountered some complications, I'm afraid. As I told you at the time of the operation, which was . . .' He consulted her dossier.

'The twenty-first of June,' she prompted him. Feast of the Sacred Heart.

'Ah, yes. June the twenty-first. As I told you, there might be need for some further treatment. Your condition has not quite developed along the lines we had hoped.'

He spoke as if it was her fault. She felt almost amused by the outrageous coldness of his manner.

'Complications are, of course, almost inevitable in cases of this kind.'

'Is this a complication that can be cured?'

'He blinked.

'I would not be suggesting treatment, Miss Cowper, if I did not think it could be of some help.' He looked at his fingernails. He disliked clever women. Even though, at this moment, he held the trump card, he could crudely tell her – YOU ARE DYING – nevertheless, he felt a cold terror; not of death, but of Pamela herself. He knew that she could get the better of him in conversation and he was determined not to let her try. The other woman had been much more sensible; she listened to what she was told and she seemed grateful. A model patient. They weren't called patients for nothing. His mind drifted wistfully back to the dry flies and the trout streams of the highlands, as he heard her ask,

'What type of treatment had you in mind, Mr Tulloch?'

Damn the woman; as if she knew one type of treatment from another.

'As you perhaps know, we have made very great strides forward in this area in recent years, very great strides. Cases where, even five years ago, complications would have been insuperable, now, very often, have a strong chance of success.'

'A strong chance? Is that ninety per cent or less?'

'I don't find it very helpful to think of percentages,' he said. 'I had in mind a course of chemotherapy, what we call a cocktail drug treatment. What we do is whip you into a ward for a wee while and give you some injections.'

'Why do I have to have them in hospital? Couldn't I have the injections and just go home?'

'We like to keep an eye on you. The treatment can have side effects. I must warn you of that.'

'What sort of side effects?'

'Nausea, tiredness, a sort of fluey feeling. A bit of tummy ache. Some people react more strongly than others. And there can be some hair loss too.'

'You mean that the drug which you are suggesting would make me bald?' There was a shrill note of rebellion in her voice. First he sliced at her breasts; now he tried to remove her hair.

194

'Yes,' he said bluntly. 'Hair loss can be total, I'm afraid.'

It was out of the question. She could not countenance such a thing. But she stared at him blankly, her lips quivering, and no words would come.

'What I suggest is that we whip you into one of the wards right away and start the treatment as soon as possible.'

'And if?'

'Yes.'

'If I don't have this treatment, I will die. That is what you have been trying to say to me.'

'That is not a way I like to look at it. You see, you really have no option in the matter as I see it.'

'Why not?'

'Because, as you must see yourself, if you don't have this treatment, your condition will deteriorate.'

'And I shall die.'

'Yes.'

He pursed his lips angrily. Even this, his trump card, had been snatched from him. He felt that she despised him. He in turn envied the comparative calmness with which she discussed the matter. Being professionally involved with the disease did not lessen its horror for him. On the contrary, not a day passed without its becoming more and more acute. He had his own plans prepared for the day when the condition developed in him. A wee bit of rubber tube; a drive to a lay-by on the Ring Road. Fit the tube to the exhaust, squeeze it in through the small window. Switch on the engine. Swig down the sleeping pills.

'How long do you think I will live if I don't have this treatment?' Her voice was perfectly calm now. Her large, moist, very blue eyes stared patiently at him as if he was a dim-witted undergraduate slow to construe a passage of Anglo–Saxon prose.

He shuffled in his chair.

'It's very difficult to say. A few months, maybe.'

She sighed, as if relieved. 'I thought you were going to say a couple of years at least.'

'I'm afraid not.'

'But, don't you see, a few months is much better than a few years . . .' She had not meant to blurt it out. It seemed rather an insult to his profession to be expressing such enthusiasm for solving the Great Mystery. But the first dawnings of something like exultation were welling up inside her and she could not conceal them. So, nature

195

was to spare her the agonizing year in the ward, with everyone pretending and getting increasingly fed up that she hovered so long. For most of her grown-up life, she had been more than half in love with easeful death, and, provided it could be easeful, she did not want to lose the opportunity of embracing it without sin. *A few months* – perhaps six, perhaps as few as three. Fear had absolutely vanished to be replaced by a sense of almost heady excitement, summoned up for her in the phrase she kept repeating inside her head, *at last, at last, at last*.

'It's my duty as your doctor to try to save your life, Miss Cowper.'

'You still haven't answered my question, Mr Tulloch. How great would my chances of survival be if I *did* have this cocktail treatment?'

'It would certainly lengthen your life. Some people have had it and gone back to leading perfectly normal lives.'

It was like the old joke – 'Doctor, doctor, when my broken arm is better will I be able to play the piano?' 'Oh, yes.' 'That's funny, I couldn't play it before.' The idea of her leading a 'normal' life almost tempted her to have a shot of the cocktail pumped into her arm at once just to study the effect. Who were these normal people? She had never met one.

'. . . It's difficult to be more specific,' he was still saying. 'Research in this field is making such strides forward that if we could keep you going for a year or two we might by that time have come up with an adequate solution.'

'You mean a complete cure?'

'I don't see why not.'

But, before that nebulous date, would stretch perhaps years of injections and spells in hospital; 'tummy ache' – why did they speak to people as if they were mental defectives? – baldness; and on top of all the physical miseries, one would live from disappointment to disappointment as hope gradually vanished altogether. By then, they would be prolonging one's life in misery as long as they could in the interests of research.

'I can't make up my mind all at once,' she said.

'Of course, I can't force you to live if you don't want to.' He stared for the first time into her eyes without blinking, and he tried to discern why she was behaving so stubbornly. 'But the sooner we start treatment, the longer our chances of arresting the disease will have to work.'

'I will write to you,' said Pamela, rising. She had made up her mind, but she could not entirely face telling him so, lest when she announced her decision to die with dignity the words sounded hollow, and she remained unconvinced by her own rhetoric.

She smiled, bloody condescendingly he thought, and as she left the room he began to arrange her notes and put them back in the folders with the negatives. He wondered, as he did so, how she could look so damnably healthy.

'I will write,' she said, when she reached the door.

'Good morning,' he said impatiently. In five minutes he would be in the theatre removing another breast.

NERVOUS ILLNESSES

Brain Tumour

A journey round my skull
by Frigyes Karinthy

After this announcement I appear to have sunk into a deep sleep, for I can remember nothing more about that evening, nor did I wake up during the night. I slept for ten hours on end and awoke next morning to find that I was being wheeled along the corridor. I was not at all drowsy, in fact my mind was abnormally clear and rational. I had not the slightest sensation of fear or any other emotion. It was the typical early morning mood when one has shaken off the night and its mysteries, and looks at the world with an almost ironical detachment. A day or two ago I had a glimpse from outside of the operating theatre to which I was now being taken. There was so large a No. 13 on the door that, half blind as I was, I could see it distinctly. I lay on my back, looking at the ceiling and waiting in the midst of a whiteness that was almost painful. People were walking close to me. I heard them speaking to one another in low tones, and their whispering struck me as distinctly comical. What could it be they were whispering about, and why had they to be so discreet about it? They had not brought me here to be discreet with me . . . I could see a white coat approaching, but I watched it only out of the corner of my eye, as I felt no curiosity about the face. They were wheeling me into the theatre now. Four hands laid hold of me by the feet and head and placed me on a narrow table like an ironing-board. They proceeded to turn me over on to my stomach, and fitted my head into an oval hollow, so as to allow of my breathing. I knew that I was to remain for hours in the same attitude, and I tried to find a comfortable position for my face and nose. Before settling down I spied out the land. To right and left of me I could just make out a corner of the sheet. Hardly anything else was visible. I stretched out my arms beside me.

They had begun to whisper once more above my head, but in a more decided tone. This was followed by another silence. I felt a cold touch of metal on the nape of my neck. A muffled whirring sound told me that they were shaving my head. This time the clippers did not stop short at the back, as when the barber uses them to smarten one up behind. They ran the whole length of my skull, removing the hair in long swathes. Afterwards, I felt them soaping my head, but by the time the razor came into play I was already bald.

For some minutes I could hear only the sound of footsteps. Then I felt a slight prick on the top of my head. No doubt they were giving me an injection. I wondered if the Professor had arrived. He probably had, because out of the corner of my eye I now saw two white coats moving. I felt them place some sort of blunt instrument against my head. This looked like the real thing . . .

There was an infernal scream as the steel plunged into my skull. It sank more and more rapidly through the bone, and the pitch of its scream became louder and more piercing every second. I had just time to say to myself that it must be the electric trephine. They needn't have bothered to be so discreet about their whispering . . .! My head throbbed and roared like a thousand-horse-power engine suddenly starting up. It thundered as if the infernal regions had opened or the earth were quaking. I never had a chance to think whether it was hurting me or not. Suddenly, there was a violent jerk, and the noise stopped. Having penetrated the skull the point was revolving freely in a space that offered no resistance. I felt a warm, silent rush of liquid inside my head, as if the blood were flowing *inwards* from the hole which had been made.

The silence lasted only a moment. An inch or so further on, the trephine struck into the skull and began again. I observed this second perforation more coldly, for it no longer came as a surprise. Again the trephine shot through the skull, and again the noise stopped. Once more, the blood seemed to rush inwards. Then I had the sensation that they were fumbling about with tubes. I wondered what was happening. Were there to be no more perforations? I heard people hurrying backwards and forwards. The two white coats had disappeared. Suddenly, the operating table began to move.

I was being gently wheeled through open doors and along passages. We went into two lifts, one of which took us up and the other down. I saw the carpet sliding past under my face, and wondered where I was being taken. An iron door closed. The freshness of the air suggested that it must be a large room.

More whispers and footsteps. Some one turned me on to my side and fixed my head. Photographic plates were lowered from the ceiling in front of my face. A violet light shone, followed by darkness and then by the light again. They turned me on to my back and fixed my head in another position. I was in the X-ray room. There were so many curtains, hangings and transverse beams attached to the ceiling that it looked like the back stage of a theatre. Everything was neatly and elegantly lowered from the ceiling as required. On the floor there was no trace of instruments or of the appliances used by this modern Inquisition. I was back once more in the taciturn, smiling Dr Lysholm's department. The perforations in my skull had therefore been made so that fresh photographs could be taken. They had drained the fluid from my brain cavities, and had filled them with air. That explained all the fumbling I had been conscious of. The actual opening of my skull had still to come. For a long time they kept turning me over, placing me in new positions and photographing me afresh. I began to wonder how long it was all going to last. Occasionally I caught sight of whole figures as they passed, but I saw nothing of Lysholm. One quarter of an hour went by after another.

At last I heard the table creak as they began to wheel me back to the operating theatre. Corridors, lifts, and corridors again. ... They closed the door of the theatre, and I felt them wheel me under the lamp.

Several minutes passed. No doubt they were examining the photographs. When they came up to me I was lying on my stomach again with my face in the hollow. Some one made my head firm by fixing broad plaster bands over my temples. He pulled them tight and attached them to the edge of the table, so that my head should be perfectly rigid, as if bound to the guillotine. Looking down, I saw a basin under my head, and I could see that as yet there was nothing in it. I felt them tightening the straps by which my hands and feet were to be secured. I tried to move the extremities of my limbs, but they refused to give a millimetre. I could not make the slightest movement of any kind. It was going to be hard work to stand it. I began breathing regularly, to a calm, even rhythm.

There was a fumbling movement about my neck and down my back. This time I knew what was happening, for I had seen it done myself. The nurses were arranging cloths around the area to be operated on. The Professor must be washing his hands, but I could not hear the splashing of water. Perhaps he was talking meanwhile to the other doctors. While I was being photographed he had surely lighted a cigarette in the next room and had laid the stub prudently on the edge of the ash-tray as soon as I was brought back. Afterwards, they would hand him his rubber gloves, put the sterilised gauze over his mouth, and attach the little electric lamp to his forehead.

Dead silence. I felt a succession of little pricks in a circle. Get on – that's enough now! My skin isn't so sensitive as all that. It didn't hurt me, but I distinctly felt the sharp point describe a wide circle on my head. It went over the same path a second time. Then, I felt one long horizontal incision at the back of my neck, though this did not hurt me, either. I heard the tinkle of forceps being jumbled up together and then being handled separately. This went on for a long while. I tried to see what was going on, and managed to make out an area as large as a handkerchief at the bottom of the white coat moving in front of me. It was bespattered with black spots like a speckled handkerchief. Of course, blood spouted from the arteries in jerks, instead of flowing evenly as from the veins. . . . I felt soft gestures, as if my flesh were being opened and folded back. The skull was certainly exposed by now, and the aponeurosis had contracted on to the nape of my neck. For the third time I heard the trephine strike my skull.

'Well, bye-bye, Frici!' I said aloud, and it did not surprise me that no one answered . . .

Yes, it had actually stopped at last. And high time, too! Don't you think that's enough, Professor? What I mean is. . . . It was more than enough for me, I can tell you! I was in an arrogant, almost bellicose mood and completely conscious. A violent contempt for myself swept over me.

There was a sudden jerk, as if he had seized the opening with a pair of forceps. It was followed by a straining sensation, a feeling of pressure, a cracking sound, and a terrific wrench. . . . Something broke with a dull noise. After a moment it began all over again. A straining sensation, a feeling of pressure, a cracking sound, and a terrific wrench. . . . This process was repeated many times. Each cracking sound reminded me of taking the lid off a jam-jar, while the process as a whole was like splitting open a wooden packing-case, plank by plank. The Professor seemed to be working downwards towards the back of my head, breaking off great pieces of bone as he went. The last one of all seemed so far down my neck that it felt like the topmost vertebra. For a long time it obstinately refused to give way, but at last he managed to wrench it out.

The brutality of the operation had begun to work me up into a frenzy. I abandoned myself to it with a savage voluptuousness, and longed to help him in his task. Gasping for breath, I urged him on with secret exhortations. A veritable fury of destruction seized hold of me. Give it socks! I wanted to shout. Break it up! Smash away! Bust it to bits! Now go for the vertebra! That's it! And again! Catch hold of it harder, man! Twist it round, can't you? You've got to break it! That's the way – it's coming! It's come! Now the next one! Smash into it, butchers! . . . I was struggling for my breath. Everything had gone red in front of my eyes. If I had had an axe or a lump of iron in my hand I should have hit out with it and smashed up myself and every one else, with the wild recklessness of a maniac.

In the midst of my rage I heard a gentle, comforting human voice. Its effect on me was like that of a cool hand on a madman's forehead, or like the calmly lifted sword of a Crusader quelling some African pagan.

'Wie fühlen Sie sich jetzt?'

Could it be Olivecrona's voice? It must have been, although I did not recognize him, for never before or since has it seemed to me so gentle and encouraging – so full of wise sympathy and kindliness. Was *this* his real nature, or was it just because the gauze softened his voice? I felt profoundly ashamed of myself. At the same moment my open head began to hurt. I was surprised to hear my lips form a polite, embarrassed answer, instead of swearing at the pain.

'Danke, Herr Professor . . . es geht gut!'

After this my mood underwent a change. Once the trephining of the skull was over there ensued a relative silence. But I did not find this silence reassuring. A feeling of weakness came over me, and at the same instant a sudden fear. Good God – I mustn't lose consciousness! What had the Professor said to my wife? 'I don't administer a general anaesthetic to Europeans, for the risk is twenty-five per cent less if a patient remains conscious.' So there *was* something in it after all – we were really co-operating. I had to look after my side of the business, as he was looking after his. It might all depend on thousandths of a millimetre. The moment I lost consciousness I should probably lose my life.

I had to be careful what I was doing. I must concentrate my attention and mechanically produce thoughts which were coherent and sensible. Whatever happened, I had to remain conscious. Let me see, what was the position? I was awake, I knew where I was, and that I was being operated on. At that very moment, in all probability, they were opening the cerebral membrane. That was quite a straightforward job – just a little slit and an application of forceps here and there, like a dressmaker fitting clips on her material. By a logical, yet unexpected process, I thought of Cushing's operation in the amateur film. Yes, that had been a nice, clean piece of work. I remembered saying, 'It looks like the kitchen of a luxury hotel, with the chef in his white coat cleaning a sheep's brains to make croquettes of them.' No, that was an absurd idea. . . . Something better, quickly! What could I think about? Ah yes, that would be an idea. If I could remember where I put my fountain-pen in the drawer of my bed table, I should know I was still conscious. No, that wasn't any good, either. I'd rather try . . . I'd try repeating . . . that Hungarian ballad. Yes, if I tried the ballad, it would help me to measure time as well, for it lasted a quarter of an hour from beginning to end. Anyhow, that would be something gained. I accordingly began: 'The Knight Pázmány strode up and down, In his gloomy castle hall. . . .'

'Wie fühlen Sie sich jetzt?'

'Danke, Herr Professor . . . es geht . . .'

This time it was not my voice at all. I heard someone answer in a high-pitched, quavering tone that came from far away in the distance. What was the use of speaking like that? I'd rather not answer at all. It wasn't worth frightening myself for nothing.

Besides, we ought to be nearing the end now. However long had I been lying strapped on the table? My hands and feet had gone completely numb. Why didn't they loosen the straps a little? Just a shade would be enough, but that shade would make all the difference. Did they think I'd throw myself about or upset the table? It was all a lot of rot! If they didn't undo them my arms and legs would be bursting soon. They'd die of suffocation. . . .

Once more there was a sound of pumping and draining, and I could hear the drip, drip of a liquid. How much longer were these gentlemen going to fumble about in my skull? They saw how quiet and well-behaved I was keeping. How long, then, did they propose to go on with their scratching and manipulating? Couldn't they do me the honour now and again of telling me what they were doing with my head? After all, I had been invited to this party, too. . . . I should be most interested to know how much longer they thought of using my brain for their soft, woolly fumblings.

Yes, *I* should be interested to know. *I* . . .

The fellow lying here on the table. . . . After all, those gentlemen and I had never been and would never again be on such confidential terms with one another as we were at that moment, for I knew that they had their fingers in my brain. They had been draining off some more fluid to get at their objective, and now they were making my brain ready for the assault. Yes, it was my brain. I fancied it must be throbbing now. . . .

Pain? No, I had no pain.

Although my brain didn't hurt at all, it did hurt me when one of the instruments fell on to the glass slab with a sharp, metallic sound. A certain idea passing through my mind hurt me, too. It had nothing to do with my present situation, but I could not get rid of the idea. It kept forcing itself on my notice, and the attempt to thrust it back was painful.

No, my brain did not hurt. Perhaps it was more exasperating this way than if it had. I would have preferred it to hurt me. More terrifying than any actual pain was the fact that my position seemed *impossible*. It was impossible for a man to be lying here with his skull open and his brain exposed to the outer world – impossible for him to lie here and live. It was impossible, incredible, indecent, for him to remain alive – and not merely alive, but conscious and in his right mind. It wasn't decent or natural – just as it wasn't natural . . . when at an altitude . . . of fifteen thousand feet . . . you had a very heavy object . . . very heavy . . . and it didn't fall . . . as it ought to do . . . No, not that . . . What was it, gentlemen, that the duckling said . . . in its quiet, apologetic way . . . when they came . . . to wring its neck . . .? 'Don't carve me with that knife . . . It might bring you . . . bad luck . . .!'

Stop that whispering, gentlemen! I could hear everything you say, if I weren't ashamed to listen . . . They were whispering continually, faster and faster. Faster and faster they kept whispering – and more and more obstinately. They were getting quite shameless about it. Don't whisper like that . . .! It isn't done, I tell you. It's not my fault. I feel ashamed of the whole thing. Get on, get on, can't you! It's time you covered up my naked brain . . .

This must have happened at the moment when they removed the band from Olivecrona's forehead, and when, thrusting a micro-lamp into the cavity, he was able to see, and even to touch, the tumour. There it was, growing on the slightly inflamed right side of the cerebellum, under the second lobe of the *pia mater*. It was now eleven o'clock, and the operation had so far been going on for two hours.

Psychological Disturbances

Hypochondria
from 'Head to Head' by Mel Smith and Griff Rhys Jones

MEL   I'm done for. I am not much longer for this world. My number's up.

GRIFF   What, you mean you're ill?

MEL   Yes, yes, I'm ill.

GRIFF   I didn't know you were sick. I mean, you look terrible, but I didn't know you were sick. You always look terrible, don't you.

MEL   Well, you know those pains I've been getting in my back . . .

GRIFF   No.

MEL   Well, I've been getting these pains in my back and they have diagnosed them now as . . . twinges.

GRIFF   Twinges? Fatal twinges, is that right? Is that what you've got, yeah?

MEL   Twinges, twinges coupled with shooting pains, tremulous palpitations and chronic drowsiness.

GRIFF   You ought to see a doctor, then.

MEL   I have seen a doctor.

GRIFF   Oh yeah.

MEL   I went down the Health Centre. I saw Frobisher.

GRIFF   What did he say?

MEL   He said, he said he couldn't help me.

GRIFF He's a terrible doctor, isn't he?

MEL Lousy.

GRIFF What's what's he . . . he's no good at all.

MEL Lousy, lousy.

GRIFF Is that all he said. I mean, you should have asked for a second opinion.

MEL Well, I did.

GRIFF And?

MEL He said I was a work-shy layabout.

GRIFF Well, that's another way of looking at it, I suppose. Is that all?

MEL He did, he did all the usual stuff: he told me to give up smoking and all the rest . . .

GRIFF Oh yeah. Did you?

MEL Well, while he was examining me, yeah. Well, I mean, it's ridiculous, isn't it, I mean, eight years at medical school drinking all those gallons of beer and playing rugby and that's the best they can come up with.

GRIFF I know, give up smoking. What do they know?

MEL They don't know nothing, these doctors. Anyway, I ended up . . . I went down to the new surgery at the bottom of the hill and I saw the doctor there, he's a nice bloke, Doctor, um, Doctor Locum. I said to him straight, I said to him straight, 'Doc, how long have I got?'

GRIFF And what did he say?

MEL Two minutes.

GRIFF Two minutes?

MEL Well, the surgery was full, I mean, there were hundreds of people waiting to see him. Anyway, he's sending me for some tests.

GRIFF Not tests.

MEL Yeah, you know, with a specialist.

GRIFF　What, a specialist in twinges?

MEL　A specialist. Well, I mean, apparently the top man.

GRIFF　Well, that's the worst thing you can possibly hear, isn't it? Isn't it, eh?

MEL　Why?

GRIFF　Well, you go to see the top man, think about it, they're not going to get old Sir Willoughby Whatsisname off the golf course just to look at any old rubbish, are they? You've got something dreadful wrong with you. You're doomed, mate, you're doomed! I mean, where are you going?

MEL　Peckham General.

GRIFF　Not Peckham General! Not Peckham General.

MEL　Peckham General. What's wrong with Peckham . . .?

GRIFF　Listen, listen, mate, right, my brother-in-law, right, he tells me that Peckham General is the filthiest hospital in the country.

MEL　What does your brother-in-law know about it?

GRIFF　He's the head cleaner.

MEL　Oh.

GRIFF　I wouldn't go in Peckham General if you paid me!

MEL　Well, they did pay you – you was a porter there for four years.

GRIFF　But I didn't go in there, did I?

MEL　No, no, you didn't, that's true.

GRIFF　No, I tell you, mate, whatever you do, whatever you do, they'll be all right, but if they tell you, right, they're putting you on Primrose Ward, don't go there. Don't go there! Don't go there.

MEL　Why not?

GRIFF　That Primrose Ward – Death Row, mate. Nobody ever comes out of Primrose Ward alive.

MEL　What, nobody?

GRIFF　Well, some of the nurses, occasionally, yes. But that's the holding bay for the mortuary, Primrose Ward.

MEL   Hold on a minute, I'm only going there for a scan.

GRIFF   Not a scan!

MEL   There's nothing wrong with a scan.

GRIFF   Oh my . . . No, go for the Barium Meal, mate, it's a bit easier. Go for the Barium Meal.

MEL   How do you know about it?

GRIFF   Well, I've had more Barium Meals than you've had hot dinners, I tell you.

MEL   Yeah, but with that Barium Meal you have to drink all that nasty horrible white gluck stuff, don't you. Yergh, it's horrible that.

GRIFF   Well, it's a treat after the hospital food, mate, I can tell you. It's a little bit of a problem you know, like, with the other, you know, when it, you know, when it comes out the other end, sort of thing, you know.

MEL   Why?

GRIFF   Well, it goes in like liquid clay and comes out like a sixty-two-piece earthenware tea-set.

MEL   What if you've got constipation?

GRIFF   Well, then you've got an early Henry Moore on your hands, ain't you?

~

Off colour
from Low Life *by Jeffrey Bernard*

I've known Aubrey since we were teenagers but I never realised until last week that he's a paranoid hypochondriac. Like most of us he's worried about pollution, excessive crop-spraying and the fast-vanishing hedgerow. The general decline of his neck of the woods and fields has got him twitching and the thing that bugs him most is the physical damage that he claims to have suffered in the last year from motor car and lorry exhaust fumes. Now, what he's done is to list his ailments on paper and circulate them to neighbours within a five-mile radius, and if they too can say they've suffered from any affliction on the list then he wants them to sign a petition asking the government to ban insecticides and cars from the said neck of woods and pastures. I shall allow Aubrey to continue this column now by simply quoting his 1982 health chart. You're not going to believe it, but I promise you this is his circular. This is what one man claims to have suffered from in one little year.

1. Lassitude (*acute* tiredness). 2. Distraction (lack of concentration). 3. Aching (heavy limbs). 4. Bouts of severe depression. 5. Back ache, shoulder ache. 6. Sudden acute pains in rib cage, limbs and extremities. 7. Lengthy headaches. Sudden sharp pains in temples and forehead. 8. Pains on inside of forearms. 9. Cystitis, difficulty and frequency in passing water. 10. Drawing sensation towards lower abdomen. 11. Aching backs of hands as with sprain. 12. Popping, aching, tickling ears. 13. General acute itching. 14. Violent sneezing. 15. Indigestion. Inflated, bloated, acidic. 16. Nausea. 17. Catarrh (not necessarily related to a cold). 18. Sore gum, tongue and inside of mouth with ulcers and cold sores. 19. Sores in nostrils. 20. Sore throats and swollen glands. 21. Bowel trouble – diarrhoea, motions in small quantities of soft consistency. 22. Very sharp hot pains of short duration in rectum. 23. Raw stinging circle around anus. 24. Eye trouble – stabbing sensation through eyeballs, pulling, drawing feeling. 25. Watery eyes, itching eyes, dry gritty eyes, itching lids, blurred vision, foggy eyes, winking eyelids. 26. Sweating, not related to exercise. 27. Runny nose. 28. Slurred speech. 29. Bad physical coordination. 30. Bleeding from rectum. 31. Irritability. 32. Dizziness. Loss of balance. 33. Continuous clearing of throat. 34. Bad breath and bad taste in mouth. 35. Heavy lump high in centre of chest. 36. Fluttering in chest. 37. Hormone trouble. 38. Erratic pulse.

Phew! Amazing, isn't it? And I thought I was dying a little too soon. But there are some lovely unconscious touches here and only a serious man could be so unintentionally funny. I particularly like 'sweating, not related to exercise' – the buff envelope-with-the-window syndrome? – and I'm not surprised that 'irritability' follows 'bleeding from rectum' although medically speaking I'm sure he doesn't know his arse from his elbow. But he's obviously taken to drink, hasn't he? (I haven't seen him for ten years.) The slurred speech, stomach pains, bad coordination and loss of balance all point to it and, speaking as a specialist, I'm rather touched to see that he's tried to go on the wagon. 'General acute itching' is merely a withdrawal symptom. The bit about bad breath leads me to suspect his tipple is white wine. People who drink wine without food smell like drains. The heavy lump and fluttering in the chest is what we call angst. As for the bouts of severe depression and acute tiredness one can only suppose that he's embarked on the *Spectator* Treasure Hunt. Why he doesn't go to a hospital God only knows. Perhaps, in spite of being a hypochondriac, he agrees with my friend Eva. She once asked a man in a pub, 'What do you do?' He said, 'I practise medicine.' She said, 'Practise? Why don't you get it right?'

~

Ode on melancholy
from Lyric Poems *by John Keats*

I

No, no, go not to Lethe, neither twist
   Wolf's-bane, tight-rooted, for its poisonous wine;
Nor suffer thy pale forehead to be kiss'd
   By nightshade, ruby grape of Proserpine;
Make not your rosary of yew-berries,
    Nor let the beetle, nor the death-moth be
      Your mournful Psyche, nor the downy owl
A partner in your sorrow's mysteries;
    For shade to shade will come too drowsily,
      And drown the wakeful anguish of the soul.

II

But when the melancholy fit shall fall
   Sudden from heaven like a weeping cloud,
That fosters the droop-headed flowers all,
   And hides the green hill in an April shroud;
Then glut thy sorrow on a morning rose,
    Or on the rainbow of the salt sand-wave,
      Or on the wealth of globed peonies;
Or if thy mistress some rich anger shows,
    Emprison her soft hand, and let her rave,
      And feed deep, deep upon her peerless eyes.

III

She dwells with Beauty – Beauty that must die;
   And Joy, whose hand is ever at his lips
Bidding adieu; and aching Pleasure nigh,
   Turning to Poison while the bee-mouth sips:
Ay, in the very temple of delight
   Veil'd Melancholy has her sovran shrine,
     Though seen of none save him whose strenuous tongue
   Can burst Joy's grape against his palate fine;
His soul shall taste the sadness of her might,
     And be among her cloudy trophies hung.

~

Manic depression
by Spike Milligan

The pain is too much
A thousand grim winters
   grow in my head.
In my ears
   the sound of the
   coming dead.
All Seasons
All sane
All living
All pain.
No opiate to lock still
   my senses
Only left,
   the body locked tenses.

214

DEAFNESS AND TINNITUS

Deafness

Paracusis Willisii

from Thomas Willis 1621–1675: His Life and Work
by J. Trevor Hughes

There is a phenomenon, well known to specialists of ear diseases, and which is experienced by certain deaf patients, whose hearing improves in the presence of noise. The deafness may be so profound as to prevent normal conversation, but in the noise, for example of a railway train, a conversation can be heard by the otherwise deaf passenger. This symptom excludes nerve deafness and indicates an obstruction in conduction. It is most likely to be due to stapes fixation and the commonest cause is otosclerosis.

Paracusis is well described in *De Anima Brutorum** in the section 'On hearing':

> For we meet with a certain kind of deafness, in which those affected, seem wholly to want the Sense of Hearing, yet as soon as a great noise, as of great Guns, Bells, or Drums, is made near to the Ears, they distinctly hear the speeches of the by-standers, but this great noise ceasing, they presently grow deaf again.

The following passage includes two cases reports, the first being:

> a Woman, tho she were deaf, yet so long as a Drum was beaten within her Chamber, she heard every word perfectly; wherefore her Husband kept a Drummer on purpose for his servant, that by that means he might have some converse with his Wife.

and the second:

> another Deaf Person, who living near a Ring of Bells, as often as they all rung out, he could easily hear any word, and not else.

* First published in 1672

217

Visible speech
from First Love *by Eudora Welty*

In Natchez it was the bitterest winter of them all.

✳

Natchez people turned silently to look when a solitary man that no one had ever seen before was found and carried in through the streets, frozen the way he had crouched in a hollow tree, gray and huddled like a squirrel, with a little bundle of goods clasped to him.

Joel Mayes, a deaf boy twelve years old, saw the man brought in and knew it was a dead man, but his eyes were for something else, something wonderful. He saw the breaths coming out of people's mouths, and his dark face, losing just now a little of its softness, showed its secret desire. It was marvelous to him when the infinite designs of speech became visible in formations on the air, and he watched with awe that changed to tenderness whenever people met and passed in the road with an exchange of words. He walked alone, slowly through the silence, with the sturdy and yet dreamlike walk of the orphan, and let his own breath out through his lips, pushed it into the air, and whatever word it was it took the shape of a tower. He was as pleased as if he had had a little conversation with someone.

∼

Sophy
from Dr Marigold's Prescription *by Charles Dickens*

You'd have laughed – or the reverse – it's according to your disposition – if you could have seen me trying to teach Sophy. At first I was helped – you'd never guess by what – milestones. I got some large alphabets in a box, all the letters separate on bits of bone, and saying we was going to WINDSOR, I give her those letters in that order, and then at every milestone I showed her those same letters in that same order again, and pointed towards the abode of royalty. Another time I give her CART, and then chalked the same upon the cart. Another time I give her DOCTOR MARIGOLD, and hung a corresponding inscription outside my waistcoat. People that met us might stare a bit and laugh, but what did *I* care, if she caught the idea? She caught it after long patience and trouble, and then we did begin to get on swimmingly, I believe you! At first she was a little given to consider me the cart, and the cart the abode of royalty, but that soon wore off.

We had our signs, too, and they was hundreds in number. Sometimes she would sit looking at me and considering hard how to communicate with me about something fresh – how to ask me what she wanted explained, – and then she was (or I thought she was; what does it signify?) so like my child with those years added to her, that I half-believed it was herself, trying to tell me where she had been to up in the skies, and what she had seen since that unhappy night when she flied away. She had a pretty face, and now that there was no one to drag at her bright dark hair, and it was all in order, there was a something touching in her looks, that made the cart most peaceful and most quiet, though not at all melancolly. [N.B. In the Cheap Jack patter, we generally sound it lemon-jolly, and it gets a laugh.]

The way she learnt to understand any look of mine was truly surprising. When I sold of a night, she would sit in the cart unseen by them outside, and would give a eager look into my eyes when I looked in, and would hand me straight the precise article or articles I wanted. And then she would clap her hands, and laugh for joy. And as for me, seeing her so bright, and remembering what she was when I first lighted on her, starved and beaten and ragged, leaning asleep against the muddy cart-wheel, it give me such heart that I gained a greater heighth of reputation than ever, and I put Pickleson down (by the name of Mim's Travelling Giant otherwise Pickleson) for a fypunnote in my will.

This happiness went on in the cart till she was sixteen year old. By which time I began to feel not satisfied that I had done my whole duty by her, and to consider that she ought to have better teaching than I could give her. It drew a many tears on both sides when I commenced explaining my views to her; but what's right is right, and you can't neither by tears nor laughter do away with its character.

So I took her hand in mine, and I went with her one day to the Deaf and Dumb Establishment in London, and when the gentleman come to speak to us, I says to him: 'Now I'll tell you what I'll do with you, sir. I am nothing but a Cheap Jack, but of late years I have laid by for a rainy day notwithstanding. This is my only daughter (adopted), and you can't produce a deafer nor a dumber. Teach her the most that can be taught her in the shortest separation that can be named, – state the figure for it, – and I am game to put the money down. I won't bate you a single farthing, sir, but I'll put down the money here and now, and I'll thankfully throw you in a pound to take it. There!' The gentleman smiled, and then, 'Well, well,' says he, 'I must first know what she has learned already. How do you communicate with her?' Then I showed him, and she wrote in printed writing many names of things and so forth; and we held some sprightly conversation, Sophy and me, about a little story in a book the gentleman showed her, and which she was able to read. 'This is most extraordinary,' says the gentleman; 'is it possible that you have been her only teacher?' 'I have been her only teacher, sir,' I says, 'besides herself.' 'Then,' says the gentleman, and more acceptable words was never spoke to me, 'you're a clever fellow, and a good fellow.' This he makes known to Sophy, who kisses his hands, claps her own, and laughs and cries upon it.

~

Laura Bridgman's story
from American Notes *by Charles Dickens*

(In his *American Notes*, Charles Dickens describes a visit which he made in 1842 to the Perkins Institution and Massachusetts Asylum for the Blind in Boston. There he met an eight-year-old girl called Laura Bridgman, whose 'sight and hearing were gone for ever'.)

[She was] a girl, blind, deaf, and dumb; destitute of smell; and nearly so of taste . . . a fair young creature with every human faculty, and hope, and power of goodness, inclosed within her delicate frame, and but one outward sense – the sense of touch – (she was) impervious to any ray of light, or particle of sound . . .

I have extracted a few disjointed fragments of her history, from an account, written by that one man who has made her what she is.

'The darkness and the silence of the tomb were around her: no mother's smile called forth her answering smile, no father's voice taught her to imitate his sounds – they, brothers and sisters, were but forms of matter which resisted her touch, but which differed not from the furniture of the house, save in warmth, and in the power of locomotion; and not even in these respects from the dog and the cat.

But the immortal spirit which had been implanted within her could not die, nor be maimed nor mutilated; and though most of its avenues of communication with the world were cut off, it began to manifest itself through the others. As soon as she could walk, she began to explore the room, and then the house; she became familiar with the form, density, weight, and heat, of every article she could lay her hands upon.

There was one of two ways to be adopted: either to go on to build up a language of signs on the basis of the natural language which she had already commenced herself, or to teach her the purely arbitrary language in common use: that is, to give her a sign for every individual thing, or to give her a knowledge of letters by combination of which she might express her idea of the existence, and the mode and condition of existence, of any thing. The former would have been easy, but, very ineffectual; the latter seemed very difficult, but, if accomplished, very effectual. I determined therefore to try the latter.

The first experiments were made by taking articles in common use, such as knives, forks, spoons, keys, etc., and pasting upon them labels with their names printed in raised letters. These she felt very carefully, and soon, of course, distinguished that the crooked lines *spoon*, differed as much from the crooked lines *key*, as the spoon differed from the key in form.

Then small detached labels, with the same words printed upon them, were put into her hands; and she soon observed that they were similar to the ones pasted on the articles. She showed her perception of this similarity by laying the label *key* upon the key, and the label *spoon* upon the spoon. She was encouraged here by the natural sign of approbation, patting on the head.

The same process was then repeated with all the articles which she could handle; and she very easily learned to place the proper labels upon them. It was evident, however, that the only intellectual exercise was that of imitation and memory. She recollected that the label *book* was placed upon a book, and she repeated the process first from imitation, next from memory, with only the motive of love of approbation, but apparently without the intellectual perception of any relation between the things.

After a while, instead of labels, the individual letters were given to her on detached bits of paper: they were arranged side by side so as to spell *book, key*, etc.; then they were mixed up in a heap and a sign was made for her to arrange them herself so as to express the words *book, key*, etc.; and she did so.

Hitherto, the process had been mechanical, and the success about as great as teaching a very knowing dog a variety of tricks. The poor child had sat in mute amazement, and patiently imitated everything her teacher did; but now the truth began to flash upon her: her intellect began to work: she perceived that here was a way by which she could herself make up a sign of anything that was in her own mind, and show it to another mind; and at once her countenance lighted up with a human expression: it was no longer a dog, or parrot: it was an immortal spirit, eagerly seizing upon a new link of union with other spirits! I could almost fix upon the moment when this truth dawned upon her mind, and spread its light to her countenance; I saw that the great obstacle was overcome; and that henceforward nothing but patient and persevering, but plain and straightforward, efforts were to be used.

The result thus far, is quickly related, and easily conceived; but not so was the process; for many weeks of apparently unprofitable labour were passed before it was effected.

When it was said above, that a sign was made, it was intended to say, that the action was performed by her teacher, she feeling his hands, and then imitating the motion.

The next step was to procure a set of metal types, with the different letters of the alphabet cast upon their ends; also a board, in which were square holes, into which holes she could set the types; so that the letters on their ends could alone be felt above the surface.

Then, on any article being handed to her, for instance, a pencil, or a watch, she would select the component letters, and arrange them on her board, and read them with apparent pleasure.

She was exercised for several weeks in this way, until her vocabulary became extensive; and then the important step was taken of teaching her how to represent the different letters by the position of her fingers, instead of the cumbrous apparatus of the board and types. She accomplished this speedily and easily, for her intellect had begun to work in aid of her teacher, and her progress was rapid.

This was the period, about three months after she had commenced, that the first report of her case was made, in which it was stated that 'she has just learned the manual alphabet, as used by the deaf mutes, and it is a subject of delight and wonder to see how rapidly, correctly, and eagerly, she goes on with her labours. Her teacher gives her a new object, for instance, a pencil, first lets her examine it, and get an idea of its use, then teaches her how to spell it by making the signs for the letters with her own fingers: the child grasps her hand, and feels her fingers, as the different letters are formed; she turns her head a little on one side like a person listening closely; her lips are apart; she seems scarcely to breathe; and her countenance, at first anxious, gradually changes to a smile, as she comprehends the lesson. She then holds up her tiny fingers, and spells the word in the manual alphabet; next, she takes her types and arranges her letters; and last, to make sure that she is right, she takes the whole of the types composing the word, and places them upon or in contact with the pencil, or whatever the object may be.'

The whole of the succeeding year was passed in gratifying her eager inquiries for the names of every object which she could possibly handle; in exercising her in the use of the manual alphabet; in extending in every possible way her knowledge of the physical relations of things; and in proper care of her health.

At the end of the year a report of her case was made, from which the following is an extract:

'During the year she has attained great dexterity in the use of the manual alphabet of the deaf mutes; and she spells out the words and sentences which she knows, so fast and so deftly, that only those accustomed to this language can follow with the eye the rapid motions of her fingers.

'But wonderful as is the rapidity with which she writes her thoughts upon the air, still more so is the ease and accuracy with which she reads the words thus written by another; grasping their hands in hers, and following every movement of their fingers, as letter after letter conveys their meaning to her mind.'

Such are a few fragments from the simple but most interesting and instructive history of Laura Bridgman. The name of her great benefactor and friend, who writes it, is Dr Howe.

∼

Deafness
by David Wright

It is quite natural. Some hear more pleasantly
with the eyes than with the ears. I do.
GERTRUDE STEIN

About deafness I know everything and nothing. Everything, if forty years' firsthand experience is to count. Nothing, when I realise the little I have had to do with the converse aspects of deafness – the other half of the dialogue. Of that side my wife knows more than I. So do teachers of the deaf and those who work among them; not least, people involuntarily but intensely involved – ordinary men and women who find themselves, from one cause or another, parents of a deaf child. For it is the non-deaf who absorb a large part of the impact of the disability. The limitations imposed by deafness are often less noticed by its victims than by those with whom they have to do.

Deafness is a disability without pathos. Dr Johnson called it 'the most desperate of human calamities'. Yet its effects are slapstick:

'Where's the baby?'

'I put it in the dustbin.'*

There is a buffoonery about deafness which is liable to rub off on anybody who comes into contact with it. Having to shout at the hard of hearing is not elegant, nor is finger-spelling or the mouthing of words to magnify lip movements for those whose eyes are their ears. Deafness is a banana skin: an aspect which may conveniently be illustrated by an anecdote I recently came across in an old memoir. It concerns the once famous but now forgotten Victorian poet, Alexander Smith. Variations of this incident, I may add, have pursued me through life. Smith, then a young man in the early bloom of literary repute, had been taken by Swinburne's friend John Nichol to pay his respects to that formidable but deaf bluestocking, Harriet Martineau:

Miss Martineau, it is otherwise well known, is a little hard of hearing. When the travellers arrived, several ladies were with her, and by the little circle of petticoats they were received with some *empressement*. Mr Nichol took up the running, and some little conversation proceeded, Smith, in the racing phrase, *waiting*. Presently he 'came with a rush' and observed it 'had been a very fine day' – an unimpeachable and excellent remark which brought

224

him instantly into difficulties. Miss Martineau was at once on the *qui vive*. The poet had made a remark probably instinct with fine genius, worthy of the author of *The Life Drama*. 'Would Mr Smith be so good as to repeat what he said?' Mr Smith – looking, no doubt, uncommonly like an ass – repeated it in a somewhat higher key. Alas! Alas! in vain. The old lady shook her head. 'It was really so annoying, but she did not quite catch it; would Mr Smith be *again* so good?' and her hand was at her eager ear. The unhappy bard, feeling, as he said, in his distress as if suicide might be the thing, shrieked and again shrieked his little piece of information – symptoms of ill-suppressed merriment becoming obvious around him. Finally the old lady's ear-trumpet was produced, and proceeding to shriek through this instrument, of which the delicate use was unknown to him, the bard nearly blew her head off.

The suffering, it will be seen, lay more to the side of Mr Smith than the deaf lady, even if she did nearly have her head blown off. Hard to bear is the devaluation of whatever one may be saying – which is almost inevitable after its fourth or fifth repetition. Yet the anecdote illustrates an undramatic but not minor disadvantage of deafness, felt less positively by the deaf than their hearing friends: having to dispense with the easy exchange of trivialities which is oil to the wheels of conversation and to the business of living. The use of language as gesture, as reassuring noise rather than an instrument of specific communication, is largely denied the deaf.

Harriet Martineau, who underwent a partial loss of hearing at the age of twenty, was one of the relatively few to write about deafness from experience. There is a surprising amount of unsentimental good sense in her *Letter to the Deaf*, bossy and dogmatic though she is. However she does put her finger on a main problem of describing deafness at first hand, when she recognises how far the experience of it must vary from one person to another. That it must differ according to the severity of the hearing loss is obvious.

Very few are absolutely deaf. Their experience must necessarily be different from that of the severely deaf, the partially deaf, and the merely hard of hearing. The partially deaf, it seems to me, have the worst of both worlds. They hear enough to be distracted by noise yet not enough for it to be meaningful. For the merely hard of hearing there is the strain of extracting significance from sounds that may be as loud as life yet out of focus; what comes through is an auditory fuzz. Of course there are hearing-aids, but not everybody can profit from these.

Yet what is crucial is the age at which hearing is lost. Those who have been born deaf, whether completely or partially, must always be at a disadvantage compared with those who lose hearing later in life. The deaf-born cannot pick up speech and language naturally like ordinary children. They have to be taught, a difficult and slow process, the slower and more difficult the later the teaching begins. For the most intense activity of the brain takes place in the first few years of one's life, and thereafter – from the age of about three – gradually decreases. That is why small children quickly and easily pick up foreign languages while older children and adults find it an effort. But the born deaf and those who become deaf in early childhood have the compensation that they do not feel the loss of a faculty they never had or cannot remember. They are at least spared the painful effort of adjustment. The later in life one loses hearing, the sharper the test of character and fortitude: because adaptability lessens with age. On the other hand the years of hearing are so much money in the bank. Those to whom deafness comes late do not have to acquire with pain and struggle the elements of language, vocabulary, speech. These assets – pure gold – are theirs already.

*To a lipreader the words *baby* and *paper* are indistinguishable.

~

Maître Florian
from Notre Dame de Paris *by Victor Hugo*

[*Quasimodo the deaf and hunchbacked bellringer of Notre Dame is charged with criminal offences in the Magistrates' Court of Paris, presided over by Maître Florian, a deaf magistrate known by the title of 'auditor'. The year is 1482.*]

... Maître Florian, the auditor, was leafing intently through the documents of the charge laid against Quasimodo, which the clerk had held out to him, and, having glanced at them, he seemed to reflect for a moment. Thanks to this precaution, which he was always careful to take when proceeding to an interrogation, he knew in advance the names, titles and crimes of the accused, could make predictable rejoinders to predictable answers, and could survive all the ins and outs of the interrogation without letting his deafness show overmuch. For him the documents of the case were like the blind man's guide-dog. If it happened now and again that his infirmity was revealed by an incoherent apostrophe or an unintelligible question, then some ascribed this to his profundity, others to his imbecility. In either case, the honour of the magistrature was preserved, since it is better for a judge to be thought profound or an imbecile than deaf. So he took great pains to conceal his deafness from the general notice, and normally succeeded so well that he had even come to deceive himself. Which is, as it happens, easier than one might think. All hunchbacks hold their heads high, all stammerers make speeches, all deaf people talk quietly. He thought merely that his hearing was somewhat rebellious. That was the one concession he made in the matter to public opinion, during those moments of candour when he examined his conscience.

Having thus ruminated on Quasimodo's case, he threw back his head and half closed his eyes, so as to look more impartial and majestic, with the result that at that moment he was both deaf and blind. Twin conditions without which there can be no perfect judge. In this magisterial pose, he began the interrogation.

'Your name?'

But here was a circumstance which had not been 'foreseen by the law', whereby one deaf man would have to question another.

Quasimodo, totally ignorant that a question had been addressed to him, continued to stare fixedly at the judge and did not answer. The judge, who was deaf and totally ignorant of the deafness of the defendant, thought he had replied, as defendants generally did, and continued, with his stupid and mechanical self-assurance:

'Good. Your age?'

Quasimodo did not reply to this question either. The judge thought it had been answered and went on.

'Now, your trade?'

Still the same silence. The audience, meanwhile, had begun to whisper and exchange glances.

'That will do,' went on the imperturbable auditor, assuming that the defendant had completed his third reply. 'You are accused before us: *primo*, of nocturnal disturbance; *secundo*, of an unlawful act of violence against the person of a loose woman, *in praejudicium mere-tricis* [to the detriment of a harlot]; *tertio*, of insubordination and disloyalty towards the archers of the ordinance of the king our master.

Justify yourself on all these points. Clerk, have you written down what the defendant has said so far?'

At this luckless question, a roar of laughter went up from clerks and spectators alike, so violent, so wild, so contagious, and so universal that the two deaf men could not but be aware of it. Quasimodo turned round with a scornful shrug of his hump-back, while Maître Florian, equally amazed and supposing the laughter to have been provoked by some irreverent rejoinder from the prisoner, made visible for him by that shrug of the shoulders, apostrophized him indignantly.

'The answer you have just given, you scoundrel, deserves the noose. Do you know to whom you are speaking?'

Which outburst was not calculated to stay the general explosion of merriment. Everyone found it so incongruous and absurd that the uncontrollable laughter spread even to the serjeants from the Parloir-aux-Bourgeois, those knaves of spades, as it were, whose stupidity was part of their uniform. Quasimodo alone remained unsmiling for the good reason that he understood nothing of what was going on around him . . .

. . . the clerk, just as Maître Florian Barcedienne was reading the sentence in his turn in order to sign it, felt moved by pity for the poor wretch who had been condemned and, in the hope of obtaining some relaxation of his punishment, he came as close as he could to the ear of the auditor and said, pointing to Quasimodo:

'The man is deaf.'

He had hoped that this common infirmity would arouse Maître Florian's interest in favour of the prisoner. But in the first place, we have already observed that Maître Florian did not like it to be known he was deaf. And he was, secondly, so hard of hearing that he did not hear a single word of what the clerk was saying to him: however, he wanted to appear to have heard, and he answered: 'Ha, ha, that's different! I didn't know that. In that case, one hour extra in the pillory.'

And he signed the sentence so modified.

Tinnitus

Internal ringing of the ears
by Celcus

Internal ringing of the ears is a different kind of disease from the fore-going; although this also impairs their power of receiving the impressions of sound. That is the slightest species which arises from gravedo: that is worse which ensues upon disease or upon chronic head-aches: but the most dangerous is that which is the forerunner of violent diseases, and particularly of epilepsy. If the affection arise from gravedo, one ought to clear out the ear, and hold in the breath until some frothy fluid proceed from it. If it owes its origin to disease, or to head-ache, so far as regards exercise, frictions, affusion, and the use of gargarisms, the same remedial measures apply as in the last-mentioned disease: all the food should be of an extenuating quality: radish-juice with rose-oil ought to be poured into the ear, or juice of wild cucumber with the radish-juice; or castor with vinegar and laurel-oil. Hellebore is also rubbed with vinegar, then incorporated with boiled honey, and afterwards introduced into the ear in the form of a collyrium. If it has begun independently of the causes just expressed, and on that account inspires us with a dread of something worse, one ought to introduce into the ear castor with vinegar, or orris-oil, or laurel-oil, or, together with this last, castor with the juice of bitter almonds, or myrrh and nitre with rose-oil and vinegar. Nevertheless in this malady more benefit is derivable from a strict regimen; and the same plan is to be pursued as above comprised, but with still greater exactitude: in addition to these, wine is to be excluded till the sound in the ears be cured. But if both a sounding and inflammation exist simultaneously, all that is requisite is to inject laurel-oil, or the expressed oil of bitter almonds, to which some add castor, or myrrh.

~

Cricket-in-the-ear
from Writings in the New Yorker 1927–1976
by E.B. White

Mid-september, the cricket's festival, is the hardest time of year for a friend of ours who suffers from a ringing in the ears. He tells us that at this season it is almost impossible, walking or riding in the country, to distinguish between the poetry of earth and the racket inside his own head. The sound of insects has become, for him, completely identified with personal deterioration. He doesn't know, and hasn't been able to learn from his doctor, what cricket-in-the-ear signifies, if anything, but he recalls that the Hemingway hero in 'Across the River and Into the Trees' was afflicted the same way and only lasted two days – died in the back seat of an automobile after closing the door carefully and well. Our friend can't disabuse himself of the fear that he is just a day or two from dead, and it is really pitiful to see him shut a door, the care he takes.

~

The bells of hell
from The Sunday Telegraph, *20 June 1993*
by James Le Fanu

'My ears whistle and buzz continuously day and night. I can say I am leading a wretched life,' poor old Beethoven complained about his tinnitus. What might have helped, had it been available at the time, was a Walkman mini-stereo for, as Aristotle observed: 'Buzzing in the ears ceases when a greater sound drives out the less.'

This was also the basis for the apparently miraculous cure for tinnitus sufferers who made the pilgrimage to the Breton town of Stival. There the handbell of the Celtic saint St Meriadec was (and, on request, still is) rung loudly in the suppliant's ears and then placed over his head. When the bell was removed, the tinnitus supposedly stopped, at least temporarily.

For the suggestible the cure may even have been permanent because there is a strong psychological component to the condition. The problem is not so much the whistling and buzzing as, according to Linda Luxon, Professor of Audiological Medicine at London University, the patient's perception of it.

Tinnitus is the amplification of the noise that can be induced by placing both hands over the ears. Many people experience it – especially those like Beethoven who have some form of hearing impairment – but few complain of it. For some, however, it comes to dominate their lives. Why?

It is easy to understand how tinnitus might be more of a nuisance for the gloomy than for the optimistic. And indeed over a half of those seeking medical help are suffering from depression. But here we are caught in a classic chicken-and-egg conundrum.

For some, tinnitus can take the form of a high-pitched whistling, or loud 'machinery' noises. Such patients seek a medical opinion, expecting there to be a reason and a solution, only to be told the cause is not precisely known and that there is no reliable remedy. This response can easily be interpreted as indifference on the part of the doctor, and the resulting frustration then causes depression. Next thing, patients are being offered anti-depressants and psychotherapy, with the obvious implication that it is their fault for not coping. This only makes them more miserable.

From this it can be fairly surmised that tinnitus is difficult to treat. A positive attitude from the doctor is very helpful – not just 'you'll have to learn to live with it', but a proper examination, an explanation and reassurance that it should get better. The use of tinnitus maskers or a Walkman to drown out the noise is useful for some, and the anti-epileptic drug Clonazepam in low dosage has its advocates. For the anxious, the much maligned Valium is the drug of choice, and for the depressed, Nortriptylene.

Professor R. Hinchcliffe, of London University recommends a form of psychological treatment called cognitive therapy, while those much afflicted by tinnitus, in bed at night can drive it out of their consciousness by simply repeating in mantra-like fashion the same words over and over again.

A number of tinnitus sufferers find yoga a relief, taking a leaf out of the book of Eastern mystics to exploit the naturally occurring tinnitus induced by placing the hands over the ears. 'The ears are closed by the fingers and attention is focused on the sounds that are heard. With practice the mind is able to hold on to progressively finer and subtler sounds until eventually liberation is reached.'

There is no doubt that the numbers complaining of tinnitus have risen markedly in recent years, which, if Professor Luxon is correct, must mean that the threshold at which people are prepared to tolerate it must have fallen. This might be because of the considerable adverse publicity tinnitus has received in the press, and the frequently repeated rumour that it can so sap morale as to lead to suicide. A few reported cases have, however, all had a severe psychiatric illness as well.

A recent health education programme focusing on the dangers of noise at work has certainly contributed, especially as those seeking compensation for occupation-related hearing loss receive much larger sums if they are also suffering from tinnitus.

According to the British National Study of Hearing 8 per cent of the population have tinnitus that is bad enough to cause 'moderate or severe annoyance'. It is, however, virtually unknown in India. Is this, Professor Hinchcliffe asks, 'because they have a lot of things to worry about, or because they have not been subject to the maleficent effects of the mass media?'

~

On his tinnitus
from Lancet: In England Now

To one who has been long in city pent
And would from all oppressive noise be free,
The forest's stillness offers sanctuary:
The mountain peaks bestow a peace heaven-sent.
These havens once I sought; as well I spent
Days by a stream, remote in deep country,
Where less the play of angling was to me
Than finding in the quietness deep content.
Now silence have I none: sounds curious,
That have no source save cells in the cochlea,
Haunt my old ears in song continuous.
In cities now I stay; always I hear
The traffic's roar, canned music far and near:
The surging noises mask my tinnitus.

TILL DEATH US DO PART

Last Words

*All say 'How hard it is that we have to die' – a strange
complaint to come from the mouths of people who have had
to live.*

Mark Twain

Death as a friend
from The Professor at the Breakfast-Table
by Oliver Wendell Holmes

No human being can rest for any time in a state of equilibrium, where
the desire to live, and that to depart just balance each other. If one has
a house, which he has lived and always means to live in, he pleases
himself with the thought of all the conveniences it offers him, and
thinks little of its wants and imperfections. But once having made up
his mind to move to a better, every incommodity starts out upon him,
until the very ground-plan of it seems to have changed in his mind,
and his thoughts and affections, each one of them packing up his little
bundle of circumstances, have quitted their several chambers and
nooks and migrated to the new home, long before its apartments are
ready to receive their bodily tenant. It is so with the body. Most persons have died before they expire – died to all earthly longings, so that
the last breath is only, as it were, the locking of the door of the already
deserted mansion. The fact of the tranquillity with which the great
majority of dying persons await this locking of those gates of life
through which its airy angels have been going and coming, from the
moment of the first cry, is familiar to those who have been often called
upon to witness the last period of life. Almost always there is a prepa-
ration made by Nature for unearthing a soul, just as on a smaller scale
there is for the removal of a milk-tooth. The roots which hold human
life to earth are absorbed before it is lifted from its place. Some of the

dying are weary and want rest, the idea of which is almost insepara-
ble in the human mind from death. Some are in pain, and want to be
rid of it, even though the anodyne be dropped, as in the legend, from
the sword of the Death–Angel. Some are stupid, mercifully narcotised
that they may go to sleep without long tossing about. And some are
strong in faith and hope, so that, as they draw near the next world,
they would fain hurry toward it, as the caravan moves faster over the
sands when the foremost travellers send word along the file that water
is in sight. Though each little party that follows in a foot-track of its
own will have it that the water to which others think they are hasten-
ing is a mirage, not the less has it been true in all ages for human
beings of every creed which recognised a future, that those who have
fallen worn out by their march through the Desert have dreamed at
least of a River of Life, and thought they heard its murmurs as they
lay dying.

The change from the clinging to the present to the welcoming of the
future comes very soon, for the most part, after all hope of life is
extinguished, provided this be left in good degree to Nature, and not
insolently and cruelly forced upon those who are attacked by illness,
on the strength of that odious foreknowledge often imparted by
science, before the white fruit whose core is ashes, and which we call
death, has set beneath the pallid and drooping flower of sickness.
There is a singular sagacity very often shown in a patient's estimate of
his own vital force. His physician knows the state of his material
frame well enough, perhaps – that this or that organ is more or less
impaired or disintegrated; but the patient has a sense that he can hold
out so much longer, – sometimes that he must and will live for a
while, though by the logic of disease he ought to die without any
delay.

~

Errand
by Raymond Carver

Chekhov. On the evening of March 22, 1897, he went to dinner in
Moscow with his friend and confidant Alexei Suvorin. This Suvorin
was a very rich newspaper and book publisher, a reactionary, a self-
made man whose father was a private at the battle of Borodino. Like
Chekhov, he was the grandson of a serf. They had that in common:

each had peasant's blood in his veins. Otherwise, politically and temperamentally, they were miles apart. Nevertheless, Suvorin was one of Chekhov's few intimates, and Chekhov enjoyed his company.

Naturally, they went to the best restaurant in the city, a former town house called the Hermitage – a place where it could take hours, half the night even, to get through a ten-course meal that would, of course, include several wines, liqueurs, and coffee. Chekhov was impeccably dressed, as always – a dark suit and waistcoat, his usual pince-nez. He looked that night very much as he looks in the photographs taken of him during this period. He was relaxed, jovial. He shook hands with the maître d', and with a glance took in the large dining room. It was brilliantly illuminated by ornate chandeliers, the tables occupied by elegantly dressed men and women. Waiters came and went ceaselessly. He had just been seated across the table from Suvorin when suddenly, without warning, blood began gushing from his mouth. Suvorin and two waiters helped him to the gentlemen's room and tried to stanch the flow of blood with ice packs. Suvorin saw him back to his own hotel and had a bed prepared for Chekhov in one of the rooms of the suite. Later, after another hemorrhage, Chekhov allowed himself to be moved to a clinic that specialized in the treatment of tuberculosis and related respiratory infections. When Suvorin visited him there, Chekhov apologized for the 'scandal' at the restaurant three nights earlier but continued to insist there was nothing seriously wrong. 'He laughed and jested as usual,' Suvorin noted in his diary, 'while spitting blood into a large vessel.'

Maria Chekhov, his younger sister, visited Chekhov in the clinic during the last days of March. The weather was miserable; a sleet storm was in progress, and frozen heaps of snow lay everywhere. It was hard for her to wave down a carriage to take her to the hospital. By the time she arrived she was filled with dread and anxiety.

'Anton Pavlovich lay on his back,' Maria wrote in her *Memoirs*. 'He was not allowed to speak. After greeting him, I went over to the table to hide my emotions.' There, among bottles of champagne, jars of caviar, bouquets of flowers from well-wishers, she saw something that terrified her: a freehand drawing, obviously done by a specialist in these matters, of Chekhov's lungs. It was the kind of sketch a doctor often makes in order to show his patient what he thinks is taking place. The lungs were outlined in blue, but the upper parts were filled in with red. 'I realized they were diseased,' Maria wrote.

Leo Tolstoy was another visitor. The hospital staff were awed to find themselves in the presence of the country's greatest writer. The most famous man in Russia? Of course they had to let him in to see Chekhov, even though 'nonessential' visitors were forbidden. With much obsequiousness on the part of the nurses and resident doctors, the bearded, fierce-looking old man was shown into Chekhov's room. Despite his low opinion of Chekhov's abilities as a playwright (Tolstoy felt the plays were static and lacking in any moral vision. 'Where do your characters take you?' he once demanded of Chekhov. 'From the sofa to the junk room and back'), Tolstoy liked Chekhov's short stories. Furthermore, and quite simply, he loved the man. He told Gorky, 'What a beautiful, magnificent man: modest and quiet, like a girl. He even walks like a girl. He's simply wonderful.' And Tolstoy wrote in his journal (everyone kept a journal or a diary in those days), 'I am glad I love . . . Chekhov.'

Tolstoy removed his woollen scarf and bearskin coat, then lowered himself into a chair next to Chekhov's bed. Never mind that Chekhov was taking medication and not permitted to talk, much less carry on a conversation. He had to listen, amazedly, as the Count began to discourse on his theories of the immortality of the soul. Concerning that visit, Chekhov later wrote, 'Tolstoy assumes that all of us (humans and animals alike) will live on in a principle (such as reason or love) the essence and goals of which are a mystery to us. . . . I have no use for that kind of immortality. I don't understand it, and Lev Nikolayevich was astonished I didn't.'

Nevertheless, Chekhov was impressed with the solicitude shown by Tolstoy's visit. But, unlike Tolstoy, Chekhov didn't believe in an afterlife and never had. He didn't believe in anything that couldn't be apprehended by one or more of his five senses. And as far as his outlook on life and writing went, he once told someone that he lacked 'a political, religious, and philosophical world view. I change it every month, so I'll have to limit myself to the description of how my heroes love, marry, give birth, die, and how they speak.'

Earlier, before his t.b. was diagnosed, Chekhov had remarked, 'When a peasant has consumption, he says, "There's nothing I can do. I'll go off in the spring with the melting of the snows."' (Chekhov himself died in the summer, during a heat wave.) But once Chekhov's own tuberculosis was discovered he continually tried to minimize the seriousness of his condition. To all appearances, it was as if he felt, right up to the end, that he might be able to throw off the disease as he would a lingering catarrh. Well into his final days, he spoke with seeming conviction of the possibility of an improvement. In fact, in a letter written shortly before his end, he went so far as to tell his sister that he was 'getting fat' and felt much better now that he was in Badenweiler.

*

Badenweiler is a spa and resort city in the western area of the Black Forest, not far from Basel. The Vosges are visible from nearly any-where in the city, and in those days the air was pure and invigorating. Russians had been going there for years to soak in the hot mineral baths and promenade on the boulevards. In June, 1904, Chekhov went there to die.

Earlier that month, he'd made a difficult journey by train from Moscow to Berlin. He traveled with his wife, the actress Olga Knipper, a woman he'd met in 1898 during rehearsals for 'The Seagull.' Her contemporaries describe her as an excellent actress. She was talented, pretty, and almost ten years younger than the play-wright. Chekhov had been immediately attracted to her, but was slow to act on his feelings. As always, he preferred a flirtation to marriage. Finally, after a three-year courtship involving many separations, let-ters, and the inevitable misunderstandings, they were at last married, in a private ceremony in Moscow, on May 25, 1901. Chekhov was enormously happy. He called Olga his 'pony', and sometimes 'dog' or 'puppy'. He was also fond of addressing her as 'little turkey' or sim-ply as 'my joy'.

In Berlin, Chekhov consulted with a renowned specialist in pul-monary disorders, a Dr Karl Ewald. But, according to an eyewitness, after the doctor examined Chekhov he threw up his hands and left the room without a word. Chekhov was too far gone for help: this Dr Ewald was furious with himself for not being able to work miracles, and with Chekhov for being so ill.

A Russian journalist happened to visit the Chekhovs at their hotel and sent back this dispatch to his editor: 'Chekhov's days are num-bered. He seems mortally ill, is terribly thin, coughs all the time, gasps for breath at the slightest movement, and is running a high tempera-ture.' This same journalist saw the Chekhovs off at Potsdam Station when they boarded their train for Badenweiler. According to his account, 'Chekhov had trouble making his way up the small staircase at the station. He had to sit down for several minutes to catch his breath.' In fact, it was painful for Chekhov to move: his legs ached continually and his insides hurt. The disease had attacked his intestines and spinal cord. At this point he had less than a month to live. When Chekhov spoke of his condition now, it was, according to Olga, 'with an almost reckless indifference.'

Dr Schwöhrer was one of the many Badenweiler physicians who earned a good living by treating the well-to-do who came to the spa seeking relief from various maladies. Some of his patients were ill and infirm, others simply old and hypochondriacal. But Chekhov's was a special case: he was clearly beyond help and in his last days. He was also very famous. Even Dr Schwöhrer knew his name: he'd read some of Chekhov's stories in a German magazine. When he examined the writer early in June, he voiced his appreciation of Chekhov's art but kept his medical opinions to himself. Instead, he prescribed a diet of cocoa, oatmeal drenched in butter, and strawberry tea. This last was supposed to help Chekhov sleep at night.

On June 13, less than three weeks before he died, Chekhov wrote a letter to his mother in which he told her his health was on the mend. In it he said, 'It's likely that I'll be completely cured in a week.' Who knows why he said this? What could he have been thinking? He was a doctor himself, and he knew better. He was dying, it was as simple and as unavoidable as that. Nevertheless, he sat out on the balcony of his hotel room and read railway timetables. He asked for information on sailings of boats bound for Odessa from Marseilles. But he *knew*. At this stage he had to have known. Yet in one of the last letters he ever wrote he told his sister he was growing stronger by the day.

He no longer had any appetite for literary work, and hadn't for a long time. In fact, he had very nearly failed to complete *The Cherry Orchard* the year before. Writing that play was the hardest thing he'd ever done in his life. Toward the end, he was able to manage only six or seven lines a day. 'I've started losing heart,' he wrote Olga. 'I feel I'm finished as a writer, and every sentence strikes me as worthless and of no use whatever.' But he didn't stop. He finished his play in October, 1903. It was the last thing he ever wrote, except for letters and a few entries in his notebook.

A little after midnight on July 2, 1904, Olga sent someone to fetch Dr Schwöhrer. It was an emergency: Chekhov was delirious. Two young Russians on holiday happened to have the adjacent room, and Olga hurried next door to explain what was happening. One of the youths was in his bed asleep, but the other was still awake, smoking and reading. He left the hotel at a run to find Dr Schwöhrer. 'I can still hear the sound of the gravel under his shoes in the silence of that stifling July night,' Olga wrote later on in her memoirs. Chekhov was hallucinating, talking about sailors, and there were snatches of something about the Japanese. 'You don't put ice on an empty stomach,' he said when she tried to place an ice pack on his chest.

Dr Schwöhrer arrived and unpacked his bag, all the while keeping his gaze fastened on Chekhov, who lay gasping in the bed. The sick man's pupils were dilated and his temples glistened with sweat. Dr Schwöhrer's face didn't register anything. He was not an emotional man, but he knew Chekhov's end was near. Still, he was a doctor, sworn to do his utmost, and Chekhov held on to life, however tenuously. Dr Schwöhrer prepared a hypodermic and administered an injection of camphor, something that was supposed to speed up the heart. But the injection didn't help – nothing, of course, could have helped. Nevertheless, the doctor made known to Olga his intention of sending for oxygen. Suddenly, Chekhov roused himself, became lucid, and said quietly, 'What's the use? Before it arrives I'll be a corpse.'

Dr Schwöhrer pulled on his big moustache and stared at Chekhov. The writer's cheeks were sunken and gray, his complexion waxen; his breath was raspy. Dr Schwöhrer knew the time could be reckoned in minutes. Without a word, without conferring with Olga, he went over to an alcove where there was a telephone on the wall. He read the instructions for using the device. If he activated it by holding his finger on a button and turning a handle on the side of the phone, he could reach the lower regions of the hotel – the kitchen. He picked up the receiver, held it to his ear, and did as the instructions told him. When someone finally answered, Dr Schwöhrer ordered a bottle of the hotel's best champagne. 'How many glasses?' he was asked. 'Three glasses!' the doctor shouted into the mouthpiece. 'And hurry, do you hear?' It was one of those rare moments of inspiration that can easily enough be overlooked later on, because the action is so entirely appropriate it seems inevitable.

The champagne was brought to the door by a tired-looking young man whose blond hair was standing up. The trousers of his uniform were wrinkled, the creases gone, and in his haste he'd missed a loop while buttoning his jacket. His appearance was that of someone who'd been resting (slumped in a chair, say, dozing a little), when off in the distance the phone had clamored in the early-morning hours – great God in Heaven! – and the next thing he knew he was being

241

shaken awake by a superior and told to deliver a bottle of Moët to Room 211. 'And hurry, do you hear?'

*

The young man entered the room carrying a silver ice bucket with the champagne in it and a silver tray with three cut-crystal glasses. He found a place on the table for the bucket and glasses, all the while craning his neck, trying to see into the other room, where someone panted ferociously for breath. It was a dreadful, harrowing sound, and the young man lowered his chin into his collar and turned away as the ratchety breathing worsened. Forgetting himself, he stared out the open window toward the darkened city. Then this big imposing man with a thick moustache pressed some coins into his hand – a large tip, by the feel of it – and suddenly the young man saw the door open. He took some steps and found himself on the landing, where he opened his hand and looked at the coins in amazement.

Methodically, the way he did everything, the doctor went about the business of working the cork out of the bottle. He did it in such a way as to minimize, as much as possible, the festive explosion. He poured three glasses and, out of habit, pushed the cork back into the neck of the bottle. He then took the glasses of champagne over to the bed. Olga momentarily released her grip on Chekhov's hand – a hand, she said later, that burned her fingers. She arranged another pillow behind his head. Then she put the cool glass of champagne against Chekhov's palm and made sure his fingers closed around the stem. They exchanged looks – Chekhov, Olga, Dr Schwöhrer. They didn't touch glasses. There was no toast. What on earth was there to drink to? To death? Chekhov summoned his remaining strength and said, 'It's been so long since I've had champagne.' He brought the glass to his lips and drank. In a minute or two Olga took the empty glass from his hand and set it on the nightstand. Then Chekhov turned onto his side. He closed his eyes and sighed. A minute later, his breathing stopped.

Dr Schwöhrer picked up Chekhov's hand from the bedsheet. He held his fingers to Chekhov's wrist and drew a gold watch from his vest pocket, opening the lid of the watch as he did so. The second hand on the watch moved slowly, very slowly. He let it move around the face of the watch three times while he waited for signs of a pulse. It was three o'clock in the morning and still sultry in the room. Badenweiler was in the grip of its worst heat wave in years. All the windows in both rooms stood open, but there was no sign of a breeze. A large, black-winged moth flew through a window and banged wildly against the electric lamp. Dr Schwöhrer let go of Chekhov's wrist. 'It's over,' he said. He closed the lid of his watch and returned it to his vest pocket.

At once Olga dried her eyes and set about composing herself. She thanked the doctor for coming. He asked if she wanted some medication – laudanum, perhaps, or a few drops of valerian. She shook her head. She did have one request, though: before the authorities were notified and the newspapers found out, before the time came when Chekhov was no longer in her keeping, she wanted to be alone with him for a while. Could the doctor help with this? Could he withhold, for a while anyway, news of what had just occurred?

Dr Schwöhrer stroked his moustache with the back of a finger. Why not? After all, what difference would it make to anyone whether this matter became known now or a few hours from now? The only detail that remained was to fill out a death certificate, and this could be done at his office later on in the morning, after he'd slept a few hours. Dr Schwöhrer nodded his agreement and prepared to leave. He murmured a few words of condolence. Olga inclined her head. 'An honor,' Dr Schwöhrer said. He picked up his bag and left the room and, for that matter, history.

It was at this moment that the cork popped out of the champagne bottle; foam spilled down onto the table. Olga went back to Chekhov's bedside. She sat on a footstool, holding his hand, from time to time stroking his face. 'There were no human voices, no everyday sounds,' she wrote. 'There was only beauty, peace, and the grandeur of death.'

*

She stayed with Chekhov until daybreak, when thrushes began to call from the garden below. Then came the sound of tables and chairs being moved about down there. Before long, voices carried up to her. It was then a knock sounded at the door. Of course she thought it must be an official of some sort – the medical examiner, say, or someone from the police who had questions to ask and forms for her to fill out, or maybe, just maybe, it could be Dr Schwöhrer returning with a mortician to render assistance in embalming and transporting Chekhov's remains back to Russia.

243

But, instead, it was the same blond young man who'd brought the champagne a few hours earlier. This time, however, his uniform trousers were neatly pressed, with stiff creases in front, and every button on his snug green jacket was fastened. He seemed quite another person. Not only was he wide awake but his plump cheeks were smooth-shaven, his hair was in place, and he appeared anxious to please. He was holding a porcelain vase with three long-stemmed yellow roses. He presented these to Olga with a smart click of his heels. She stepped back and let him into the room. He was there, he said, to collect the glasses, ice bucket, and tray, yes. But he also wanted to say that, because of the extreme heat, breakfast would be served in the garden this morning. He hoped this weather wasn't too bothersome; he apologized for it.

The woman seemed distracted. While he talked, she turned her eyes away and looked down at something in the carpet. She crossed her arms and held her elbows. Meanwhile, still holding his vase, waiting for a sign, the young man took in the details of the room. Bright sunlight flooded through the open windows. The room was tidy and seemed undisturbed, almost untouched. No garments were flung over chairs, no shoes, stockings, braces, or stays were in evidence, no open suitcases. In short, there was no clutter, nothing but the usual heavy pieces of hotel-room furniture. Then, because the woman was still looking down, he looked down, too, and at once spied a cork near the toe of his shoe. The woman did not see it – she was looking somewhere else. The young man wanted to bend over and pick up the cork, but he was still holding the roses and was afraid of seeming to intrude even more by drawing any further attention to himself. Reluctantly, he left the cork where it was and raised his eyes. Everything was in order except for the uncorked, half-empty bottle of champagne that stood alongside two crystal glasses over on the little table. He cast his gaze about once more. Through an open door he saw that the third glass was in the bedroom, on the nightstand. But someone still occupied the bed! He couldn't see a face, but the figure under the covers lay perfectly motionless and quiet. He noted the figure and looked elsewhere. Then, for a reason he couldn't understand, a feeling of uneasiness took hold of him. He cleared his throat and moved his weight to the other leg. The woman still didn't look up or break her silence. The young man felt his cheeks grow warm. It occurred to him, quite without his having thought it through, that he should perhaps suggest an alternative to breakfast in the garden. He coughed, hoping to focus the woman's attention, but she didn't look at him. The distinguished foreign guests could, he said, take breakfast in their rooms this morning if they wished. The young man (his name hasn't survived, and it's likely he perished in the Great War) said he would be happy to bring up a tray. Two trays, he added, glancing uncertainly once again in the direction of the bedroom.

He fell silent and ran a finger around the inside of his collar. He didn't understand. He wasn't even sure the woman had been listening. He didn't know what else to do now; he was still holding the vase. The sweet odor of the roses filled his nostrils and inexplicably caused a pang of regret. The entire time he'd been waiting, the woman had apparently been lost in thought. It was as if all the while he'd been standing there, talking, shifting his weight, holding his flowers, she had been someplace else, somewhere far from Badenweiler. But now she came back to herself, and her face assumed another expression. She raised her eyes, looked at him, and then shook her head. She seemed to be struggling to understand what on earth this young man could be doing there in the room holding a vase with three yellow roses. Flowers? She hadn't ordered flowers.

The moment passed. She went over to her handbag and scooped up some coins. She drew out a number of banknotes as well. The young man touched his lips with his tongue; another large tip was forthcoming, but for what? What did she want him to do? He'd never before waited on such guests. He cleared his throat once more.

No breakfast, the woman said. Not yet, at any rate. Breakfast wasn't the important thing this morning. She required something else. She needed him to go out and bring back a mortician. Did he understand her? Herr Chekhov was dead, you see. *Comprenez-vous?* Young man? Anton Chekhov was dead. Now listen carefully to me, she said. She wanted him to go downstairs and ask someone at the front desk where he could go to find the most respected mortician in the city. Someone reliable, who took great pains in his work and whose manner was appropriately reserved. A mortician, in short, worthy of a great artist. Here, she said, and pressed the money on him. Tell them downstairs that I have specifically requested you to perform this duty for me. Are you listening? Do you understand what I'm saying to you?

The young man grappled to take in what she was saying. He chose not to look again in the direction of the other room. He had sensed that something was not right. He became aware of his heart beating

245

rapidly under his jacket, and he felt perspiration break out on his forehead. He didn't know where he should turn his eyes. He wanted to put the vase down.

Please do this for me, the woman said. I'll remember you with gratitude. Tell them downstairs that I insist. Say that. But don't call any unnecessary attention to yourself or to the situation. Just say that this is necessary, that I request it – and that's all. Do you hear me? Nod if you understand. Above all, don't raise an alarm. Everything else, all the rest, the commotion – that'll come soon enough. The worst is over. Do we understand each other?

The young man's face had grown pale. He stood rigid, clasping the vase. He managed to nod his head.

After securing permission to leave the hotel he was to proceed quietly and resolutely, though without any unbecoming haste, to the mortician's. He was to behave exactly as if he were engaged on a very important errand, nothing more. He *was* engaged on an important errand, she said. And if it would help keep his movements purposeful he should imagine himself as someone moving down the busy sidewalk carrying in his arms a porcelain vase of roses that he had to deliver to an important man. (She spoke quietly, almost confidentially, as if to a relative or a friend.) He could even tell himself that the man he was going to see was expecting him, was perhaps impatient for him to arrive with his flowers. Nevertheless, the young man was not to become excited and run, or otherwise break his stride. Remember the vase he was carrying! He was to walk briskly, comporting himself at all times in as dignified a manner as possible. He should keep walking until he came to the mortician's house and stood before the door. He would then raise the brass knocker and let it fall, once, twice, three times. In a minute the mortician himself would answer.

This mortician would be in his forties, no doubt, or maybe early fifties – bald, solidly built, wearing steel-frame spectacles set very low on his nose. He would be modest, unassuming, a man who would ask only the most direct and necessary questions. An apron. Probably he would be wearing an apron. He might even be wiping his hands on a dark towel while he listened to what was being said. There'd be a faint whiff of formaldehyde on his clothes. But it was all right, and the young man shouldn't worry. He was nearly a grown-up now and shouldn't be frightened or repelled by any of this. The mortician would hear him out. He was a man of restraint and bearing, this mortician, someone who could help allay people's fears in this situation, not increase them. Long ago he'd acquainted himself with death in all its various guises and forms; death held no surprises for him any longer, no hidden secrets. It was this man whose services were required this morning.

The mortician takes the vase of roses. Only once while the young man is speaking does the mortician betray the least flicker of interest, or indicate that he's heard anything out of the ordinary. But the one time the young man mentions the name of the deceased, the mortician's eyebrows rise just a little. Chekhov, you say? Just a minute, and I'll be with you.

Do you understand what I'm saying, Olga said to the young man. Leave the glasses. Don't worry about them. Forget about crystal wineglasses and such. Leave the room as it is. Everything is ready now. We're ready. Will you go?

But at that moment the young man was thinking of the cork still resting near the toe of his shoe. To retrieve it he would have to bend over, still gripping the vase. He would do this. He leaned over. Without looking down, he reached out and closed it into his hand.

∼

As I lay dying
from An Almanac of Words at Play *by Willard Espy*

The last words of James Croll, the teetotalling Scots physicist, were, 'I'll take a wee drop o' that. I don't think there's much fear o' me learning to drink now.'

Dr Croll's farewell fittingly rounded off his life; and I treasure several other deathbed statements for the same reason. Thus Dr Joseph Green, a surgeon, said to his physician, 'Congestion.' He then took his own pulse, murmured, 'Stopped,' and died. As professional to the last was the Swiss physiologist Albrecht, who checked his pulse and said, 'Now I am dying. The artery ceases to beat.'

Dominique Bonhours, the grammarian, commented, 'I am about to – or I am going to – die; either expression is used.'

Wilhelm Hegel, the philosopher, also stayed in character. 'Only one man understood me,' he sighed . . . 'and he didn't understand me.'

Less admirable, but equally apt, were the last words of Dylan Thomas: 'I've had eighteen straight whiskies. I think that is the record.'

Asked whether he would prefer to have his niece or his nurse spend the night by his bedside, the playwright Sir Henry Arthur Jones replied: 'The prettier. Now fight for it!'

I like Arthur Roth's list of apocryphal last words:

A judge: 'I have no precedent for this.'

A believer in reincarnation: 'Intermission time already?'

A lawyer: 'My final brief.'

A mortician: 'I'm off on a busman's holiday.'

A childless railroad conductor: 'End of the line.'

A philosopher: 'No cogito, ergo no sum.'

An atheist: 'I was kidding all along.'

A student: 'I fail.'

A bridge player: 'I pass.'

A gossip: 'I'm just dying to tell someone.'

An elevator operator: 'Going up?'

My wife: 'I'm not ready yet, give me another five minutes.'

~

Why me?

from Written in Sickness *by Damon Runyon*

When physical calamity befalls, the toughest thing for the victim to overcome is the feeling of resentment that it should have happened to him.

'Why me?' he keeps asking himself, dazedly. 'Of all the millions of people around, why me?'

It becomes like a pulse beat – 'Why me? Why me? Why me?'

Sometimes he reviews his whole life step by step to see if he can put his finger on some circumstance in which he may have been at such grievous fault as to merit disaster.

Did he commit some black sin somewhere back down the years? Did he betray the sacred trust of some fellow human being? Is he being punished for some special wrongdoing? 'Why me?'

He wakes suddenly at night from a sound sleep to consciousness of his affliction and to the clock-like ticking in his brain – 'Why me? Why me? Why me?'

He reflects, 'Why not that stinker Smith? Why not that louse Jones? Why not that bum Brown? Why me? Why me? Why me?'

Was he guilty of carelessness or error in judgment? 'Why me? Why? Why? Why?'

It is a question that has been asked by afflicted mortals through the ages. It is being asked more than ever just now as the maimed men come back from war broken in body and spirit and completely bewildered, asking 'Why me?'

I do not have the answer, of course. Not for myself nor for anyone else. I, too, am just a poor mugg groping in the dark, though sometimes I think of the words of young Elihu reproving Job and his three pals: 'Look into the heavens, and see; and behold the clouds which are higher than thou.'

The Book of Job may have been an attempt to solve the problem why the righteous suffer and to point out that such suffering is often permitted as a test of faith and a means of grace. They sure put old Job over the hurdles as an illustration.

He was a character who lived in the land of Uz, 'way back in the times recorded in the Old Testament. He had more money than most folks have hay and he was also of great piety. He stood good with the Lord, who took occasion to comment favourably on Job one day to Satan, who had appeared before Him.

'There is no one like Job,' remarked the Lord to Satan. 'He is a perfect and upright man. He fears God and eschews evil.'

'Well, why not?' said Satan. 'You have fixed him up so he is sitting pretty in every way. But you just let a spell of bad luck hit him and see what happens. He will curse you to your face.'

'You think so?' said the Lord. 'All right, I will put all his belongings in your power to do with as you please. Only don't touch Job himself.'

Not long afterwards, the Sabeans copped all of Job's oxen and asses and killed his servants and his sheep were burned up and the Chaldeans grabbed his camels and slaughtered more of his servants and a big wind blew down a house and destroyed his sons.

But so far from getting sore at the Lord as Satan had figured would happen after these little incidents, Job rent his mantle and shaved his head and fell down upon the ground and worshipped and said:

'Naked I came out of my mother's womb, and naked shall I return thither; the Lord gave, and the Lord hath taken away; blessed be the name of the Lord.'

Now had I been Satan I would have given Job up then and there but lo, and behold, the next time the Lord held a meeting Satan again appeared and when the Lord started boosting Job for holding fast to his integrity, Satan sniffed disdainfully and said:

'Skin for skin, yea, all that a man has he will give for his life, but just you touch his bone and his flesh and see what your Mr Job does.'

'All right,' the Lord said, 'I will put him in your hands, only save his life.'

Then Satan smote poor Job with boils from the soles of his feet to the crown of his head. I reckon that was the worst case of boils anyone ever heard of, and Job's wife remarked:

'Do you still retain your integrity? Curse God, and die.'

'Woman,' Job said, 'you are a fool. Shall we receive good at the hands of God and not evil?'

But when those pals of Job's, Eliphaz, Bildad and Zophar, came to see him he let out quite a beef to them and in fact cursed the day he was born. In the end, however, after listening to discourses from his pals of a length that must have made him as tired as the boils, Job humbly confessed that God is omnipotent and omnipresent and repented his former utterances and demeanour 'in dust and ashes' and the Lord made him more prosperous than ever before.

'Why me?'

'*Therefore have I uttered that I understood not; things too wonderful for me, which I knew not.*'

Biographical Notes

Asher, Richard (1912–1969)
Educated at Lancing and the London Hospital, he graduated in 1934. In 1942 he was appointed as physician to the Central Middlesex Hospital, and ten years later he was elected a Fellow of the Royal College of Physicians of London.

He was an eccentric.

Barbirolli, Sir John (1899–1970)
Born in London and christened Giovanni Battista, Barbirolli studied the cello, but became famous as the conductor of the Hallé Orchestra in Manchester, from 1943 to 1968. He married Evelyn Rothwell, an oboist, in 1939.

He received many honours and medals, was knighted in 1949 and became Companion of Honour in 1969.

A cricket fan.

Bernard, Jeffrey (1932–   )
A journalist with an 'unswerving dedication to booze, fags, the horses, unsuitable women, overspending and the law courts', who most weeks for several years 'managed to get himself off the bar stool to write the "Low Life" column' for the *Spectator* magazine.

According to the playwright John Osborne, Jeffrey Bernard belongs to the band of heavy drinkers 'not to be confused with alcoholics or modern drug-addicts', though drinking has been responsible, directly or indirectly, for most of his meetings with the medical profession.

Blum, Alan (dates unknown)
Associate Professor in the Department of Family Medicine at Baylor College of Medicine in Houston, Texas.

Bosman, Herman Charles (1905–1951)
Born in a village near Cape Town, this South African writer soon

251

moved with his family to Johannesburg. As a student at Witwatersand University he wrote both prose and poetry, but as a youth he had become acquainted with the work of American humorists and short story writers, and it is as a short story writer that he is remembered.

After serving a four-year prison sentence for murdering a step-brother, he spent almost a decade in Europe.

Shortly after the Second World War, Bosman returned to South Africa.

He died of a stroke.

Brain, Lord Walter Russell (1895–1966)
Doctor of Medicine, Fellow of the Royal College of Physicians. A distinguished neurologist, consultant to the Maida Vale Hospital, the London Hospital and Moorfields Eye Hospital.

President of the Royal College of Physicians, 1950–1957. Knighted, 1952; baronet, 1959; baron 1962.

Became a Quaker.

Caldwell, Vice Admiral Sir Dick (1909–   )
Born in Edinburgh, where he qualified as a doctor. M.D. 1950; F.R.C.P. (Edinburgh) 1962; F.R.C.P. (London) 1967. C.B. in 1965; Knighted (KBE) 1969.

Medical Director-General of the Royal Navy 1966–1969; Executive Director, Medical Council on Alcoholism, 1970–1979.

Carver, Raymond (1939–1988)
Born in Clatskanie, Oregon, he lived most of his life in Port Angeles, in the state of Washington.

He was a Guggenheim Fellow in 1979, and in 1983 he received the Mildred and Harold Strauss Living Award.

In 1988 he was elected to the American Academy and Institute of Arts and Letters and was awarded a Doctorate of Letters from Hartford University.

Celsus, Aulus Cornelius (25BC–AD50)
A learned Roman who wrote treatises on rhetoric, history, jurisprudence, agriculture and the military arts as well as on medicine.

Although he 'was not a money-making physician' and 'not a Hospital Physician', he held an influential position in the history of medicine.

His '*De Medicina*' was published in AD30.

Chekhov, Anton Pavlovich (1860–1904)

The son of a small shopkeeper and the grandson of a serf, after finishing school in his native town of Taganrog, Chekhov moved to Moscow, whither his father had fled earlier to escape a debtor's prison. With the aid of a scholarship, he entered the university there to study medicine.

To help pay his way through medical school, he began to write short stories, and it is as a short story writer – arguably the greatest ever – that he is best known.

However, he was also a distinguished playright – of, among others, *The Three Sisters* and *The Cherry Orchard* – and in 1901 he married Olga Knipper, an actress at the Moscow Art Theatre.

Chekhov suffered from tuberculosis for much of his life, but he did not succumb to the disease until 21 years after the first symptoms appeared, before he graduated in medicine.

He died in the Black Forest with a glass of champagne in his hand and his coffin was transported to Moscow in a green van marked 'For Oysters'. That story is retold, with embellishments, by Raymond Carver in his short story 'Errand'.

Dalrymple, Theodore (1953–   )

This is the pen name of a 'psychiatrist and prison doctor in an inner city slum.' Having worked in several countries of the so called Third World, he is convinced that 'the poverty of spirit to be found in an English slun is the worst to be found anywhere'.

If Symptoms Persist, a collection of pieces from his column of that name in the *Spectator*, is now available in book form.

Dickens, Charles (1812–1870)

One of the world's greatest novelists, his childhood experiences were similar to those depicted in *David Copperfield*.

His best-known works are *A Christmas Carol*, *Oliver Twist* and *A Tale of Two Cities*.

Dickens popularized cheap serial publication, as in *Sketches by Boz* and the *Pickwick Papers*

Espy, Willard (1910–   )

Reared in Oysterville in the State of Washington, Willard Espy became a public relations counsel in New York City.

He 'has long accompanied his more serious endeavours with a delight in the frivolity of language'.

Gopaleen, Myles na (1911–1966)
Under this pseudonym, Brian O'Nolan wrote a column, the 'Cruiskeen Lawn', in the *Irish Times* for 25 years. His other pseudonym was 'Flann O'Brien'.

The Keats and Chapman anecdotes were among the best.

Harris, Walter (1647–1732)
Educated at Oxford and qualifying as a doctor at Bourges in France, he became a physician to King William III.

He wrote a treatise on diseases of childhood.

Hartston, William (1947–   )
An international Chess Master and former British champion.

The idea for writing *Drunken Goldfish and Other Irrelevant Scientific Research* came to him whilst browsing in the university library in Cambridge, 'when I came across a research paper about the effect of alcohol on the ability of goldfish to remember things.'

Although admitting that 'on the one hand I have great admiration and love of research for its own sake', he 'cannot help feeling . . . that there might be too much research going on, and much of that is taken far too seriously.'

Hippocrates, (born 460BC)
Known as the 'Father of Medicine', Hippocrates was born on the island of Cos. He was a member of the 'sect' known as the Asclepiadae, son of Asclepios, who is mentioned in the *Iliad* as a physician.

The 'Hippocratic Oath', in which doctors undertake not to divulge confidential information about their patients, is named after him.

His age at the time of his death has been variously estimated at between 85 and 110!

Holmes, Oliver Wendell (1809–1894)
Physician, poet and humorist. Born in Cambridge, Massachusetts, he was professor of anatomy and physiology in Harvard University from 1847 to 1882.

The Professor at the Breakfast Table was published in 1860.

Horder, Lord Thomas Jeeves (1871–1955)
Educated at St Bartholomew's Hospital in London, he became a consultant physician there. He had an extensive private practice, which included the British royal family.

He travelled widely, wrote much and lectured in many parts of the world.

Hughes, J. Trevor (1928–   )
Dr Hughes is a distinguished neuropathologist in Oxford, where he qualified as a doctor in 1951. He has written many papers on his own specialist subject and on medical history.

Hugo, Victor (1802–1885)
The most prolific and versatile of nineteenth-century French authors, he wrote costume dramas, verse, political and other journalism, and several novels.

Notre Dame de Paris was published in 1885.

Huxley, Thomas (1825–1895)
English biologist and philosopher who graduated in medicine from Charing Cross Hospital in London in 1845. After leaving service with the Royal Navy in 1854, he became a lecturer in natural history and was one of the earliest supporters of Charles Darwin's *The Origin of Species*.

Elected Fellow of the Royal Society (FRS) in 1851.

Grandfather of Julian and Aldous Huxley.

James I, King (1566–1625)
King of Great Britain and Ireland, and James VI of Scotland, he was the son of Mary Queen of Scots by her second husband Henry Stewart, Lord Darnley, who was murdered.

His 'Counter–Blaste to Tobacco' was published in 1604.

Jones, Griff Rhys (1953–   )
The slimmer member of the comedy duo of Smith and Jones.

Educated at Emanuel College, Cambridge, he is an actor, writer and producer.

Karinthy, Frigyes (1887–1938)
Born in Budapest, Karinthy spent most of his life there.

He was one of the outstanding writers of the first half of the twentieth century, writing poems and plays as well as short stories, humorous sketches and numerous newspaper articles.

In 1936 a brain tumour was diagnosed and it was removed by the pioneering Swedish neurosurgeon, Professor Herbert Olivecrona in Stockholm. Karinthy made a good recovery from the surgery, which was performed under local anaesthesia but he died one-and-a-half years later, apparently from a stroke while bending down to tie his shoelaces.

Keats, John (1795–1821)
An English poet who has been ranked among the greatest of the Romantic era.

He studied medicine at Guy's Hospital in London but never practised it.

He died of tuberculosis at the age of 26.

Lancet
A registered newspaper.

In England Now – 50 Years of Peripatetic Correspondence was published in 1989.

Leacock, Stephen (1869–1944)
Born in Britain but brought up and educated in Canada, he became Professor of Political Economy to the McGill University in Montreal. He wrote several books on this subject but it is as a humorous writer that he is remembered.

According to the old *Morning Post*, he was 'the subtlest of all transatlantic humorists and might almost be defined as the discoverer of a method of combining English and American humour'.

Lear, Edward (1812–1888)
Artist and traveller – to Italy, Albania, Corsica, Egypt, the Holy Land, Greece and India – he was best known as a writer and illustrator of nonsense verse and limericks.

He suffered from epilepsy for most of his life and he died in San Remo, Italy.

Le Fanu, James (1950–   )
A member of the Royal College of Physicians, he is a general practitioner in London.

He is medical correspondent of *The Sunday Telegraph*.

L'Etang, Hugh (1917–)
Educated at Oxford University, St Bartholomew's Hospital in London and Harvard University.

Editor of *The Practitioner* 1973–1982, and author of *Pathology of Leadership* (1969) and *Fit to Lead* (1980).

Maugham, W. Somerset (1874–1965)
Son of a solicitor for the British Embassy in Paris after the Franco-Prussian War, Somerset Maugham had lost both his parents by the time he was ten.

After attending King's School in Canterbury, he studied medicine at St Thomas's Hospital in London but, after qualification, he very soon turned to writing as his chosen profession. He is admired particularly as 'a consummate master of the short story'.

Of Human Bondage, he wrote, 'is not an autobiography but an autobiographical novel; fact and fiction are inextricably mingled.'

Milligan, Spike (1919–)
Born in India, Milligan graduated to Lewisham Polytechnic after attending a series of Roman Catholic schools in India and England.

He first appeared on stage at the age of eight, in a nativity play at his convent school in Poona, but he began his career in show business as a band musician. He was one of the main figures in and behind the famous *Goon Show*.

This manic-depressive comic has produced many books, notably war memoirs and books of verse, much of the latter for children.

Narayan, R.K. (1906–)
Born in Madras, India, he is known particularly as the creator of the fictional territory of Malgudi.

He has written several collections of short stories, travel books and essays, and has retold the classical legends of *The Ramayana* and *The Mahabharata*.

In 1980 he was awarded the A.C. Benson Medal by the Royal Society of Literature and in 1982 he was made an Honorary Member of the American Academy and Institute of Arts and Letters.

Nightingale, Florence (1820–1910)
An English nurse, she is generally regarded as the originator and founder of modern nursing. When she began her nursing career, in

1844, nursing was considered disreputable and many nurses were 'drunken prostitutes'. In 1854 she sailed for the Crimea, during the war with Russia, and working day and night, she brought order out of chaos.

The Nightingale training school for nurses at St Thomas's Hospital in London was opened in 1860.

She received the Order of Merit (OM) in 1907.

Paget, Sir James (1814–1899)
British surgeon, physiologist and pathologist who, with his friend Rudolf Virchow, is regarded as the co-founder of the science of pathology.

Elected Fellow of the Royal Society (FRS) in 1851, President of the Royal College of Surgeons in 1875, and Vice-Chancellor of London University in 1883.

Pasteur, Louis (1822–1895)
One of the exceptionally few great scientific geniuses, Pasteur was a French chemist who, after early researches in crystallography, turned his attention to the causation and control of silk-worm disease, anthrax and hydrophobia (rabies). Following experiments on rabid dogs, he produced an effective inoculation against hydrophobia, and later an anti-diphtheritic serum.

Pepys, Samuel (1633–1703)
Educated at St Paul's School in London and Magdalene College, Cambridge, he kept company with many famous scientists such as Isaac Newton and Robert Boyle.

'Learned in many things, skilled in music', he is remembered for his diary, which opened on 1 January 1660 and closed on 31 May 1669.

Perelman, S.J. (1904–1979)
Born in New York, Perelman attended Brown University and began his professional career as a writer for *Judge* and *College Humour*. Subsequently, as a scenario writer, he worked for the Marx Brothers, and several of his plays were produced on Broadway. He was a member of the National Institute of Arts and Letters.

He described himself as 'button-cute, rapier-keen, wafer-thin and pauper-poor'.

Pythagoras (Active c. 530BC)
Best known for his contributions to geometry, Pythagoras was a Greek philosopher, who gave his name to an order of scientific and religious thinkers.

The 'Mathematicians' had a special interest in mathematical and musical theory.

Randolph, Vance (dates unknown)
This author first visited the Ozark region of Missouri and Arkansas in 1899 and he spent most of his life there after 1920. The Ozark 'hill-billies', who have been described as 'the most superstitious people in America' are thought to come from British stock. Although many Ozarkers boast of Cherokee blood, and some of their superstitions may be of American Indian origin, Vance Randolph believed that 'most of the hillman's folk beliefs came with his ancestors from England or Scotland'. His paper 'Ozark superstitions' was published in the *Journal of American Folklore* in 1933.

Richards, Peter (1936–   )
Master of Arts (MA), Doctor of Medicine (MD), Doctor of Philosophy (PhD) and Fellow of the Royal College of Physicians (FRCP).

Pro-Rector (Medicine) of Imperial College and Dean and Professor of Medicine at St Mary's Hospital Medical School in the University of London.

Peter Richards has written extensively on medical education and student selection.

Rufus of Ephesus (98–117)
His *Dietetics*, in five books, was much studied and quoted.

He wrote a treatise on anatomy and several contributions on the pulse.

Apparently he knew how to control haemorrhage – by compression, styptics, cautery and ligature.

Runyon, Damon (1884–1946)
At the age of fourteen, he enlisted in the Spanish–American War.

He began his writing career as a journalist, but was known particularly for his short stories of sleazy New York life. He was the creator of such infamous characters as Harry the Horse, Izzy Cheesecake and the Lemon Drop Kid.

During his final illness, he wrote a group of eight short stories under the title *'Written in Sickness'*, a record of human courage in the face of death.

Shaw, George Bernard (1856–1950)
Born in Dublin, he moved to England twenty years later.

Although known especially as a playwright, he consciously created his own image as 'showman, satirist, controversialist, critic, pundit, wit, intellectual buffoon and dramatist'.

The term 'Shavian' has entered the English language as a term which embraces all those qualities.

Smith, Mel (1952–   )
The plumper member of the Smith and Jones duo.

Educated at New College, Oxford, he is an actor, writer and director.

Snow, Lord C.P. (1905–1980)
Educated at University College, Leicester and Christ's College, Cambridge, he was a scientist and writer.

At one time he was parliamentary secretary to the Minister of Technology and is best known for his book *The Two Cultures*. He was also a novelist, reviewer and public figure.

Commander of the Order of the British Empire (CBE) in 1943, he was knighted (KBE) in 1957 and created a baron (Life Peer) in 1964.

He also received honorary doctorates and other awards from American, Canadian, English, Scottish and Soviet universities, colleges and academies.

Solzhenitsyn, Aleksandr (1918–   )
After graduating in mathematics at Rostov University and taking a correspondence course in literature, he was called up for the army, in which he served with some distinction. However, early in 1945 he was arrested and charged with making derogatory remarks about Stalin.

Released in 1953 on Stalin's death, he was in further trouble with the Soviet authorities in 1969 and, although he was awarded a Nobel Prize for Literature in 1970, he was deported in 1974.

After living for several years in Vermont USA, Solzhenitsyn returned home when Soviet citizenship was restored in 1990, and in the same year he was awarded the Russian State Literature Prize.

Speight, Johnny (1920–   )
Writer and creator of the working-class racist bigot Alf Garnett, who featured in many television series of *Till Death Do Us Part* (which won the Screenwriters' Guild Award in 1966, 1967 and 1968) and of *In Sickness and in Health*.

Thomas, Lewis (1913–   )
Son of a general practitioner in Flushing, Long Island (New York), Lewis Thomas has written several collections of essays in popular science, including *The Lives of a Cell, The Medusa and the Snail*, and *The Youngest Science*.

A member of the National Academy of Sciences, he is Chancellor of the Memorial Sloan–Kettering Centre in New York City.

Timbs, John (1801–1875)
Apprentice to a printer and druggist, he was an author but was not medically qualified.

He edited *Mirror of Literature* and a number of periodicals.

Trollope, Anthony (1815–1882)
Born in London, Trollope became a clerk in the post office in 1834 and he is remembered as the inventor of the letterbox.

In addition to several volumes of short stories, he wrote nearly 50 novels. *The Chronicles of Barchester* formed one of the first novel-series in English, and *Dr Thorne* was the third of them.

He died of a stroke.

Twain, Mark (1835–1910)
Born Samuel Langhorne Clemens, he moved to Hannibal, Missouri, on the Mississippi River when he was four, and he spent most of his life there.

Although he began to write humorous sketches when he was still young, he began to train as a river-boat pilot in 1857, and it was from this experience on the river that he took his pen-name Mark Twain, that being the cry of the river-boat men to indicate that there were two fathoms clear ahead, i.e. that the boat could pass with safety.

He returned to journalism after a period of silver prospecting and he published his first short story in 1865.

He is best known as the creator of *Tom Sawyer* and *Huckleberry Finn*.

He was awarded honorary degrees from Yale University, the University of Missouri and Oxford University.

Updike, John (1932–   )
After attending schools in Shillington, Pennsylvania, where he was born, he attended Harvard College and the Ruskin School of Drawing and Fine Art in Oxford, where he spent a year on a Knox Fellowship.

One of his novels won the Pulitzer Prize for fiction and he has written several volumes of short stories.

Usaybia, Ibn Abi (1203–1270)
Born in Damascus, this highly cultured Arab physician, after studying at Damascus and Cairo, lived at the court of Sarkhad in Syria.

His major work, *Uyam al-Aba*, was a collection of biographies of 400 Arab and Greek physicians and scientists.

Waugh, Evelyn (1903–1966)
Born in London, he was educated at Lancing and Hereford College, Oxford.

He travelled widely in Europe, the Near East, Africa and tropical America and was well known as a travel writer, but he was also a biographer and, in particular, a novelist.

Vile Bodies appeared in 1930.

Welty, Eudora (1909–   )
Born in Jackson, Mississippi, where she has lived all her life, Eudora Welty is especially well known as a writer of short stories.

She has received many honours and awards, including the National Medal for Literature, the Pulitzer Prize and the Presidential Medal of Freedom, as well as honorary degrees from Yale and Harvard Universities, and from Washington University.

White, E.B. (1899–1985)
Best known perhaps as the author of the delightful children's story, *Charlotte's Web*, and as co-author of Strunk and White's brilliant *Elements of style* – arguably the best of all short works on English syntax – E.B. White wrote many essays and magazine articles, and he contributed regularly to the *New Yorker* for half a century.

Williams, William Carlos (1883–1963)
This American poet, now established as one of the masters of 'Modernism' was also a novelist and short story writer.

Until the end of his life he practised as a general practitioner/paediatrician, in his home town of Rutherford, New Jersey.

He wrote a group of *Doctor Stories*.

Wilson, A.N. (1950–)
Educated at Rugby School and New College, Oxford, A.N. Wilson was a lecturer at the University of Oxford for five years and was at one time literary editor of the *Spectator*.

He has written several biographies and many novels, and *The Healing Art* won the Somerset Maugham Award in 1980.

He was elected a Fellow of the Royal Society of Literature in 1981.

Wodehouse, P.G. (1881–1975)
Born in Guildford, Surrey and educated at Dulwich College, he first went into journalism. Moving to the USA before the First World War, he had most of his writings published in the *Saturday Evening Post* for 25 years and he took American citizenship in 1955.

Creator of Psmith, Jeeves and Bertie Wooster, he was made an honorary Knight Commander of the British Empire (KBE) in 1975.

Wright, David (1920–1994)
Born in Johannesburg, he became totally deaf after scarlet fever at the age of seven. Educated at Northampton School for the Deaf and Oriel College, Oxford, he won one of the last Atlantic Awards in Literature.

He has published several books of poems, among them *Monologue of a Deaf Man* (in 1958) and *Nerve Ends* (in 1969).

Young, Francis Brett (1884–1954)
After education at Epsom College and Birmingham University, Francis Brett Young qualified as a doctor but soon turned to writing as a career, ultimately becoming an honorary Doctor of Literature (D. Litt).

Although he wrote a few poems, plays and critical studies, it is as a novelist that he is remembered.

His 30-odd novels included *The Young Physician* (in 1919) and *Dr Bradley Remembers* (in 1938).

Index by Author

Asher, Richard   32–8
Barbirolli, Sir John   157
Bernard, Jeffrey   42–3, 97–9, 130–32, 154–6, 211–13
Blum, Alan   172–4
Bosman, Herman Charles 85–8
Brain, Lord Walter Russell   70
Caldwell, Sir Dick   127–9
Carver, Raymond   236–47
Celsus, Aulus Cornelius 147–8, 229
Chekhov, Anton   50–54, 77–81, 132–7
Dalrymple, Theodore   94–5
Dickens, Charles   4, 218–23
Espy, Willard   108–9, 247–8
Gopaleen, Myles na   40–41
Harris, Walter   164
Hartston, William   137–8
Hippocrates   3, 10
Holmes, Oliver Wendell   103, 235–6
Horder, Lord   68
Hughes, J. Trevor   217
Hugo, Victor   226–8
Huxley, Thomas   67
James I, King   139
Jones, Griff Rhys   208–11
Karinthy, Frigyes   201–7
Keats, John   213–14
Lancet   139–40, 232

Leacock, Stephen   21–4, 105–7, 123, 140–43
Lear, Edward   147
Le Fanu, James   165–6, 230–32
L'Etang, Hugh   123–7
Maugham, W. Somerset   4–5
Milligan, Spike   70–71, 119, 214
Narayan, R.K.   75–7
Nightingale, Florence   157
Paget, Sir James   44
Pasteur, Louis   67
Pepys, Samuel   164–5
Perelman, S.J.   41–2, 57–60
Pythagoras   164
Randolph, Vance   167–8
Richards, Peter   7–9
Rufus of Epheseus   75
Runyon, Damon   88–9, 103–4, 248–50
Shaw, George Bernard   38–9, 68–9
Smith, Mel   208–11
Snow, Lord C.P.   24–32
Solzhenitsyn, Aleksandr 174–86
Speight, Johnny   xi–xiv, 89–93, 162–3
Thomas, Lewis   5–6, 44–9, 103, 110–18, 168–71
Timbs, John   129–30
Trollope, Anthony   10–14

Twain, Mark   50, 67, 103,
   123, 148–54, 158–62, 235
Updike, John   60–66
Usaybia, Ibn Abi   3
Waugh, Evelyn   50
Welty, Eudora   218
White, E.B.   54, 96–7, 157–8,
   230

Williams, William Carlos   6–7,
   15–20, 81–4
Wilson, A.N.   186–97
Wodehouse, P.G.   55–7
Wright, David   224–6
Young, Francis Brett   164